The Jews of Italy,
1938–1945

The Jews of Italy, 1938–1945

An Analysis of Revisionist Histories

CHARLES T. O'REILLY

McFarland & Company, Inc., Publishers
Jefferson, North Carolina, and London

Charles T. O'Reilly is the coauthor with William A. Rooney of *The* Enola Gay *and the Smithsonian Institution* (McFarland, 2005)

LIBRARY OF CONGRESS CATALOGUING-IN-PUBLICATION DATA

O'Reilly, Charles T., 1921–
   The Jews of Italy : an analysis of revisionist histories / by Charles T. O'Reilly.
      p.   cm.
   Includes bibliographical references and index.

   ISBN-13: 978-0-7864-3002-4
   softcover : 50# alkaline paper ∞

   1. Jews — Italy — History — 20th century.   2. Jews — Italy — Historiography.   3. Holocaust, Jewish (1939–1945) — Italy — Historiography.   4. Pius XII, Pope, 1876–1958 — Relations with Jews.   5. Judaism — Relations — Catholic Church.   6. Catholic Church — Relations — Judaism.   7. Christianity and antisemitism — History — 20th century.   8. World War, 1939–1945 — Religious aspects — Catholic Church.   9. Italy — Politics and government —1922–1945 — Historiography.   10. Italy — Ethnic relations.   I. Title.
   DS135.I8O74   2007
   305.892'404509044 — dc22   2007019384

British Library cataloguing data are available

©2007 Charles T. O'Reilly. All rights reserved

No part of this book may be reproduced or transmitted in any form or by any means, electronic or mechanical, including photocopying or recording, or by any information storage and retrieval system, without permission in writing from the publisher.

On the cover: Mussolini, 1940 ©2006 Pictures Now; Jewish children ©2006 Clipart

Manufactured in the United States of America

McFarland & Company, Inc., Publishers
   Box 611, Jefferson, North Carolina 28640
      www.mcfarlandpub.com

In memory of thousands of Italians
who risked their lives to help Jews escape
the Nazi-Fascist Holocaust

Table of Contents

Preface   1

1. Italy's Jewish Community   3
2. The Royal Italian Army and the Jews   13
3. The Vatican and the Pope   27
4. Papal "Silence" and "Fear of Communism"   75
5. Afterword   115

Appendix A: On Historiography   157
Appendix B: The Vatican Archives   179
Chapter Notes   191
Selected Bibliography   213
Index   219

When it comes to dealing with the past each individual and organization has a responsibility, especially with regard to written records, to ensure that the historical truth (what has happened) remains unadulterated.*

---

*Sigfried Büttner, "The Treatment of Enemy Archives in the Third Reich," *Washington Conference on Holocaust-Era Assets, November 30-December 3, 1998* (Washington, D.C.: U.S. Government Printing Office, 1999), 743.

Preface

Much of the history of the Holocaust in English centers on what happened in Germany and Eastern Europe, often with less attention given to what happened elsewhere in Europe including in Italy. This book presents an overview of the travail of Italy's Jewish community from the beginning of Mussolini's anti–Semitic policies in the late 1930s, through the increasing danger it faced with the opening of World War II and then under German occupation from September 1943 to May 1945. The chapters focus primarily on what happened in Italy and the roles played by the Royal Italian Army and the Vatican. The Italian Army deserves attention for its often humanitarian treatment of Jews, both Italian and non–Italian. The portions about the Vatican and Pius XII make no pretense to systematic coverage of one of the major postwar controversies of World War II, his alleged "silence" in the face of Nazi atrocities and the Holocaust. Instead, attention is given to aspects of the role of the Vatican during the war that are seldom heeded by authors writing about that time. Two appendices complement the main text. The first explores the pitfalls that have entrapped many historians, in particular those writing about Pius XII and the Vatican's role in World War II. Preconceptions, credulous acceptance of unreliable ore clearly inaccurate sources and a host of other problems inherent in many of the "canonical" works on the subject have led to a self-perpetuating cycle of historical writing of highly questionable accuracy and merit. Unfortunately, many of these works also form the basis of the public's understanding of this facet of World War II history. The second appendix is an article by Pierre Blet, S.J., first published in response to outright and implied criticism of *Actes et documents du Saint-Siège relatifs à la seconde guerre mondiale* (Records and Documents of the Holy See Regarding the Second World War), a work that he and others spent years compiling in an effort to shed light on the Vatican's role in World War II.

Preface

Pius XII was honored after the war for his efforts to save Jews. Paradoxically, while his contemporary, the American poet Ezra Pound — who applauded Nazism and Fascism as models for America to emulate during the war and reveled in denouncing Jews before, during and after the war, as well as favoring a pogrom against them — today is an honored icon in American letters, Pius XII is castigated for his alleged silence and accused of collaboration with Hitler. To question the truth of such a matter should not be construed as defending anything but Clio's virtue by recalling that facts and truth are, or should be, stronger than fiction.

As always when studying the past, one must depend on the knowledge and help of others. Whether in agreement with them or not, I am grateful to all who have written about the topics covered here. The research was made possible by the help of the excellent professionals of the Archivio, Ufficio Storico, Stato Maggiore del Esercito, Rome, and the Biblioteca Militare Centrale, Rome; the Biblioteca Nazionale, Rome; the Biblioteca, Centro di Cultura Ebraica, Rome; Antonio Carrozza of the Biblioteca, Istituto Nazionale di Statistica, Rome; the Biblioteca Istituto Storico della Compagnia Gesù, Rome, and the Biblioteca della *Civiltà Cattolica*, Rome. Appreciation also is due to the experts at the National Archives, College Park, Maryland; the Library of Congress; the United States Army Institute of Military History, Carlisle, Pennsylvania; Yale University Beinecke Rare Book and Manuscript Library, the librarians of the Wilmette Public Library, which is one of the nation's best smaller libraries, and above all to the librarians of Loyola University Chicago. I also am grateful to Dr. John Felice, Director of Loyola's Rome Center, for his hospitality several times at the Rome Center when doing research in Rome.

– 1 –
Italy's Jewish Community

> The Jews neither constitute a race nor do they have unique characteristics.
> —*Enciclopedia italiana*, 1932

> The Jews do not belong to the Italian race.
> —*Il manifesto della razza*, 1938

In 1936 Jews were a small minority in Italy's population of 43,799,000, making up perhaps one-tenth of one percent of the population. Although often suffering discrimination, they were in Rome before the time of the Caesars. At the time of the emperor Nero, for example, an estimated 30,000 Jews were living in Rome. Giuliana Albini Mantovani found that in the 1400s, "Jewish communities were rather numerous in Northern Italy: among the major ones were those of Milan, Pavia, Como, Vigevano, Brescia, Bergamo, Venice, Padua, Vicenza and Mantua." Tracing the demographics of the Italian Jewish community from the twelfth century to the 1970s, Sergio Della Pergola found that there always was a Jewish presence in the peninsula, reaching as high as 120,000 in 1500. Not only was there a Jewish presence in Italy, Joachim Prinz tells of popes in the early Middle Ages — Gregory VI, Gregory VII and Anaclet II — who reportedly had Jewish backgrounds.[1] According to Andrew Canepa, "The Israeli historian Raphael Mahler has pointed out that as early as the period of Haskalah and the French Revolution, the Jews were better integrated into the surrounding population in Italy than they were anywhere else in Europe." By the 1890s, informed observers commented that the Italian Jewish community was the most assimilated in Europe.[2]

Although they were a part of the Italian landscape for millennia, Jews suffered persecution and, as in Venice and Rome, were often segregated in ghettos. That began to change in the 1800s, and after the unification of

Italy in 1870 Jews played distinguished roles in the nation's cultural and political life. Paolo Bernardini found: "After 1870, Jews became more and more involved in politics especially as liberals, public life, the press and academia, as well as in the army." Lois Dubin showed how the small Jewish community in Trieste played a role in the overall intellectual life of European Jewry. The Jewish community gave Italy the artist Modigliani, Olivetti the industrialist, and the nation's thirteenth prime minister, Luigi Luzzati. The mayor of Rome before World War I, Ernesto Natan, was Jewish. Barbara Armani and Guri Schwarz introduced "Ebrei Borghesi" by discussing the varied roles of Jews in Italian society. The contributors who wrote about the Jewish middle class represent an increasing interest in the study of the multiple dimensions of Jewish life in Italy. One focused on the cost and the benefits of being Jewish in Florence in the 1800s; another on the history of the Franchetti family in liberal Italy; a third on Jewish philanthropy in France, Italy and England; and the last on Jews in business experiencing reality and prejudice. A similar series, "Ebrei sotto Processo" (Jews on trial), dealt with Jewish encounters over the years with the criminal justice system, in which, at times, they won their cases.

A good example of the integration of Italian Jews into Italian life is found in Philip Cannistraro and Brian Sullivan's description of the wealthy and influential Sarfatti family of Venice. For many years their daughter Margherita was a political confidant and mistress of Mussolini. The cultural and religious richness of Italian Jewish life is illustrated in Vivian Mann's *Gardens and Ghettos: The Art of Jewish Life in Italy*, while what H. Stuart Hughes called the "Silver Age" of Italian Jews is a good overview of Jewish life in Italy. Indeed, according to Meir Michaelis, "Prior to Hitler's rise to power there was no 'Jewish Question' in modern Italy. It is no exaggeration to say that until 1936 there was less anti–Semitism there than in any of the Western democracies." There were observant Jews, secular Jews, ardent Zionists and all combinations thereof who sometimes debated whether there were Italian Jews or Jewish Italians. Most were comfortable in a nation that provided them opportunity and political rights. That sense of security was to be sorely tested and have fatal consequences for many in the community.[3]

The 1924 edition of the *Enciclopedia Italiana* reported 54,000 Jews in Italy and the 1932 edition confirmed what Meir Michaelis said about a "Jewish Question." It had a fifty-four page article on Jewish history and the Jewish religion and asserted, "To begin it is necessary to state the nonexistence of a race or type of Jew that is a combination of bodily characteristics limited to the Jewish people.... The Jews neither constitute a race nor do they have unique characteristics." When the notorious anti–Semite Albert Rosenberg gave a lecture in 1931 in Italy on the purity of blood, a member of the Royal Academy, Professor Francesco Orestano said, in German so Rosenberg would clearly understand him, that Rosenberg's remarks were nonsense and that every nation was a hybrid. A further indication of the Italian attitude in the early 1930s was reported by Indro Montanelli in a 1932 interview with Mussolini who told him, "racism is for blonds," referring to the Germans. For opportunistic reasons those references to Jews changed in 1938.[4]

The Italian census routinely gathered information about various religious groups and in 1931 found, "More than 85 percent of the Jews in Italy lived in large cities: Rome, 14,000; Milan, 7,000; Trieste, 4,500; Turin, 3,800; Florence, 3,000; Genoa, 3,000; Leghorn, 2,000; Venice, 1,800; Fiume, 1,600. There also were between 30,000 and 40,000 Jews in the Italian colonies." Also, "Non Catholics are concentrated in the larger Comunes, especially the Jews, who for centuries are preeminently city residents. Of the 11,600 Jews in Lazio, 11,280 were counted in Rome." The regular 1936 census provided information on the number of Jews in Libya, then an Italian colony, but not for mainland Italy or other Italian possessions. Libya's population of 750,851 included 28,299 Jews, 3.7 percent of the population.[5]

Like other Italians, many Jews were not averse to joining the Fascist Party. The number enrolled in the party swelled from 750 in 1922 to about 7,300 in 1933. In the mid 1930s Hitler began to press Mussolini to do something about the Jews, and the Fascists changed their attitudes and policies about Jews. An anti–Semitic campaign began with the publication of the Protocols of the Elders of Zion and similar works that claimed there was a Zionist conspiracy to dominate the world. The government-controlled press and books and articles sought to provide a "scientific" rationale for the anti–Semitic campaign. On July 14, 1938, newspapers carried a "Manifesto of the Race" that proclaimed an Aryan Italian Race and claimed that Jews did not belong to the Italian race. A book by Aldo Capasso held that Jews, unlike the Germans and Italians, were a non–European race and could not be assimilated into other races.

Although distinguishable by physical characteristics, their difference was predominantly religious, and "the baptized Jew always remains a Jew." On the other hand, Ugo Andalo, when explaining how Jews were different, affirmed that the idea of an "Italian race is not based on a confusing biological concept, or a historical-linguistic idea of People and Nation, but on the ties of blood that unite today's Italians to past generations."[6] With the way prepared by such propaganda, there followed the infamous "racial" census of August 22, 1938, that found 58,412 persons of *razza ebraica* in Italy, a minuscule minority in the population. It happened that 10,380 of them were foreigners. When Michele Sarfatti analyzed the census, he discovered that although listed as Jewish in the census, 11,756 actually were not Jewish. Some 7,000 were children of mixed marriages and another 2,563 had left the Jewish religion.[7]

Several royal decrees affecting Jews were issued between September and November 1938. One decree denied Jewish children access to all levels of education and another expelled foreign Jews from Italy, Libya and the Italian islands in the Aegean. A third decree prohibited the marriage of Italians and foreigners, Hamites and Semites. It also defined who was Jewish and excluded them from the military, public and quasi-public employment, banking and other positions. In addition, it limited the size of Jewish business and imposed other restrictions as well as effectively expropriating much Jewish business. A more detailed decree on education excluded Jewish faculty from universities and Jewish students from academies of art and music. It also prohibited the public schools from using books written or edited by Jews, although an exception was made for their use in the private Jewish schools that were authorized. Somewhat paradoxically, in October 1938, the Fascist Grand Council issued a declaration on race that covered most of the legislation but said that Jews who lost their jobs retained their pension rights and that any pressure to force Jews to renounce their religion would be rigorously repressed. Ugo Caffaz's book also described the toll exacted from the Jewish community by the confiscations authorized by the racial laws.

The Fascists did not leave the promotion of anti–Semitism to chance. Giorgio Sacchetti told how one small town was taught about the laws of 1938. In Arezzo not far from Florence, in 1938–1939, there was intensive public instruction about the Jews through courses and lessons organized by the National Institute of Fascist Culture. Lectures were given on "racial studies" and Jewishness in the world and in Italy in a community with no more than one hundred Jews in 1938. Arezzo had a small Jewish community in the area at least since the mid–1700s that ranged from thirty to perhaps 130 persons, a minuscule part of the area's population. For more than a century they had been tolerated if not fully accepted. That changed with the racial laws.[8]

According to David Kertzer in his well-written and heavily documented *The Popes Against the Jews*, "The Italian racial laws, in particular, have been strangely and disturbingly ignored, almost as if they should be excused in retrospect for being so mild compared with the actual massacre of the Jews." He then went on to say, "The racial laws have an uncannily familiar ring to them, for they differed little from those that the Church itself had employed when it was in power in Italy." Kertzer correctly identified the historian's tendency to ignore Italy's racial laws, which, had Italy not been invaded by the Allies, probably would have had a draconian enforcement as German policy increasingly dominated Fascist Italy. There can be little question that the potential for what happened to Jews in Vichy and Hungary also existed in Mussolini's Italy. On the matter of the "familiar ring" to the racial laws of 1938, Kertzer argued his case based on the situation in the country a century earlier and on several articles in *La Civiltà Cattolica* that were anti–Jewish, and also on the remarks of the notorious anti–Semite and prominent Fascist Roberto Farinacci. That conclusion could be reached only by overlooking all the contrary evidence from sources with which he demonstrated his familiarity.

It should not be overlooked that when the racial laws were implemented in Italy, many Catholics may have considered them unexceptional insofar as they comported with an antipathy toward Judaism based upon a lengthy tradition in their church. That did not mean, as Giovanni Miccoli pointed out, that they necessarily approved of the measures used against the Jews. However, it led to not taking responsibility as persecution became more extreme. Although many Catholics aided the Jews, they lacked "that mobilization that alone, perhaps, would have limited if not impeded movement toward the 'final solution.'"[9]

At the Armistice that ended hostilities between the Allies and the Royal Italian government in September 1943, about 39,000 Jews lived in northern and central Italy and came under German occupation. The deportation of 8,566 Jews to Germany began September 16, 1943, and ended on February 24, 1945. Liliana Picciotto Fargion listed those who were deported during the existence of Mussolini's puppet Repubblica Sociale Italiana (RSI) (Italian Social Republic), better known as the Republic of Salo, which existed during the German occupation of central and northern Italy. In *Black Sabbath* Robert Katz told how over 800 Roman women and children and 327 men were hunted down by the Nazis on October 16, 1943, and deported to Auschwitz. Only fifteen of the Roman Jews returned home. About 250 of all those deported from Italy returned home.[10]

Italy's anti–Jewish laws imitated those of Germany although their enforcement did not reach Hitlerian extremes. However, despite Arthur Butz's claim that the Fascist treatment of Italy's Jews was "mild," the 1938 laws imposed terrible hardships upon the Jewish community. The racial laws revoked the citizenship of Jews who received it after January 1, 1919, and expelled foreign Jews from Italy within six months. Careers were destroyed, property expropriated, jobs lost, education denied, families separated and ultimately the laws had fatal consequences for many of its victims. The consequences for five Jewish families are told by Alexander Stille in *Benevolence and Betrayal,* which followed mostly assimilated families of different social classes as they experienced what Butz and others have called the mild or half-hearted enforcement of the racial laws before and after the German occupation.

Far from mild were the experiences of Giancarlo Sacerdote, who recalled his life as a young Jewish boy in Bologna during the war. In a non-dramatic way he told of the teachers in his Jewish school who lost their jobs as librarians and professors and how daily life was shaped by persecution. In October 1943, "Something terrible happened to the grandparents of Sergio and Maria Grazia Rossi who had remained in their home certain that their baptism would save them, but that was not to happen. I saw the Germans arrive at the house on Via Putti. Too late the two old people realized what was happening and attempted to escape through the back of the house but were knocked down and killed like rabbits." Sacerdote went to live in the country with farmers to escape deportation, and fortunately his family survived.

A similar story was told by Paolo Ravenna, who was twelve when he was expelled from school in Ferrara. He went to a Jewish school and recounted the hurt of a child who could not understand why he had been expelled from his school. While he remembered many small acts of kindness, such as that of the school's principal who told him she would always be his teacher, he also recalled the many friends and schoolmates who disappeared. One not so petty rule for a child was that although Jewish students were allowed to take examinations for promotion, the Ministry of Education required that they be separated from the other students, who were given precedence in taking oral examinations.[11]

The Jewish community made an effort to have its children live as "normally" as possible under the restrictions imposed by the racial laws. The schools at various levels were part of this effort. In his "quasi-novel," *The Tiber Afire*, Fabio Della Seta told about Jewish children who went to the equivalent of a Jewish high school in Rome and after graduation enrolled in the first year of an engineering program. Some attended a Pontifical institution for legal education that was open to Jews. All of this happened after the racial laws that excluded them from high schools and universities were enforced and before the German occupation.

The tenor of the restrictions placed on Jews can be seen in a regulation prohibiting kosher slaughter. Jewish newspapers were forbidden, and obituaries and funerals could not be reported in newspapers. Jews could not get telephone service, and gradually, in addition to exclusion from the professions such as medicine and law as well as teaching, matters became even more restrictive. Internment camps were established throughout Italy to hold first foreign Jews and then other categories of Italian Jews. It should be realized that as Jews fled Austria, Germany and Czechoslovakia before war began in 1939, they went to Italy, hopefully as a transit point to go abroad. With Italy's entry in the war, the hope of leaving disappeared, and they were stranded in an increasingly hostile Italy and were moved to Italian concentration camps. Beginning in November 1943, the Republic of Salo under Mussolini defined all Jews of whatever nationality as enemies and ordered them into concentration camps. In addition, all their property was subject to confiscation.

Perhaps 6,000 Jews were able to emigrate, and Vera Jarach and Elenora Smolensky told about the 2,000 who went to Argentina between 1937 and 1943. Most of them were in families headed by middle-aged professionals who told of the persecution they suffered because of Italy's racial laws and what it meant to leave homes in places like Venice or Milan. They were fortunate to find a large Jewish and Italian community in their new country. Between 1934 and 1945, 24,488 Jews, many of them German speaking, migrated to Argentina.[12] Trieste is an example of what happened in a city in which there had been a Jewish presence for hundreds of years. Although Trieste was under the Hapsburgs until World War I, Angelo Ara found that like most residents of Trieste, Jews identified with Italy and spoke Italian. "The racial laws of 1938 struck a socially assimilated group that could not imagine being objects of discrimination and persecution." Of 390 physicians and dentists in the city, 90 were Jewish, as were 40 of the 310 lawyers. They lost their professions, and the city's foremost newspaper passed into "Aryan" hands. Of the more than 5,000 Jews in Trieste before the war, fewer than half remained when the Germans took over. "During the whole period of German occupation some 600 Trieste Jews were deported and only 400 or 500, living in great destitution were discovered after the entry of the Eighth Army on May 7th, 1945."[13]

Mussolini's regime brutalized Italy's Jews although it did not demonstrate Nazi fervor, but that should not lead anyone to ignore or discount anti–Semitism within the Fascist movement. Luigi Villari, an early postwar apologist for Fascism, discounted the influence of Germany's policies on what happened in Italy. Instead he traced Mussolini's Jewish policy to his long-standing suspicion of Zionism and Jewish international finance. Although mildly critical of the anti–Jewish laws of 1938, Villari argued that, "While the existence of a Jewish problem demanding some solution was generally admitted, the measures enacted by the Italian Government did not help to solve it, but they brought much odium on Mussolini and on Italy in general.... The activities of international Jewish finance, which were undoubtedly dangerous and do serve to explain Mussolini's attitude, might have been dealt with in other and better ways."

As an unabashed apologist for the Italian Social Republic, Villari hurried past what really happened to the Jews in Fascist Italy. He also was more than understanding of why the Germans took a savage reprisal for the Via Rasella incident that led to the Ardeatine Caves massacre, as well as their reaction to other actions by partisans. Villari's claim that Mussolini's 1938 policies reflected a long-standing antipathy toward Zionism and "international Jewry" found support in Gene Bernardini's thoughtful study of the relationship between Fascism and anti–Semitism, as well as in Michael Ledeen's review of the development of anti–Semitism in Fascist ideology. Bernardini noted that in 1919, writing in *Il popolo d'Italia*, Mussolini had inveighed against "the great Jewish bankers ... [who] seek their revenge against the Aryan race." That rhetoric changed when he assumed power. However, that such elements of Fascism would have led to the events of 1938 is questionable. Mussolini was a ruthless pragmatist in matters political and a charismatic master showman, just as was Hitler. Yet he was too practical to turn cynically against the Jews until he joined Hitler's vision of Europe as the junior partner in the "Pact of Steel."

Although Mussolini's anti–Semitism may have been more opportunistic than ideological, that did not make it any less heinous because its consequences could be fatal. It should not be surprising that many years later, Villari was quoted by "Blood-Honor," a white supremacist group, as saying that Mussolini was "sincerely opposed to Jewish influence in Italy but did everything to prevent interference with Italian Jews." Such revisionism of Mussolini's legacy also heralds Il Duce's early social programs and the draining of the Pontine Marshes, which improved the lot of many of Italy's poor. However, to mention such in order to burnish his image for a later generation is akin to talking about Hitler's autobahns as somehow relevant when discussing Auschwitz. Still, some writers persist in finding something positive in the lives and work of dictators like Hitler, Mussolini, Stalin and Pol Pot. Nicholas Kristof did this when reviewing a biography of Chairman Mao in the *New York Times*. After describing Mao as a monster and saying that his "ruthlessness was a catastrophe at the time," Kristof continued, "Mao also helped lay the groundwork for the rebirth and rise of China after five centuries of slumber." Kristof belongs with progressives who, while regretting the fatalities, can appreciate the leader's contribution to building for tomorrow.

Despite the efforts of historian Renzo De Felice and others to be more "objective" about Mussolini's legacy, there is no way to revise the fact that Il Duce was ultimately responsible for sending his ill-prepared military into a doomed war that cost the lives of at least 330,000 men, not including POWs who did not return from German and Soviet captivity and may have numbered more than 300,000. He ruined his nation and caused the death of 80,000 of his fellow citizens and sent his fellow Italians who were Jews to death camps. Between emigration and casualties before the war, and mass murder during the war, the Jewish community lost 45 percent of its members. While the *Annuario statistico italiano* reported 51,893 persons identified as Jewish in Italy in 1938, by 1948 the number dropped to 28,482. Those missing numbers will forever burden the memory of Benito Mussolini. Thanks to ordinary Italians, although the loss of Jewish lives was grievous, many survived. How they survived is the subject of the chapter "Survival in Italy" in Professor Susan Zuccotti's book *Italians and the Holocaust*. Without the help of many Italians it would not have been possible for Leon Poliakov to say, "It is to the imperishable glory of Italy that in all circles and in all administrative divisions there was evident, from the start, a tenacious resistance to the racial policy of Fascism and its consequences."[14]

– 2 –
The Royal Italian Army and the Jews

> I have always regarded it a duty of conscience to remember how much the Italian army did in 1941 to help persecuted Jews and to save them from extermination camps.
> — Chief Rabbi of Rome, Professor Elio Toaff

The tragedy of the Holocaust was so immense and pervasive that the West's failure to do more for the Jewish community before the war will continue to be questioned. What happened when war began is another historical question for which some answers are possible. In Italy the entire society was affected by the anti–Semitism promulgated by Benito Mussolini in 1938, and the then Royal Italian Army was no exception. Leon Trotsky said that the army reflects its society; thus, as a cross section of Italian society it is useful to examine how the military, as a social institution, reacted to the tragedy played out in its presence. This essay is not an apologia for an army whose members often acted atrociously; on the other hand when it treated Jews humanely, that deserves recognition. Ivo Herzer asked why "the role of the Italians in saving and protecting Italian and foreign Jews has been left in a dark corner of Holocaust historiography for so long." He gave several reasons, and then added: "It is now established, based on thorough research, that the Italian army and foreign ministry protected foreign Jews everywhere in Italian-occupied territories." What that army did should not be forgotten.

The Italian Army was ill-equipped for war by any standard and too often led by political generals. Despite such handicaps, its soldiers fought well although they were outmatched in both equipment and leadership by the Allies in the air and at sea as well as on land. According to military historian MacGregor Knox, "The troops themselves in any event did not necessarily show in 1940–41 the readiness to surrender of popular legend. Units in North Africa, Albania, and Russia held together in conditions — usually deriving from the army's logistical inadequacies — that would have caused soldiers of the industrial democracies to quail." By 1942, however, military leaders knew that their war was hopeless, and they pushed for the removal of Mussolini and an end to the war.

Mussolini was deposed and arrested on July 25, 1943, and replaced by Marshal Pietro Badoglio as prime minister. This effectively ended hostilities between the Allies and Italy, although an Armistice with the Allies was not announced until September 8, 1943. Italy declared war on Germany on October 13, 1943, joining the Allies in the war against Germany. However, hostilities with Germany began immediately after the Armistice between elements of the Royal Army and the Germans in Rome, Sardinia and Corsica as well as on islands in the Aegean, with resultant heavy Italian casualties. One of the most notorious atrocities happened after the Armistice on the island of Cefalonia. From September 15 to September 22, the Acqui Division resisted overwhelming German forces. Compelled to surrender, over 5,000 of its men were executed by the Germans following the "Führer Order" that Italians who resisted joining the Germans were to be killed.

By December 1943, the First Italian Motorized Group was fighting the Germans and eventually about 100,000 men served in several combat divisions with the British and American armies. There also were small air force and naval units. The story of the men in combat units is well told by Richard Lamb in *War in Italy: A Brutal Story*. Hundreds of thousands of other men served in support units in Italy, France, Britain, India, and North Africa, with more than 30,000 in Italian Service Units in the United States. The story of Italy's role in the Italian Campaign is little known outside of Italy and too little known in Italy.[1]

How the Royal Army related to the Jews is told in Menachem Shelah's *Un debito di gratitudine* and Jonathan Steinberg's *All or Nothing: The Axis and the Holocaust, 1941–1943*, each an important source for a thorough coverage of the topic. In *Il libro della memoria*, Liliana Picciotto Fargion comprehensively covers the fate of the Jewish community from the fall of Mussolini until the end of the war. A more general treatment of the situation of Jews in Italy is found in Professor Susan Zuccotti's *The*

2—The Royal Italian Army and the Jews

Italians and the Holocaust: Persecution, Rescue, and Survival. Richard Lamb recounted both the efforts made by the Germans to deport Italian Jews and, without minimizing the too frequent collaboration with the Germans by some Italians, the sometimes successful efforts of even Fascist officials to protect the Jews. His chapter "Italian Jews Under the Nazis" must be read to know the details of the army's role in protecting the Jews. Earlier books by Gerald Reitlinger, for example, also are useful for background. Perhaps the most useful shorter overview of the experience of Italian Jews before and after the racial laws is found in Meir Michaelis's chapter on the Holocaust in Italy, which comments on the origins of the racial laws, the role of the Vatican, and the Italian army's efforts to protect Jews in areas it occupied.[2]

In November 1937, the Ministry of War informed the military academies not to admit Jewish students, although Jewish cadets already admitted were allowed to remain for the academic year. Jewish cadets were well motivated and had no academic problems, but none were to be admitted for the next academic year. In October 1938, however, the immediate discharge of all Jewish cadets from the military schools and academies was ordered. Another indication that the racial program was anticipated is found in a June 1938 memo from the Ministry of War to Mussolini that asked what to do about General Ugo Levi. When he was promoted to general of division in July 1937, *per ovvie ragioni* (for obvious reasons) he was not considered for the command of a division, but continued as assigned to the Inspectorate of Engineers. As in the case of the military academies, there were "obvious reasons" for different treatment of Jewish members of the army in 1937 before the official anti–Semitic campaign began.

A census of the military in September 1938 was similar to the infamous and more general "racial" census of Jews. Among other questions it asked whether the respondent's father and mother belonged to the Jewish "race," whether one belonged to the Jewish community and if one professed the Jewish religion. There were successive redefinitions of who was to be considered Jewish, although none were as detailed as Germany's Nuremberg Laws. In the beginning Jews were persons with both parents who were Jewish, as well as those whose father was Jewish and the mother a foreigner, and those in mixed marriages professing Judaism. In December it was decided that if either parent was Jewish and the other a foreigner, even if the latter was an Italian citizen, a child was Jewish. Then on December 10, 1938, the Ministry of War ordered that within that month all Jewish enlisted men were to be separated from the army.³

There were about 700 Jewish officers in the Italian army in 1895, according to E. Rubin, and World War I saw a number of Jewish generals and admirals in the Italian military. Jewish officers continued to serve until excluded by the Royal Decree of November 17, 1938 (Number 1728, Chapter II, Article 10a) that said, "Italian citizens of the Jewish race cannot undertake military service in peace and in war." Luciano Tas found that the 1938 "racial" census identified 150 army officers while Sergio Della Pergola's study of the number of Jews in various occupations discovered that relative to the size of the Jewish community, the percentage of Jews in the military was higher than it had been in the early 1900s. Rubin reported that about ten Jewish generals and an admiral were forced out of service by the racial laws. The admiral may have been Admiral Pugliese, a distant relative of Giancarlo Sacerdote who was mentioned earlier. One retired Jewish general and one admiral died in Auschwitz and another retired general died while fighting with the Partisans.⁴

The manner in which the law was interpreted caused Bruno Segre, who had a Jewish father and Catholic mother, but was not baptized, to be classified as Jewish, while his brother, who was baptized, was classified as Aryan. Giancarlo Finzi was separated from the army in 1938 because his grandmother was Jewish. His grandfather, who was baptized in 1844, had King Victor Emanuele II as his godfather and the family had been Catholic for four generations. When Finzi requested restoration to the army following Mussolini's overthrow, he and seven other officers were turned down because in August 1943 the racial laws were still in effect. In addition, a memo of August 29, 1943, said Jews were forbidden to work in war industry. At the time, the Badoglio government that replaced Mussolini was playing a cautious game with the Germans and believed that abrogating the racial laws would have heightened their suspicion.⁵

Article 31 of the "Long Form" of the September 1943 Armistice required the recision of all laws discriminating on the basis of race, color, creed or political opinion. Some amends to the victims of the racial laws began to be made by the Badoglio government in 1944 with Royal Decree Number 6 of January 20, 1944. Lt. Col. Moise Cohen, a victim of the 1938 racial laws, was reinstated in the army at his former rank and with seniority rights. That law only began a process that lasted more than twenty years and took more than eighty-nine separate laws and regulations to remove, to some degree at least, the impact of the 1938 laws on property rights, job rights, validation of diplomas, and countless other matters, including a Treasury Ministry decree as late as February 1989 regarding pensions. Mario Toscano's compilation of those laws showed the complex process of restoring, insofar as possible, what was lost by the victims and their families.[6]

Guido Bedaria noted the rarity of anti–Semitism in the 1930s until it was introduced by the Fascists and claimed that the help given to the Jews by Italians was "the best anti-fascist and anti-racist plebiscite ever seen." Professor Susan Zuccotti also felt that so many Italian Jews survived due to the commendable attitudes and behaviors of many Italians. Dan Vittorio Segre described how his family was sheltered in their village: "This grotesque situation, which lasted until the end of the war combined a deep sense of human solidarity with an equally deep hate for the Germans and the Fascist Republicans.... It was a situation in which, because of the war, but not only because of it, all social relationships and economic barriers were removed and replaced by a visceral, almost animal solidarity that I do not think existed, as far as the Jews are concerned, anywhere else in the Western world."

In *Un debito di gratitudine*, Menachem Shelah recounted the efforts of the Italian military to protect the Jews in its zone of occupation in Yugoslavia. The importance of that effort cannot be denied, but Antonello Biagini, in the preface to Shelah's book, does not hide the fact that there were "cases in which because of failure to receive refugees or turning over of small groups of Jews to the Ustachi, as did the Italian questor of Susak, and of the military headquarters at Pristina and Dubrovnik, or because of the passivity of the headquarters at Pago, Italians contributed to the 'final solution.'" Some Italians were strongly anti–Semitic. General Renato Coturri, who commanded the V Corps at Cirquenizza, sought permission to turn over Jews to the Croats, but the headquarters of the 2nd Army refused his request.

The Italian army had occupied part of Croatia, and when the Germans began to deport Jews in their occupation zone, they wanted the Italians to turn over the Jews in the Italian zone. According to General Mario Roatta, who commanded the Second Army, "The Ustase began to carry out a massive extermination of the Serbian Orthodox population ... and of the Jews." He went on to say "the Army saved the lives and possessions of numbers of Serbian Orthodox (their authorities put the number at 600,000). It also took under its protection some thousands of Jews who had fled from Zagreb and parts of Croatia under German occupation." One of the most notorious episodes in Croatia was the Jasenovac concentration camp whose commandant was a former Franciscan friar, Fra Filipovic, who had been expelled from the order for taking part in attacks on Serbian villages. He has been justifiably excoriated for his atrocities, but most writers fail to add that he was no longer a Franciscan friar. After the war he was tried and executed for war crimes. Like too many others he had subordinated religious commitment to a ruthless, murderous nationalism.

The Croatian government wanted a census of the Jews and their transfer to Croatian custody, but aware of what was happening, the Italians procrastinated, claiming that they could not identify who was Jewish. Roberto Ducci, who was with the Italian foreign ministry in Croatia, explained that the matter was referred to Mussolini who replied, "*nulla osta*," meaning he was not opposed to the transfers. However, the military interpreted his response not as an agreement or an order, but merely that he was not opposed, and continued to refuse to transfer Jews to the Germans. Meir Michaelis quoted Siegfried Kasche, who was the German envoy in Croatia, saying that Mussolini's decision to turn over the Jews was disregarded by his subordinates, some of whom were apparently influenced by "Vatican opposition to the German brand of anti–Semitism." The refusal continued until the Armistice on September 8, 1943, when the Germans took complete control of the area.[7]

* * *

The Army's attitude toward the Jews is revealed by small incidents that are often ignored. After three Italian soldiers on duty in Poland in September 1942 promised to help several Jews escape to Hungary, they were betrayed to the Germans, who then shot the Jews. The soldiers' commanding general regretted that the men could not be tried locally because it would upset relations with the Germans, but he sent them to Rome for court-martial. The wife of one man wrote to Mussolini's sister asking her to intercede with Il Duce, pointing out that her husband was a longtime, loyal Fascist. The wife's letter has the notation, "The Duce says, he took the money." However, Mussolini later intervened, and the most serious charges were dropped although the men received some punishment.

The Weisers, a Jewish couple from Florence, were trapped in Poland when war began. Both were pharmacists, and the husband a member of the Fascist Party. Thanks to the intervention of the Duke of Bergamo, they were smuggled back to Italy on an army hospital train. During an investigation of this "illegal" smuggling, the officer in charge of the train said that it was well known what was happening in Poland. If the Weisers were not allowed on the train, they probably would have been killed the next day. The Weisers left the train when it arrived in Italy and what happened to them is not in the record. Such incidents reflected the attitudes many Italians had about Jews.[8]

Branko Bokun also told something that revealed the attitudes of many Italians toward the Jews. Bokun was helping two Jewish men from Zagreb who were hiding in an Etruscan tomb in Cerveteri, a town near Rome. Three other refugees arrived, one of whom was Jewish, and when Bokun asked how they knew where to come, they said the local police told them that two foreign Jews who were hiding in an old tomb would help them. If the local police knew where the men were hiding, the police were not the only ones because in a town like Cerveteri what is known to anyone is (literally) known to everyone. The episode represented an aspect of Italian culture that meant survival for many Jews and escaped prisoners of war.[9]

After the war the former Italian ambassador in Albania, Francesco Jacomoni, was charged among other matters of having aided in the assassination of King Alexander of Yugoslavia and of the French Minister of Foreign Affairs Barthou. At his trial a deposition by the Rev. Giuseppe Valentini, S.J., head of the Liceo di Scutari, claimed that Jacomoni "always was opposed to the racial laws and I know that he saved many Jews that came into Italian territory from the German zone. He helped them to leave and told the Germans searching for them that they could not be found."[10]

A reminder of that Italian attitude was found at the Ardeatine Caves. Of the 335 men killed at the Ardeatine Caves in a reprisal on March 24, 1944, seventy-seven were Jews who, along with others, were added to the list of hostages when not enough men who the Germans said were guilty of capital offenses were available for execution. A Catholic victim managed to write a short note before his death. "God, great Father, we pray that you will protect the Jews from barbarous persecution. An Our Father, ten Hail Marys, a Gloria." The list of such incidents could be multiplied many times but still could not meet the desperate need for help. Although too much should not be made of similar incidents, that some help was forthcoming, often at high risk, should be acknowledged.[11]

When the Germans sought the expulsion of Croatia's Jews to Germany, "There was, however, one complication; the several thousand Jews in the Italian zone.... The Italian commander in Mostar, for instance had promised equal treatment, and had even refused to evict Jewish tenants to make room for the German organization Todt. When asked for an explanation, he declared that anti-Jewish measures were incompatible with the honor of the Italian army." Menachem Shelah said, "The story here is of the military of Italy, a nation allied with Nazi Germany, and therefore interested in Axis victory. Fascist Italy was dominated by an extremely nationalistic totalitarian ideology that was opposed to any show of the humanitarianism of the 'decadent western democracies.' In Fascism the State was all and a citizen's civil rights were considered unimportant. But in precisely this Nation, under a Fascist regime, many of its high functionaries and even more the officers of the army unhesitatingly opposed the Nazi work of extermination and placed themselves in open opposition to a more powerful ally in order to save the lives of some thousands of Jews who were not even their fellow citizens." Martin Gilbert's account of the efforts of Italians to help Jews highlighted what some Italians did to help Jews although some with good reason might say too little and too late. An outstanding example was, of course, what the Italian military did in the occupied zone in France. Both on the initiative of individuals and on the orders of Rome headquarters, the effort made the difference between life and death for many Jews. After the September 8th Armistice, the Germans took over the Italian zone and captured those who had found refuge there. Susan Zuccotti has a good account of what happened as the Germans moved into the Italian zone of occupation.[12]

What the Italian military did to help the Jews in occupied Yugoslavia and France is outlined in John Bierman's description of how the Italians frustrated the German effort to deport Jews from France and ended thus: "The record surely provides a prime example of how Italians at all levels and by all variety of means sabotaged the murderous racial policies of the

Nazis and their surrogates." The help the Italian military gave the Jews in the Italian occupation zone in France from 1940 until September 1943 is the subject of several books, with Leon Poliakov one of the earliest to tell the story of Italian protectiveness in its zone of occupation. Luciano Tas wrote, "Italian occupation troops first in France and later in Greece and Yugoslavia defended the local Jews against the racist Germans. Especially in Southern France their work was methodical, preordered and undoubtedly directed by higher command, and it saved thousands of Jewish lives." A few days before Mussolini fell, a German official reported that, "The Italian military authorities and the Italian police protect the Jews by every means in their power. The Italian zone of influence, particularly in the Cote d'Azur, has become the Promised Land for the Jews in France. In the last few months there has been a mass exodus of Jews from our occupation zone into the Italian zone." German requests to seize and deport Jews were refused or delayed long enough to frustrate Adolph Eichman who was responsible for their deportation. On occasion the military forced the release of hundreds of Jews who were to be deported to Germany. Nora Levin described how the Italians confounded their ally until the drastic change when Italy left the Pact of Steel on September 8, 1943, which placed the Jews at the mercy of the Germans.[13]

On August 28, 1943, the Badoglio government, which still was formally allied with Germany, agreed that it would not be opposed to the entry of Jews from France but this was not announced until September 7th, on the eve of the Armistice. Had the move from France to Italy been possible, perhaps as many as 20,000 Jews could have entered Italy. But after the Armistice the Germans took over the Italian occupation zone and began hunting for the more than 50,000 Jews that sought shelter there. Alberto Cavaglion described how many of those who had escaped from France to Northern Italy after the Armistice were caught by the Germans and deported to extermination camps. Some managed to remain in Italy and survive, thanks to the help of the local people. Although eventually the efforts of the Italian military came to naught for most of the Jews in France, their willingness to resist German pressure and attempt to help the Jews who managed to enter their zone was impressive. Much the same happened in the Balkans in the area under Italian occupation. There some Jews were brought to southern Italy and survived the war. For most, however, the Armistice spelled the end of hope as the Germans took over with brutal efficiency. Too seldom these efforts of the Italian military, which might have saved thousands of lives of non–Italians, are unrecognized although they represent the best in the Italian character. [14]

The island of Corfu had a Jewish community since the thirteenth century and, according to Pearl Preschel, during the Italian occupation was home to about 2,000 Jews. "The Italians occupied the island in April 1941. Under their domination peace and tranquillity prevailed. Many Jews from the German-occupied mainland found refuge in Corfu." The Germans installed themselves on the island on September 27, 1943, and the deportation of the Jewish community began in June 1944. Colonel Friederich Jaeger, the German commander on Corfu, spoke of his abhorrence for the deportation of the Jews that the army was carrying out. Sixteen hundred of Corfu's Jews were sent to Auschwitz where they died in the gas chamber in June 1944. In 1982, Preschel found only seventy Jews remained on Corfu.[15]

On the island of Rhodes, General Ulrich Kleeman, who commanded the German forces, ordered the evacuation of the Jews to be pursued by his troops "with National Socialist zeal." Because of the lack of sufficient ships to transport the refugees, they seem to have been deliberately drowned. What would happen if Germany occupied the islands was certain, and Giuseppe Mayda criticized the Badoglio government for not finding a way to evacuate the Jews on the islands during the forty-five days between Mussolini's fall and September 8th. He also criticized Badoglio for suspending but not eliminating Mussolini's racial laws, although he admitted that Badoglio played a cautious game in order to avoid alienating the Germans. Harriet Pass Freidenreich found that in Yugoslavia under Italian military occupation, "The Jews who managed to escape to those regions under Italian control fared relatively better than Jews in other parts of the former Yugoslav kingdom. While most ... were eventually interned in Italian camps, they appear to have received better treatment. The Italian authorities saved them from deportation to the Reich as long as they were in command."[16]

In Greece, "From 15 March onwards Jewish Salonika was in the toils of the Rosenberg Commission. Members of the Jewish community were loaded into cattle wagons and sent in convoys of several thousand at a time to 'colonize the spaces of the East.... 55,000 Jews had made Salonika a Jewish city in the same tradition as Alexandria, Toledo and Livorno.

46,061 of them went off to the ovens. Before the war, 77,000 Jews had lived in Greece without experiencing or causing the slightest racial problem. 68,000 were arrested and 66,000 of these were murdered." A lengthy report to the Vatican on the situation in Greece was made on May 15, 1943, by the Nuncio in Greece, Angelo Roncalli. It mentioned the appeals of Jews to go to Italy to escape the "harsh and hateful treatment of the Jewish community in Salonika." The report said the Italian authorities behaved very differently from the Germans in regard to the Greek population and especially in regard to the persecuted Jews. "The Italians, civilian and military, in general show understanding and are rather well disposed."

Although Deborah Dwork and Richard Jan van Pelt considered the Italian army useless as a fighting force, they said, "The entire Italian Army in Italian-occupied Croatia, Greece and France ... flouted the Germans.... They found their Teuton partners overbearing and barbaric." The went on to say, "The Italians took solace in their civilization and their humanity. Their army, unique among the Axis forces, protected the Jews in its domain." That was the same conclusion reached by historian Charles Delzell, that while the Fascists were in power no foreign Jews in the French occupied zone were turned over to the Germans.[17]

Historian Renzo De Felice estimated that about 1,000 Jews joined the Resistance. One of them was Isidor Gottlieb, who brought his family to Italy from the Italian-occupied zone in France after the Armistice. He joined the Partisans of Valcasotto and took part in numerous fire fights with the Germans. "During one of these operations on March 17, 1944, he was wounded and captured by the Germans along with six other Partisans. That same day, Gottlieb and his six companions were shot in the piazza of Ceva," a town located between Mondovi and Savona. Gottlieb had been a lieutenant in the Polish army and was known as "tenente Berto" among the Partisans.[18]

Aided by the Germans, Mussolini's Republic of Salo continued to pursue Jews in its territory. According to Richard Lamb, "The Nazi persecution of Italian Jews was shocking; fortunately, neither Mussolini nor his Salo Ministers were anti–Semitic, with the exception of the poisonous Preziosi. Many Fascist officials, and the Italian people, generally protected the Jews from what would otherwise have been wholesale slaughter. However, no one should underestimate the grave harm done to Italian Jews by the anti–Semitic laws of 1938 and 1943." Philip Cannistraro and Brian

Sullivan also noted that Mussolini often opposed the German efforts to destroy Italian Jewry and adopted a moderate stance toward the Jews. Il Duce was perceived as being afraid that the Germans would think he had lost his nerve, but in fact his attitude "represented the reassertion of a deep Italian virtue: the triumph of old humanitarianism values over Fascist principles." On the other hand, when the Fascist Party convened at Cremona, it said in its "Manifesto di Cremona" on November 1943, "Those of the Jewish race are foreigners. During this war they belong to an enemy nationality." That went far beyond the racial laws of 1938 and justified ruthless hunts for Jews to be turned over to the Germans for deportation to death camps. In this regard Mussolini's republican guard that cooperated with the Germans was considered a terrorist organization by SS Colonel Eugen Dollman. Until the final days of the war, the "Brigate Nere" in Milan continued to hunt Jews and rewarded informants who identified them. Finally, with the war clearly lost, Giovanni Preziosi, the director of the RSI's agency for racial matters and a violent anti–Semite, "who was the most tenacious enemy of the Jews in Italy," committed suicide along with his wife.[19]

Considering the Racial Manifesto and Il Duce's "*nulla osta*" to turning over Croatian Jews to the Germans, it seems that Lamb and Cannistraro and Sullivan were overly generous in their estimates of Il Duce's anti–Semitism. Whatever Benito Mussolini's intentions for the social republic or his private opinion of the Jews may have been, or his abhorrence of the "final solution," it was his cynical exploitation of public policies in 1938 that was relevant for the Jews who suffered under his regime both before and after September 8th, 1943.

Italian school textbooks in the 1980s virtually ignored what the Italian army did during the war to protect Jews. Salvatore Loi commented on that lack of attention: "I must add that to the silence of many analysts one can contrast the recognition from the Chief Rabbi of Rome, Professor Elio Toaff. Recently he wrote to me, 'I have always regarded it a duty of conscience to remember how much the Italian army did in 1941 to help persecuted Jews and to save them from extermination camps.' Unfortunately, few want to remember those times, almost as if it was inopportune and inconvenient to revive an episode that compels admiration." A similar fate waited for the more than 600,000 soldiers who were captured by the Germans after the Armistice. Imprisoned under harsh conditions, at least one in ten did not survive. For the survivors, according to Enrico Deaglio, "When the war ended, for months and months, the Italian soldiers who had been deported to the Nazi camps after September 8 returned home. There were six hundred thousand of them, and they had been offered the chance to return home as free men if they would agree to wear the uniform of the Wehrmacht or the Republic of Salo. Only an infamous few accepted the offer, but their stories were not told. They were considered "strange beasts" that the postwar could not figure out how to categorize, and their collective experience has still not found its place in the history books." Unfortunately too little is known about how these soldiers expressed their contempt for Nazism at the cost of great personal sacrifice.[20]

German extermination units were made up of ordinary Germans, according to Daniel Goldhagen. He was convinced that Italians would not have acted as did the Germans executioners, saying that the notion that they would, "not only strains credulity beyond the breaking point but is also falsified by the actual historical record." That is a generous gesture toward the Italian military whose army often waged a brutal war, witness its conduct in Ethiopia. In many places, however, the Italian army recognized a common humanity that needed protection and contributed to a moral history of Italian society. The sharp difference between the German and Italian military when it came to their treatment of the Jews gives credence to the notion that the military reflected the wider society of which it was a part. With notable exceptions, the Italian military tried to help the Jews; with notable exceptions the German military participated in their destruction. Although echoes of anti–Semitism in contemporary Italy are disturbing, today's fringe anti–Semitism should be seen against the backdrop of what Leon Poliakov called "the imperishable glory of Italy that in all circles and in all administrative divisions there was evident, from the start, a tenacious resistance to the racial policy and its consequences."[21]

− 3 −
The Vatican and the Pope

> The effectiveness of a papal denunciation cannot be answered with absolute certitude. One thing is clear, however, by maintaining its thunderous silence and refusing to act, the Vatican bestowed a certain degree of legitimacy on Nazi atrocities.
> — Deborah Lipstadt, 1983

> They [the Italians] know exactly and fully about the atrocities taking place in Poland. We would like to utter words of fire against such actions and the only thing restraining Us from speaking is the fear of making the plight of the victims even worse. Where is Italian honor?
> — Pius XII, 1941

This chapter discusses only a few of the controversial issues surrounding the papacy during World War II. The "silence" of Pius XII has been examined by many historians, some sympathetic if not always kindly in their assessment of what they saw as his passiveness. Others go for the jugular, so to speak, giving him no leeway or credibility. An example of the former is *The Hidden Encyclical of Pius XI* by Georges Passelecq and Bernard Suchecky, and of the latter, John Cornwell's *Hitler's Pope*, closely followed by Michael Phayer's *The Catholic Church and the Holocaust 1930–1965* and Daniel Goldhagen's *A Moral Reckoning*. Michael O'Carroll's *Pius XII: Greatness Dishonored* may seem overly protective of Pius's reputation but, on the other hand, he deals with facts ignored by Pius's severe critics. To the extent possible, and in the words of the International Catholic–Jewish Historical Commission, these essays seek a more nuanced understanding of the role of the papacy during World War II and the Holocaust.

A bibliography of what has been written in English since the end of

World War II on this topic would be exhaustive. Adding what was written in Europe would make it encyclopedic. Fortunately, a good beginning has been made by William Doino in his annotated bibliography of many of the works, in English and several other languages, on Pius XII, World War II and the Holocaust. In this chapter the range of issues covered about the Vatican during the war is limited to some of the most salient ones, and the focus is mostly upon Italy. Other important issues that form the context of the Vatican's relationship with the Jewish community, such as the Vatican's relationship to the armed Italian resistance during the war and its role as mediator between the nascent political parties during the war remain in the background. Regardless of the scholarly and public interest in what the Vatican did, or did not do, during the war, this essay attests to the salience and importance many writers ascribed to the Papacy. Certainly it shows how the assessment of Pius XII has changed, most notably since the 1960s. Various reasons are given for the change, including anti–Catholicism. Whether that motivates some writers, one dynamic is clear: the rise of "revisionist" history. To appreciate the dramatic change in the historiography of the war, it is important to understand its context, which was a radical shift in the approach to interpreting World War II by a new generation of historians. Their approach went well beyond the usual and ordinary differences in historical interpretation commonly found among historians in the past.

The "revisionist" approach to history was allied with a literary theory of the 1960s called deconstruction that quickly spread into other academic disciplines. By focusing on what they called the "indeterminacy" of texts and therefore the importance of the writer assigning meaning to texts and events, deconstructionists taught an academic generation that all meaning was relative and "truth" was at best elusive and always subjective. Emphasis on the point of view of the historian's gender, class, race, and ideology enabled one to assert that history really is a form of identity politics and that any statements about the past were expressions of power. This meant that the so-called truths of yesterday were essentially political. The primacy of the individual's subjective vision of events denied there was something called "objectivity." An example of the result of this approach to reality was the comment by a prominent literary theorist, Professor Stanley Fish, who said that the death of objectivity "relieves me of the obligation to be right."

3—The Vatican and the Pope

Rolf Hochuth, whose drama *The Deputy* played such a large part in the revision of Pius XII's reputation, did not need formal instruction in deconstruction to achieve this ability: "To intuitively combine the already available facts into a truthful whole becomes the noble and rarely realized function of art.... The writer must hold fast to his freedom, which alone empowers him to give form to the matter." In other words, the writer can "intuitively" organize the facts into his "truthful whole," unhampered by whatever would limit his freedom. This was further explained in his "Sidelights on History" (an addendum to *The Deputy*) in which Hochuth noted that it was unusual "to burden a drama with an historical appendix," but he wanted the reader to know that he made extensive use of historical resources, although he said that "anyone who makes even the most modest effort to pick his way through the rubble ... of so-called historical events in order to reach the truth, the symbolic meaning—will find that the dramatist cannot use a single element of reality as he finds it; his work must be idealized in all its parts if he is to comprehend reality as a whole." While Hochuth claimed considerable knowledge of the relevant literature that was available before he wrote *The Deputy*, the paucity of references in "Sidelights" make it impossible for anyone to back up that claim, or to discover how he idealized the "single elements of reality" he mentioned in creating a drama allegedly based on historical sources. Hochuth deserves major credit for revising the reputation of Pius XII by writing for a popular audience interested in sensation and scandal, and influencing revisionist journalists like John Cornwell and Gary Wills as well as historians. Thanks to his success they now had carte blanche to follow the profitable trail blazed by Hochuth.

How this could be done was described by a former president of the American Historical Association, Professor Eric Foner of New York's Columbia University: "In the past twenty years American History has been remade. Inspired initially by the social movements of the 1960s and 1970s.... American historians redefined the very nature of historical study.... The study of American history today looks far different than it did a generation ago." Foner was not writing about the way history has changed (or been revised) over the centuries as new facts have been discovered. Nor was he referring to adapting knowledge about the past to a contemporary audience. For the benefit of a more readable text for contemporary readers, a writer might decide to replace the capitalized words in an eighteenth century text with lower case letters. Purists might object but the content of the revised text would be true to the meaning of the original. Contemporary "revisionists," on the other hand, have attacked the very meaning of what happened in the past based on their vision of what could or should have happened. When this is coupled to the widespread focus of academic history on issues of gender, class and race, there is the absence of careful and objective study of matters of international politics and the leaders of yesterday.

When discussing the development in history "of the revisionism in process during the late sixties," Professor Barton Bernstein, a prominent practitioner of the new history, said this new breed of historians "emphasize the ideological cleavages of the past more than did the historians of the fifties." The latter were so-called consensus historians who represented a more traditional approach to history although they often embraced sharply different interpretations of the past. In another context, referring to war in the Pacific, the influential historian John Dower said, "Participants in the events of a half century ago are still alive to tell their emotional tales." They are confronted by the skepticism and detachment of younger generations without memories of the war and historians "who develop new perspectives on the dynamics and significance of what took place." Later it will be evident that Dower's view of the memories of veterans also applies to Holocaust victims and others whose memories conflict with the claims of critics of the Vatican. Such revisionist history occurs even in the absence of evidence that the survivors' accounts are inaccurate because accuracy means less to a younger generation focused on what they believe are the dynamics and significance of what happened.

In another exegesis on revisionism Jack Davis said, "The mere selection of truths, an unavoidable process in doing history, jeopardized the objectivity of even the most conscientious historian." He decried "fact fetishists" who allow facts to get in the way of discerning what really happened, and claimed that the meaning of events depended on the subjective understanding of the commentator. This approach to history allows the creativity of the writer free rein. A notable practitioner of this style of history is Professor Susan Zuccotti who has been dismissive of what Dower called participants' emotional tales. Knowing better, Dower could dismiss the tales of veterans who claimed to know something about the war while Zuccotti dismissed the accounts told by Jewish survivors of Nazi ferocity.

3—The Vatican and the Pope

In both cases the scholars vigorously asserted the kind of historical conjectures usually found in historical novels, only to have them become part of the academic "consensus" about the war.

Revisionist historians in the West have changed the assessment of many aspects of World War II and the origin of the Cold War, emphasizing what they considered the excesses of American imperialism. The result in many ways parallels not only the way history was written and taught behind the Iron Curtain but how the Vatican's role in the war began to be reinterpreted. Progressive Western revisionist diplomatic historians accused the United States of heavy culpability for the Cold War, stemming from its failure to accommodate what they considered the legitimate interests of the Soviet Union, as well as because of America's imperialistic ambitions. In their view the Marshal Plan was not a generous, if not entirely altruistic, effort to restore Europe, but as did Stalin, they considered it a cynical plan to isolate the Soviet Union. Sidney Lens, one of many articulate proponents of such an interpretation of postwar history, found the United States had isolated the Soviet Union and ended any chance of an effective United Nations controlling the atom. The two foremost problems Soviet communism contended with since its revolution were, he said, "the threat of intervention by the Western powers and the need to acquire capital for reconstruction and development. It was from these earthy concerns, more than from ideology or the character of its leaders, that the communist system took shape."

In a surprising departure from his earlier radicalism, the novelist James T. Farrell, a prominent New York intellectual, countered, "The simple and blunt fact of the matter is that nothing stands in the way of the Stalinization of Europe but American power.... For thousands and millions of others, the question concerning Stalinism is a matter of actual survival. For the American capitalists, in effect, it's the same issue. It is for different reasons, but it is a question of survival." Farrell's was a dissident minority voice among intellectuals in the 1950s and remained as such in the reinterpretations of the past that became fashionable, and indeed dominant, in the historical profession in the decades to follow. While revisionists like Gabriel Kolko downplayed any threat from the USSR, contending that it was only interested in its own security, someone who was on the scene, John McCloy, who succeeded General Lucius Clay as military governor and high commissioner for Germany from 1949 to 1952, saw it differently.

McCloy pointed "to the spur which we always had at this stage — the fear of the Soviet Union, the fear of the Russians. There they were, across the way in Berlin, pressing. In those days we were always on an alert — reports always were coming down the line that a column was coming toward our eastern borders. Would they come through?" Soviet security was hardly compromised by the presence of the French, British and Americans in Berlin, but in an effort to have complete control of the city, the Soviets began a blockade of Berlin in April 1948 that led to the Berlin Airlift, which continued until September 1949. Conveniently consigned to the black hole of history, such matters can be ignored when writing history for today. It is little wonder that a changed historiography became the context for a similar approach to recasting the past in a niche area of history by academic Vaticanologists.

History was not the only academic discipline transformed by a new revisionist approach to the past. The flavor of what was happening in political science in the 1960s is found in a collection of dissenting essays about political science. The editors, Philip Green and Sanford Levinson, spoke of a new political science that "must be able to focus its vision on important political issues and events and it must be willing to confront rather than ignore the political ills of our own kind of social order." They went on to speak of "our own unwillingness to accept any longer the myths by which social order has been maintained." Just as in history, this approach became dominant in political science and served as the context for the analysis of domestic and foreign policy. Because it is often difficult to tell where one discipline ends and another begins, the revisionism of each is mutually reinforcing, and the reader is confronted by what seems to be a consensus of supposed authorities on the events of the war and its aftermath.[1]

* * *

When writing about what happened during the war, historians switch easily between the words "the Church," "the Vatican," and "the Pope." Although used interchangeably for convenience, or obfuscation, they refer to different entities. Very often a reference to the Vatican actually is intended for Pope Pius XII. Institutionally, some writers consider him responsible for all that happened in Vatican City and the Catholic Church on his watch, but it is important to distinguish between what an individual did or did not do, and what was done or not done by others in the institution. However, leaving such matters vague and ambiguous has the advantage of being able to imply guilt or responsibility without hard evidence.

Although repetitive, it is necessary to constantly be aware of the context in which the Vatican made decisions. Much of that context is the structure and mode of operation of the Vatican. They may be antediluvian and they certainly strike most observers as arcane, but they have been a crucial part of the Vatican's operations for centuries and change slowly if at all. An astute, and candid, reporter who covers the Vatican said what might have been said about the wartime Vatican. John Allen cautioned that, "For one thing, most business is conducted in Italian. Beyond that, there's the question of context. On the White House beat, a reference to something that happened in the Clinton administration is considered ancient history. Around the Vatican, it's nothing for officials to cite decisions made by regional church councils in the fourth century. If a reporter doesn't have at least some background in Church history and theology to make sense of such things, its a prescription for misunderstanding The result is that English-language reporters tend to rely on a stock set of great myths about the Vatican, recycling them endlessly in different combinations." What Allen said about reporters can apply even more strongly to historians.

Whenever the alleged "silence" of the Vatican is mentioned, the clear implication is that Pius XII was the guilty party. It also should be clear that in a manner not satisfactory to critics, many clergy and laity in the Church throughout Europe, and in the Vatican, including the Pope, did condemn Axis policies and atrocities during the war. And although the Vatican harbored both Axis and Allied sympathizers, the latter far outnumbered the former, so much so that like Ireland, the Vatican was considered neutral in favor of the Allies. A minor example was that during the war no American military, for example aviators who crashed or were forced to land in Ireland, were interned, although nationals of other belligerents were interned. In the Vatican, according to Anthony Cave Brown, "the Catholic hierarchs had entered into a friendly but unofficial liaison with Donovan and the OSS." Furthermore, persons in the Vatican gave the U.S. government's Office of Strategic Services reports of the Vatican's representatives in enemy countries, including Japan.

Another example of the Vatican's apparent tilt toward the Allies, as well as its nuanced attitude toward the USSR, appeared when President Roosevelt sought the Vatican's help because of American Catholic opposition to extending aid to Russia in the same manner as to Great Britain. The Vatican Secretariat of State told the Apostolic Delegate in Washington to have the American bishops explain that the encyclical *Divini Redemptoris*, which enjoined Catholics not to cooperate with Communist parties, did not apply to American help to Soviet Russia's war against Germany.

An instance of the Vatican seeking to facilitate peace efforts, as well as its neutrality in favor of the Allies, was told by Martin Quigley, an OSS agent in Rome. In late May 1945, he spoke to Msgr. Egidio Vagnozzi, a Vatican diplomat, about opening a discussion about peace through the Japanese ambassador to the Vatican. Vagnozzi did so and although skeptical, the Japanese ambassador to the Vatican, Ambassador Ken Harada, informed Tokyo about the overture on June 3, 1945.

Washington had broken the Japanese diplomatic code, and the result was called MAGIC; thus, Washington was aware of the matter as soon as Tokyo. For five days Ambassador Harada vainly waited for a reply from Tokyo and then on his own initiative asked Vagnozzi to contact Quigley about possible surrender terms. On his own, Quigley outlined some terms and they were sent to Tokyo on June 12. That the two cables were received in Tokyo was confirmed in 1972 in a letter to Quigley from Harada. However, Harada said Tokyo was determined to seek peace through the mediation of Moscow, an effort that he said began on July 12. Even more important was the intransigence of the Japanese army, which refused to surrender until the Emperor intervened and ended the war on August 14, 1945.

An earlier Vatican effort to end hostilities that favored the Allies involved Giuliano Vassalli, who belonged to a militant socialist resistance unit in Rome. Arrested in April 1944, he was held in the infamous SS Via Tasso prison awaiting execution. Through the intervention of the Vatican he was freed, but why is part of the story of papal effort to end hostilities. As early as May 1944, SS General Karl Wolff, who commanded the SS in Italy, approached the Vatican to discuss ending hostilities in Italy. As a sign of good faith, he was asked to free Vassalli and did so. Wolff's efforts then continued sporadically, but finally he met to negotiate surrender terms with Allen Dulles, the OSS chief in Switzerland. Objections by Stalin halted negotiations for a time, but with Operation SUNRISE the Germans were surrendered in Italy by Wolff a few days before Hitler's suicide. Vatican involvement leading up to SUNRISE was low key but consonant with its efforts to seek peace. Many years later revisionists saw the surrender as did Gabriel Kolko who considered SUNRISE politically inspired, arguing that it contributed to the Cold War. It was strange that he ignored that surrender negotiations began on the initiative of the German commander in Italy, so the "political" aspect, if any, began with a German. Lisle Rose saw it as "a clandestine surrender of Nazi forces," perhaps because he preferred to have such matters conducted in public. And Dante Puzzo believed that "London's apprehension of Soviet intrusion into Italian affairs was groundless." Behind the criticism of the "clandestine" surrender was the regret that the Soviets were not actively involved in the surrender as well as the belief that it was a factor in starting the Cold War because it exacerbated Soviet concerns about Allied intentions. That overlooked the fact that the Soviets, to their advantage, failed to alert their Allies to the surrender and occupation of Romania and Hungary. Bradley Smith and Elena Aga Rossi said that "we discovered few, in any of the revisionist contentions about Sunrise and the general characteristics of wartime policy, were borne out by the records of the policy makers.... There was, for example, no sign of significant influence from the State Department planners, who revisionists contended, were at the time preparing a bid to establish a worldwide system of American capitalistic influence in the post-war world."

Had Stalin not intervened, the German surrender in Italy might have occurred weeks earlier, as a result saving Allied, Italian civilian and German lives. Although criticized by some historians as too belated a surrender that did little to affect the war's outcome, an account by Allen Dulles reveals the complexity of the lengthy negotiations that ended hostilities. Wolff initiated the negotiations at considerable risk to himself, which led to his not being charged as a major war criminal, which he was. He did serve a sentence, however, although not long enough to satisfy those who wanted to see him in the dock at Nuremberg. Did his effort warrant the consideration he received despite his activities elsewhere? Dealing with Wolff saved the industrial infrastructure in Northern Italy, stopped the killing of Italian civilians and ended the Allies' daily casualty lists at least a few days earlier than anticipated. The soldiers who died fighting the Germans in the last few days of the war in the Po Valley would have had a more personal view of the importance of the surrender than historians Gabriel Kolko and Lisle Rose.

SUNRISE was one of many controversial deals the Allies made during the war that continue to disturb some historians. Another was the deal with Admiral François Darlan, the second in succession to Marshal Pétain in Vichy. When Operation TORCH began in November 1942, Darlan was in North Africa and, after fighting and negotiations, agreed to cooperate with the Allies, enabling them to land and to occupy French North Africa. Initially, large French naval, land and air force units had opposed the landing, causing heavy Allied losses. Dealing with Darlan was criticized because he was considered a French fascist. According to A.E. Campbell, Eisenhower entered the negotiations with Darlan "reluctantly and only in order to ease the landing of his forces.... The affair left a nasty taste in the mouth, contributed to a reputation for political naivete which dogged Eisenhower for years, and led many people in the United States, and in Britain, to wonder whether their leaders were losing sight of the object of the war." On the other hand, President Roosevelt, who had authorized dealing with Darlan, considered that the deal saved the lives of ten thousand American soldiers. Critics decry dealing with men like SS General Wolff and Admiral Darlan, what Italians call supping with the devil with a long spoon. Such deals continue to stalk the Allies, who were in a life or death struggle in which they balanced saving the lives of their men against tolerating dealing with unsavory, even despicable men. In quiet, risk-free seminar rooms it is easy for historians to say why they were wrong.[2]

* * *

The indictment of the "silence" of Pius XII about Nazi treatment of the Jews supposedly can be traced to his experience in Germany where he served as nuncio (Vatican representative) from 1917 to 1930. A persistent legend holds that Pacelli's fear of Communism can be traced to the Communist inspired riots he saw in Munich in the aftermath of World War I. According to historian John Lukacs, when Hitler invaded Russia, "Pope Pius XII, fearful of Communism ever since his experience in Munich in 1919, remained silent, as did the entire diplomatic and bureaucratic staff of the Vatican." Evidence of his positive feelings toward Germany reportedly are found in the concordat he negotiated with Germany in 1933 on behalf of Pius XI. There was nothing unusual about concordats, which existed between the Vatican and the earlier German states, as well as with many other countries. Pius XI wanted to have a formal, juridical relation with Germany, and when the new German government of Adolph Hitler signaled interest in drafting a concordat or treaty with the Vatican, after considerable negotiation one was signed in 1933. It was an effort to spell out the reciprocal rights and obligations of both parties regarding religious schools, hospitals and other Church institutions. This concordat has been source of endless debate and criticism of Pacelli, who had followed the orders of Pius XI to negotiate the agreement. John Cornwell's *Hitler's Pope* considered that the concordat was Pacelli's idea and "created a trust that was particularly significant in the developing struggle against international Jewry." It drew the Church into "complicity with the darkest forces of the era" and in the process destroyed the Catholic Center Party. In Italy the concordat called the Lateran Pact, according to David Kertzer, helped Mussolini because the Vatican, "decided that its best bet was to pull the plug on its own Catholic party and support Mussolini's more effective efforts to rid Italian society of the scourge of socialism." Both authors fail to inform their readers that in the later 1800s in Germany, France and Italy, anti-clerical governments were hostile to the Catholic Church, which perforce shaped Vatican policies vis-à-vis those governments. After World War I, Pius XI decided it was time for a strategic change.

In the background of the two controversial concordats was a change in Vatican policy regarding its so-called "confessional" political parties. For years in Germany, France and Italy there were Catholic political parties that contested with secular parties and governments to defend the interests of the Church as well as its social policies and programs. Pius XI sought, according to Anthony Rhodes, an end to reliance on the religious parties and to rely instead on Catholic Action, a new form of religiously inspired participation in society that he believed was more in the spirit of the times. His initiative led to the demise of the Catholic parties in France, Italy and Germany and reliance on formal agreements related to specifically Church-related matters. To the extent that the concordat with Germany and the one with Italy removed Church support for Germany's Catholic Center Party and the Catholic Popular Party in Italy, Cornwell has a point, in a sense they were a quid pro quo, but not to support Hitler or Mussolini. In each case the dissolution of the Catholic parties had unanticipated and unintended consequences that seem clear in hindsight. But the concordats were not intended to support the Nazis or Fascists and, in any event, it was inevitable that the Catholic parties would soon have been suppressed by the dictators. Instead of being applauded for assuming that the Vatican would rely on the rule of law, and advance the separation of Church and State by abstaining from politics, since clergy were told to stay out of politics, the concordats have been portrayed as collaboration with Fascism and Nazism.

Professor Michael Phayer's *The Catholic Church and the Holocaust* expressed a negative opinion about the German concordat, beginning his book with a jacket photo titled "The Concordat," showing a storm trooper with a whip and a man in red vestments (evidently a cardinal?) standing on a prostrate body with a Star of David on its chest, thus of a Jew. The message was clear: The German concordat opened the door to the Holocaust. It was an astute selling point that quickly told a reader what the book was about. The same was true of the jacket of John Cornwell's *Hitler's Pope,* which set the book's tone with a photo of the future Pius XII seemingly receiving the salute of two German soldiers in Berlin. Actually the photo was taken at a diplomatic reception in 1927. Giovanni Miccoli provided ammunition for both sides of the debate about the Pope's "silence," but his conclusions would disappoint John Cornwell and the others. The cover of Miccoli's book reproduced the 1927 picture of Pacelli on Cornwell's book, but shows clearly that the saluting "officer" really is a chauffeur and has other details that, strangely, are absent from Cornwell's picture. Miccoli might be faulted because few of the 492 items in his bibliography are by American or British writers. On the other hand 252 of them are in German and the rest are French (about 15 percent) and Italian (about 35 percent) Most of them could be relevant to an understanding of Vatican behavior during the war. The time Cornwell spent finding the deceptive photo was worthy of a paparazzi, and its use was hardly coincidental as he began a jeremiad.

One result of the concordat was, according to Anthony Read, "Cardinal Faulhaber who had been an outspoken critic of the Nazis was now ready to turn a blind eye to their excesses." That judgment was excessive and unwarranted but typical of the approach of many critics of the concordat. Anthony Rhodes also was critical of the German bishops and found the majority of their clergy wanting when it came to protesting what was happening to the Jews. On the issue of the concordat, however, he believed that it "brought some advantages, or at least prevented worse evils. In fact, in spite of all the violations to which it was subjected, it gave German Catholics a juridical basis for their defense, a stronghold behind which to shield themselves in the opposition to the ever-growing campaign of religious persecution."[3]

The German concordat was not the only "evidence" of Pius XII's alleged pro–German attitude. More came from what happened to the allegedly "secret" encyclical of his predecessor, Pius XI. For many years it has been known that Pius XI intended to issue an encyclical condemning racism that would supplement his encyclical of March 1937, *Mit Brennender Sorge* (With Burning Sorrow), that was a rejection of Nazism. Earlier, in 1931 his encyclical *Non abbiamo bisogno* was directed against Italian Fascism. The encyclical called it "a regime based on ideology which clearly resolves itself into a true and pagan worship of the state." His Christmas message of 1938 continued with the theme: "What is anti–Christian is inhuman: whether it is a matter of the common dignity of the human race, or a matter of the dignity, the freedom, or the integrity of the individual." On July 14, 1938, the Italian government publicized the "Manifesto della razza," signaling the beginning of its campaign against the Jews. On July 17, 1938, *L'Osservatore Romano* carried an article calling the Manifesto a form of apostasy and contrary to the faith of Christ. That clear rejection of anti–Semitism positioned the Vatican in opposition to the new Fascist campaign against the Jewish community.

The trajectory of Pius XI's thinking was clear and found expression in the draft of his new encyclical, some of which was prepared by an American Jesuit, John LaFarge, S.J. But the so-called secret encyclical was not issued because Pius XI became ill and died on February 9, 1939. So much has been known about what was a supposedly "secret" and "hidden" document that critics are stretching when they claim that Pius XII suppressed it to avoid offending Hitler. If that was his intent, he did not succeed because it was replaced by *Summi Pontificatus* in which Pius XII went beyond Pius XI in condemning racism.

As Pius XI's health declined, so did the political climate in which he thought about a document he commissioned months earlier. He died in early 1939, a turbulent year in which Germany annexed Austria and took the Sudetenland. Prime Minister Chamberlain went to Munich with all that implied, and, if any more evidence was needed of Nazi intentions, Kristallnacht signaled how Germany treated Jews. Pius XI was succeeded by Pius XII, who became pope on March 2, 1939. Also in March 1939 Czechoslovakia was dismembered, in August the Nazi-Soviet Pact was signed and then Germany invaded Poland on September 1, 1939, beginning World War II. The two popes were very different men who, as far as we know, worked together harmoniously for years. Pius XI was outspoken about the evils of Nazism, not hesitating to confront what he saw as a threat to more than the Church. Had he lived would he have continued that path and broken papal "silence?" His executive assistant chose not to follow that path when he became pope. Many attribute that to his positive attitude toward Germany and fear of bolshevism. Had Pius XI lived, they believe he would have continued to boldly confront Germany, but that is too simple because it does not consider that Pius XI would have had to deal with the war, something that drastically changed the situation for the Church and everyone else.

The new pontificate may have been fateful for the proposed encyclical not because of its content or fear of further alienating Germany, or the new pope's alleged pro–German attitude, but because of the times. Pius XII was said to have been unaware of the proposed encyclical, which is improbable because of his position close to Pius XI and because it was consonant with his thinking. That he had a hand in it is more plausible, according to Robert Leiber, S.J., who was private secretary and adviser to Pius XII on Germany. Referring to *Mit Brennender Sorge*, he wrote, "For that encyclical the then Cardinal Secretary of State Pacelli had almost the same responsibility as Pope Pius XI." If that was the case with the earlier encyclical, it is likely that he was more than aware of what was proposed by Pius XI in the new one. Furthermore, he would have known about it in order to be involved in the decision to shelve it.

Parts of the proposed encyclical's draft emphasized the unity of the human race while others return to philosophical and theological differences between Jews and Christians. Andrea Tornielli argued that, "Despite many clear paragraphs that condemned anti–Semitism and racism, the 'secret' encyclical repeated the traditional religious anti–Judaism of Christianity." Tornielli went on to say that propagandists in both Italy and Germany could have found elements in the draft encyclical to support their racial programs, the direct opposite of what had been intended. In any event, Pius XII did not chose to make it his own. Why a version of the "secret" encyclical was not issued led to David Kertzer's guess that the new pope "was eager to repair relations with Hitler, decided it was best to avoid any criticism of Nazi anti–Semitism." Saul Friedlander blamed the Jesuit General, Father Wladimir Ledochowski, for delaying sending the draft of the encyclical to the pope. Ledochowski was a fanatical anti–Communist, according to Friedlander and hoped, "some political arrangement with Nazi Germany remained possible." He supposedly held the draft until Pius XI was ill and unable to act on it. The same story was told by Gitta Sereny, who also blamed Father Ledochowski, whose fear of communism led him to hold the draft until it was too late to show to the pope before he died. Daniel Goldhagen weighed in with basically the same speculation, that the then Cardinal Pacelli negotiated "a treaty of cooperation" with Germany, and then when he became pope buried the "hidden encyclical" in the archives, thus "telling us a great deal about Pius XII, and about the dissimulations that have surrounded that Pope's and the Church's relationship to the Holocaust." Apart from Goldhagen's lurid prose, Tornielli and others hailed the decision to shelve a draft that attempted to straddle a gulf, retaining a traditional view of Judiasm yet condemning racism and persecution of the Jews.[4]

One also might consider that events outside the Vatican moved too fast, that Pius XII had other problems and priorities to deal with and those played a role in the decision to consign this not so "secret" document to the archives. From what is known about the might-have-been encyclical, thanks to Georges Passelecq and Bernard Suchecky, some have reason to believe the decision to shelve it regrettable. In view of what was happening in Europe and Asia, however, others may assume that the call was made for what seemed good reasons at the time. More than sixty years later anyone can speculate about the decision but might profit from what I.S.O. Playfair suggested to military historians, to avoid "the cloudy land of might-have-been, and not mistake our desks for the battlefield."[5]

With the advantage of access to hitherto unavailable Vatican records, Peter Godman documented that Pius XI and the future Pius XII, whatever else they may have done or not done, in the 1930s were well aware of the nature of Nazism and knew and scorned its racism as anti–Christian.

Reports prepared for Pius XI, and known to Pacelli, had recommended strong condemnation of the basic tenets of Nazism. There were internal debates about the wording, if, how and when the condemnation should be promulgated. Given the nature and importance of what was proposed, such deliberation was to be expected. Why the condemnation and the following "secret" encyclical were not promulgated is an important, but separate, issue. Godman shows beyond question that in the 1930s Pius XI and Pacelli were not in Hitler's corner and were not anti–Semitic. At the same time Godman was critical of their failure to publically and sufficiently assert what they knew was contrary to Catholic doctrine, more than once referring to the "notorious silence" of Pius XII.

Shortly after becoming Pope, in October 1939 Pius XII issued his first encyclical, *Summi Pontificatus*, that contained, according to Andrea Tornielli, many of the ideas of American Jesuit John LaFarge who worked on the "secret" encyclical of Pius XI. Unlike the earlier work, however, this one condemned racism and said nothing about anti–Judaism. The comparison between the draft "secret" encyclical and what was endorsed by the new pope is striking, and the latter must be considered his mature position and one that persisted throughout his tenure. There can be a debate whether he was articulate enough about his position, but the fact of his commitment to this philosophical and religious policy is undeniable.[6]

* * *

It also is undeniable that there were Catholic anti–Semites and age-old tensions between Jews and Catholics. That undoubtedly lessened the impact of formal papal pronouncements against anti–Semitism. Yet there are notable examples of Catholic clergy and laity, as well as Protestants and others, who risked their lives to help Jews. Convents, monasteries and churches sheltered Jews in Rome and elsewhere. My elderly Jewish landlord in Rome told me that he lived as a monk in a monastery for six months during the German occupation until Rome was liberated. In Milan, Odaliso Galli of the Psychology Laboratory of the Catholic University in Milan, told of hiding a Jewish engineer, Gino Sacerdote, during a visit by Roberto Farinacci, the viciously anti–Semitic editor and advisor to Mussolini. In Assisi the rescue work organized by Padre Rufino Niccacci saved scores of Jews. Nicola Caracciolo, who interviewed Jewish survivors who were helped in Assisi, reported the experiences of about fifty other Jews who received help elsewhere in Italy. These instances of aid are important but could do little to ameliorate the consequences of the massive attacks on Jews by the Germans and their Fascist allies.

The work of the Jewish underground in Genoa during the German occupation has been told in detail by Alexander Stille. Much of that was made possible because of the cooperation of the archbishop of Genoa and several of his priests who arranged hiding places for Jews and helped others escape to Switzerland. That several thousand Jews were saved from deportation and death was due to the bravery of scores of people, some of them Fascists, who risked their lives in the process.

The Vatican was able to assist many of Rome's Jews and others sought by the Germans through Father Pankratius Pfeiffer's intervention with the Germans. Father Pfeiffer, a German, served as the Pope's liaison between the Vatican and the Germans during their occupation of Rome. His work was recounted by Robert Graham, who wrote extensively on the Vatican's role in World War II. It is strange that Graham is rarely mentioned by writers about the Vatican during the war, perhaps due to the fact that much of his writing is in Italian. It is even stranger that Professor Phayer's companion piece to John Cornwell's *Hitler's Pope* referred to him as a Vatican "operative." Given the word's connotation, that depreciation of Graham's scholarship is unfortunate.[7]

An example of Vatican involvement in protecting Jews came from a November 1943 report by the Information Office of the Jewish Agency. It referred to the plight of Jewish refugees interned in a camp south of Naples at Ferramonti di Tarsia. "The internees were effectively protected by the Vatican against German interference. The camp was situated on the high road along which large German troop movements to and from the South took place, passed frightful days from the end of August until the arrival of the British troops on the 14th September 1943.... When retreating German troops attempted to enter the camp, they were opposed by Italian clergymen who explained to the Germans that the internees had been placed under the protection of the Vatican."

It should not be forgotten that Vatican intervention in Hungary at least moderated that government's treatment of the Jews until the German occupation. The story of Swedish diplomat Raoul Wallenberg overshadows that of other diplomats in Hungary who worked with him to rescue

Jews. Among them was Msgr. Gennaro Verolini of the Vatican nuncio's staff who, along with Wallenberg and others, saved some 120,000 Hungarian Jews. The efforts made by Wallenberg and other diplomats to save Hungary's Jews are a shining example of what could be done in some places.

Those efforts were outlined by Per Anger, who was Wallenberg's colleague in Budapest. Along with other diplomats, according to Anger, "Ever since the German occupation began, the nuncio, Bishop Angelo Rotta, had been making energetic representations to the Hungarian government to help the Jews. Rotta's actions were in stark contrast to the passivity shown by his chief, Pope Pius XII. During the persecution of the Jews in Italy, his silence was notable. As regards Hungary, Rotta had to work alone, without any particular support from the Vatican." Anger had no ax to grind but obviously was uninformed about the mandate Rotta received from Pius. It is clear that Anger believed Wallenberg was effectively abandoned by his government, and he did not like that policy, although as an insider intimately familiar with diplomacy, he understood it. He also did not like what he believed was Vatican policy, which he viewed as an outsider unaware of what the nuncio had been told by Rome.

Unfortunately, the legend of the lack of Vatican support persists in a book that honors Wallenberg's heroism. Anger served forty years in the Swedish diplomatic service and was candid when explaining the sometimes frustrating policies of his masters. That certainly was the case with the Wallenberg disappearance. The Swedish handling of their missing diplomat is a case study of how and why a nation acts for understandable if questionable reasons often with harsh consequences for individuals and their families. In Soviet occupied Hungary, conditions for foreigners deteriorated because of Soviet suspicion that they were Western spies. When the Swedish diplomats were allowed to leave, and by that time Wallenberg was imprisoned in the infamous Lubyanka prison in Moscow, they did not know if they would go to Siberia or go home. For diplomatic reasons Anger was told by the head of the Swedish mission in Moscow, "When you get home to Sweden — not one harsh word about the Russians." The Swedish government seemed loath to press Moscow for information about Wallenberg after Soviet Deputy Foreign Minister Vishinsky in 1947 said he was not on Soviet territory. Later it "seemed as though the new government came to feel that the Wallenberg matter was unpleasant, an especially disturbing factor in our relations with the Soviets." That situation continued for decades.[8]

Accounts of the Vatican's aid to the Jews, such as its willingness to contribute to the ransom the Nazis demanded from Rome's Jews, as well as its sheltering of many Jews, are often countered by writers as too little and too late. Knowing about the Vatican's intelligence network in the past, they assumed that early in the war the Vatican was well aware of what was happening in Poland and elsewhere, and contend that yet the pope did nothing. Robert Katz was critical of the pope in *Black Sabbath* and renewed his criticism in *The Battle for Rome*, while Rolf Hochhuth's play *Der Stellvertreter* (*The Deputy*, 1963) portrayed the pope guilty of silence in the face of the persecution of the Jews. Speaking of Hochhuth, SS Colonel Eugen Dollman, who was Himmler's representative in Rome during the German occupation, said, "The thesis of that comedy is inconsistent. Nobody did more for the Jews than the Pope.... One ought to add another consideration, keeping in mind Borman's plan: to take the Pope to Germany, which is that a public protest by the Vatican in defense of the Jews would have been a futile gesture. In fact, Hitler would have arrested and deported Eugenio Pacelli within twenty-four hours and the Jews would have suffered infinitely worse than what had happened until then."

That the abduction of the pope was more than a rumor is outlined by Giorgio Gariboldi in considerable detail. And according to Richard Lamb, there was incontrovertible evidence that Hitler was determined to occupy the Vatican. Lamb also considered Pius's opposition to Hitler impressive despite his refusal to risk a confrontation. After mentioning numerous actions by the pope in this regard, he said that the decision not to make a formal protest provided grounds for massive criticism of his silence, but ended by saying, "For better or worse, fear of reprisals governed Pius XII's actions during the German occupation of Rome from September 1943 to June 1944." It should be understood that the feared reprisals involved the citizenry and not the pope.[9]

Critics of the pope's "silence" probably would not be interested in the notes made by Msgr. Montini on May 13, 1940, when the pope met with the Italian ambassador to the Vatican. Ambassador Alfieri complained about telegrams of sympathy the pope sent to Belgium, Holland and Luxembourg when they were invaded by Germany. Mussolini saw them as a move against his policies, but the pope said, "The Italian Government knew that Germany intended to invade those countries; in fact they were aware of this since January." Montini went on to report, "The Holy Father also called attention to the fact that Italian honor itself was at stake. 'They [the Italians] know exactly and fully about the atrocities taking place in Poland. We would like to utter words of fire against such actions and the only thing restraining Us from speaking is the fear of making the plight of the victims even worse. Where is Italian honor?" *L'Osservatore Romano* published the messages on May 12 and also printed the pope's response to Ambassador Dino Alfieri on May 13, saying "We are not afraid of the concentration camp" (*"Non temiano di andare anche in un campo di concentramento"*). The government ordered the confiscation of copies of the paper, and its circulation in Italy fell from a hundred and fifty thousand to ten thousand. Even considering the privileged position of the Vatican, the consequences of crossing the Axis could be severe.

When Ambassador William Bullitt, the American ambassador to France, met with Cardinal Maglione on May 15, 1940, he spoke of anticipating Italy's entry into the war. To forestall that danger, Bullitt suggested that the pope threaten Mussolini with excommunication, and to excommunicate him if he dragged Italy into war. Aware of the perception of the excommunications of public figures, the more sophisticated diplomat told Bullitt that the pope should not be asked something impossible, which had been ridiculed for more than a century. A nuanced view of the Vatican's policy is found in Robert Graham's account of a February 1943 proposal by British intelligence to induce the pope to have the German and Austrian Bishops denounce the German government. When the British ambassador to the Vatican, d'Arcy Osborne, was asked his opinion he replied, "I believe there is not the most remote possibility of inducing the pope to take this step," adding that it would mean abandoning the jealously guarded principle of Vatican neutrality, as well as violating the caution and "passivity" of the pope. Graham said that Osborne might have added that the pope's policy was exactly the one that Osborne sought to persuade the Pope to follow since the early days of the war as the correct policy for the Vatican.

The question of Vatican neutrality became a moral issue for Professor Phayer as he recounted instances in which the Vatican acted as an intermediary to facilitate communication between Britain and German anti–Nazis but failed to condemn the German invasion of Poland, although in effect the pope condemned the invasion of the Low Countries much to the displeasure of Hitler and Mussolini. Of course, Phayer could have added to the Vatican's "violation" of neurality other examples, such as its covert neutrality in favor of the Allies, and other instances in which the Vatican acted counter to what some imagine "strict" neutrality would have required. The question will remain whether the Vatican's tilt in such cases made it wrong to practice a stricter neutrality vis-à-vis Germany. Purists like Professor Phayer ponder issues from an invulnerable ivory tower; pragmatists in the Vatican might have argued that in the latter case, assured Nazi retribution required a non-proactive stance. When Americans and British were not happy with a Vatican policy, they were not about to create more lebensraum to remind Rome who held the high cards.[10]

In December 1942 the Vatican was approached by groups seeking the elimination of Italy's Fascist government. While aware of the grave situation facing the nation, Vatican officials refused "any interference in the internal affairs of the Italian State." That neutral stance had been followed in Spain during the civil war. Despite the attacks on the Church by supporters of the Loyalist government, the Vatican kept its nuncio in Madrid until the war ended and only then recognized the Franco government.

As will be seen several times in the discussion of neutrality, the Vatican was not alone in trying to adhere to this policy. Historians might recall that in the first Roosevelt administration, neighboring Mexico engaged in a severe repression of the Catholic Church, something that evoked strong protests not only among American Catholics who were an important constituency of the President. Congressional and public pressure to act was rebuffed by FDR, whose Secretary of State said: "It would put our government in the position of claiming the right to say what the laws of another country should be in controlling internal affairs." In this case good relations with the rest of Latin America helped explain a policy that was seen as compromising by many of the president's constituents. It is instructive to compare that American policy with Giovanni Miccoli's view of a similar situation involving the Vatican as Nazi persecution of the Jews increased. After a Jewish appeal to the pope to protest what was happening, the Vatican asked Cesare Orsenigo, its nuncio in Berlin, what was happening. Miccoli saw as especially troubling the nuncio's response that it was because of a new law and that a protest would be seen as intervention in German affairs. Obviously people will differ in opinion whether the Vatican should have protested, even though in a similar circumstance, President Roosevelt did not.

Before the "phoney war" between the invasion of Poland and the war in the west in the spring of 1940, there was another attempt by the Vatican both to be neutral and to restore peace. In December 1939, influential Germans approached the Vatican with a plan to overthrow Hitler and seek peace. The pope passed a message to the British minister to the Vatican, "but made it clear that, while he felt it was his duty to transmit the message, his action must not be taken as implying any personal opinion in the matter." Nothing came of the approach, but British records show that the pope acted as a conduit between the parties and at the same time emphasized his neutrality.

The pope's insistence on neutrality was made clear to the Italian ambassador to the Vatican, Bernardo Attolico. When Mussolini sent his troops on their ill-fated mission to Russia, every effort was made to portray the campaign as a crusade against Bolshevism. Although many of the bishops, clergy and people were persuaded of this, the pope gave no indication of favoring the war in Russia. According to Attolico, "I can affirm that today the Italian Catholic world is with the Regime in the fight against Bolshevism. All, that is, except Pius XII."

However, not all Attolico's colleagues agreed with his optimistic view of support by the clergy, as was evident from complaints by the Minister of the Interior and the Minister of Education about lack of support by the clergy. Little wonder that Fascist officials were not as optimistic as the ambassador. The archives are replete with reports by the Italian military intelligence service (SIM) and the police about public attitudes about the war, the government, and so forth. Many reports gave government officials in a police state a candid if unwelcome overview of public opinion.

The Vatican knew that Hitler continued the persecution of the German Church and that the Germans forbade Italian and German military chaplains to hold services in churches in the occupied areas and otherwise hampered their work. The anti-religious policy of the Soviets was being continued by the Nazis. But when the Fascists encouraged churchmen to preach against the Soviets, the pope discouraged the Italian bishops from participating in anti–Communism manifestations. Not only did that reinforce the Vatican's stance of neutrality, it was at odds with the popular "fear of communism" theory presumed to explain the pope's "silence."

3—The Vatican and the Pope

Strict adherence to neutrality was evident from Giovanni Sale's description of Marshal Rudolfo Graziani's effort to obtain Vatican support for Mussolini's new Repubblica Sociale Italiana on September 25th, after he was rescued by the Germans. Meeting with a member of the Vatican's secretariat of state in mid–October 1943 while the Germans patrolled the walls of the Vatican, Graziani denounced the Armistice of September 8 as treason and also the Vatican's orientation toward the Allies. He acknowledged that Germany could not be "a paladin for a new Christian order" and that it was anti–Catholic and anti–Christian, but resolving relations with it could be left until after the war. Because the Allies were enemies of the Church, the Vatican should support or show sympathy for the Axis instead of waiting for the Allies. Graziani was told that the Vatican would remain neutral and could not enter so delicate and complex a political situation. That happened while Rome was occupied by the Nazis and the Fascists were in powerful positions in the city.[11]

To understand the context for that exchange, it helps to review what confronted the Vatican when the Germans occupied Rome on September 10, 1943. After Mussolini was deposed on July 25, the new government continued its formal alliance with Germany but secretly moved toward ending the alliance. Negotiations with the Allies continued until the Armistice of September 8, 1943, ended hostilities between the Allies and Italy. The Germans and many Italians saw that as a treasonous betrayal of an ally and the nation. After more than six decades it continues to be seen that way by a hard core of neo-fascists. Italy did not declare war on Germany until October 13, but the Armistice and the shift in allegiance to the Allies created terrible confusion among many Italians and resulted in divided loyalties that led to a civil war. Many Italians supported Mussolini's puppet Repubblica Sociale Italiana (Italian Social Republic or RSI), which was formed after Mussolini's rescue by the Germans. The RSI is better known as the Republic of Salo from the northern town that was Mussolini's headquarters. The RSI army was headed by Marshal Rudolfo Graziani and was an adjunct to the German army that occupied northern and much of central Italy. The Vatican, Spain and most foreign governments declined to recognize the Salo government although it was recognized diplomatically by Germany and its satellites. The Royal government headed by Marshal Pietro Badoglio fielded its own army that fought against the Germans. During the Allied occupation, first of southern and later of central Italy, its authority was gradually restored. But Rome remained in the hands of the Germans from September 1943 until June 1944.

The day after Mussolini's fall from power, Hitler broached the idea of seizing the Vatican and the pope because of suspected involvement in the coup that removed Il Duce. The idea was dropped, but not because of Vatican neutrality. Diplomats were unhappy with the idea, but their objections were ignored. Hitler was dissuaded by his military advisors because it could complicate the military occupation of the country. Seizing the pope was put on hold for a short time, but Hitler returned to it in September 1943 when he told SS General Karl Wolff, who headed the SS in Italy, to make plans to invade the Vatican and take the pope into custody. In December Hitler was persuaded that the idea would interfere with military operations and agreed to cancel the operation. Early in the planning phase the Vatican became aware of the plan when Wolff confided in the German ambassadors to Italy and the Vatican as well as Father Pancratius Pfeiffer, the pope's advisor on German matters. Wolff met with the pope in December 1944 to reassure him that the plan would not be activated.[12]

* * *

More context for understanding what influenced the Vatican's policies is the fact that there was an active, organized armed resistance against the Germans and Fascists in northern and central Italy. The Italian Communist Party (PCI) had joined with members of bitterly opposed political parties in a fragile coalition during the war, with most of them wanting to replace the monarchy when the war ended. For better or worse the Vatican faced not only the Germans and Fascists who were well-known quantities, but the emerging force of the resistance that formed part of the context with which the Allies and the Vatican had to deal from 1943 to 1945. The Communists were perhaps the largest and best organized element in the Resistenza. Robert Katz found that the Resistenza not only played an important role fighting the Germans: "In Italy in the last year of the war, a true reordering of social power had taken place. The Resistanza ... had become the de facto ruler of Italy. The socialist orientation of the institutions of the Resistenza had brought the country to the threshold of a full-scale, Bolshevik-style revolution. Indeed, the first phase of the revolution — the coming to power — had already been won, and only the 'Whites' remained to be subdued." There was more than a little hyperbole in that statement of the goal of the leftists in the coalition but for the extreme left it seemed possible.

A similar theme was sounded by Dante Puzzo in a well-written but tendentious book that maintained there was no mass insurrection in Rome because the Vatican sought to have Rome declared an open city, not to save the city but for fear that as the Germans retreated, the Partisans would take power before the Anglo-Americans arrived. He saw the liberation of Rome as marking the beginning of the real war in Italy. His account of the Resistance resembles that of Roberto Battaglia and others who saw the Resistanza as a revolutionary vanguard: "It was the working class and its vanguard party, the PCI — that conducted the basic offensive against the social demagogy of the so-called Republic of Salo." And according to Palmiro Togliatti, who headed the Italian Communist Party (PCI) after his return from the Soviet Union, "The working class saved the nation because that was its historic function as the soul and the moving force of the people" (quoted in Luigi Longo, *Chi ha tradito la resistanza*, p. 16). In the 1960s and 1970s that viewpoint was popular in Italy, with writers speaking of the Resistance betrayed because it did not achieve radical social change. The term "rivoluzione mancata" (failed revolution) faulted the leadership of the resistance for failing to seize the revolutionary moment in Northern Italy. The *Journal of Modern Italian Studies* in 1999 had several articles about the Resistance in Italy after September 1943. They are not as detailed but are more accessible than the many works in Italian on the subject and provide some background about the military and political roles the Resistenza played during the war. They also touch on what Spencer DiScala called "resistance mythology." That refers to the political coup by the Communist Party in claiming preeminence in the Resistance. Heated debates between political factions and academicians ensued that may be never ending. Such articles provide an overview of the context in which the Vatican maneuvered during the war and in the uncertain immediate postwar period.

In reality, according to Guido Quazza, "the rule of unity, imposed during the struggle against Nazism and fascism by the ever-present military dangers, prevented the left-wing parties from putting forward revolutionary objectives for the war of liberation. We must always bear in mind this basic point, in order to avoid making pointless criticisms of the

Resistance as a failed revolution: what never was a revolution cannot be a failed revolution ... despite the existence of genuine revolutionary ideas and forces within it. Judging by the percentage of left-wing participants, the Resistance was certainly a largely progressive movement. Not only were the communists, socialists and actionists in the majority, but they were also certainly the most active groups." Although it was true that resistance groups under Communist and Socialist auspices were the largest, their membership was not necessarily made up of party stalwarts. That in no way detracts from the contribution they made to the nation's liberation.[13]

What Puzzo said in 1992 about a failed opportunity for revolution ignored the reality of the situation in 1945. The Allies would have intervened forcefully had an insurrection been attempted, but factually the resources and conditions for one were not present even if absent the will of the Allies. That was known to the PCI leadership and the Committee of National Liberation that led the coalition. Those who regret a *rivoluzione mancata* might ponder the cases in which one did occur, in Poland, Czechoslovakia, and other places that ended behind the Iron Curtain. All of this was a prelude to postwar Italian politics, which continue to baffle political scientists who find it hard to understand a nation that from 1945 to the end of the century had fifty changes of government, yet remained a vital democracy.

The Vatican was well aware of the internal politics of the anti–Fascist resistance, partly because it played host to some of its leaders during the German occupation. It also was aware of Hitler's hostility toward the Church and had good reason to suspect that it might be occupied and the pope taken into German custody. That did not happen because the German military foresaw the negative consequences of such an action and advised against it. Although Stalin knew the pope had no divisions but only the Swiss Guard, his allies knew that obtaining any measure of public support from the Vatican would be priceless for propaganda purposes. The Germans knew the same and were aware that they could not expect Vatican support but at a minimum wanted no public criticism of their policies. In the face of all that was happening in Italy and elsewhere during the war, the Vatican maintained its formal policy of neutrality despite pressure from both sides.

The level of Vatican concern over its future appears in an exchange of messages between Ambassador Myron Taylor and the secretary of state

3—The Vatican and the Pope

in September 1944. On September 4, 1944, Ambassador Myron Taylor wrote the State Department that the Vatican asked about joining the new United Nations. Secretary Hull's response was that the question was premature. On September 18, 1944, Taylor asked a hypothetical question: If the Vatican applied, could it be denied and if admitted and its integrity was threatened by forcible aggression through Italian revolution or otherwise, would it be entitled to protection by armed forces? Hull answered that it would be undesirable to raise membership questions now but a lengthy cable made it clear that there would be opposition from the USSR and other places, as well as within the United States. However, if the Vatican State was victim of an aggressor it would be entitled to assistance, whether a UN member or not. The hypothetical question included a voicing of the Vatican's concern about the outcome of the war in Italy and its awareness of the understandable aim of the Communist Party to control the country, a concern that was hardly hypothetical at the time.

The assertion of Vatican neutrality was nowhere more evident than in March 1942 when the Vatican and Japan established formal diplomatic relations at the initiative of Japan. It is easy to understand why there were vigorous protests by the American and British governments. From a Vatican perspective, however, this was not a new or sudden move by Japan because in 1922 the Japanese government, which favored such a relation, had initiated talks about the arrangement, an effort that failed because of domestic opposition. Talks began again in 1939 and were finalized in March 1942. Although fully aware of Japanese aggression, the Vatican saw the move as favoring the interests of the 120,000 Catholics in Japan as well as the possible use of its good offices to seek peace.

* * *

Not at all defensive of Vatican policy was an account of Vatican diplomacy during the Holocaust by John Morley. His well-researched study raises serious questions about the Vatican's strategy in the face of what it knew about what was happening in Europe. According to John Pawlokowski, Morley interpreted the Vatican response to the attack on Poland, "as resulting from a certain primacy of the relationship with Germany in Vatican diplomatic circles." Morley had concluded that "reserve and prudence were the criterion of papal diplomacy, according to both the Pope and his secretary of state. It was a criterion that could not coexist with humanitarian concern." Further, "It must be concluded that Vatican diplomacy failed the Jews during the Holocaust by not doing all that it was possible for it to do on their behalf.... In neglecting the needs of the Jews, and pursuing a goal of reserve rather than humanitarian concern, it betrayed the ideals that it had set for itself." In a critical review, Robert Graham cited Morley's failure to mention the Jewish testimony about Vatican aid and referred to his oversimplification of the situation at the time.

One of Morley's most serious charges was that the pope's "reserve" was a betrayal of the Church's ideals. In other words, Pius XII was a moral failure. Regardless of the consequences, he should have damned the Nazis. Morley was not alone in this opinion. Professor Jose Sanchez thought that a strong papal protest against the destruction of the Jews very possibly would have had no effect upon their fate. However, "there can be no question that such a protest would have preserved the moral integrity of the papacy." And further, he asked if the pope protected German Catholics from persecution "at the cost of losing his moral reputation by not speaking out against the Nazis?" While serious scholars like Meir Michaelis have described the dire consequences of such an action, and how Pius's decisions saved lives, Morley and Sanchez preferred a dramatic gesture despite the probability that more innocents would suffer. Giovanni Macalli is another critic who provides a detailed history of the role of the Italian Church in relation to the racial laws and critically discusses the posture of Pope Pius XII.[14]

John Pawlikowski also faulted the pope's behavior, or lack thereof, during the war. He sought to place the Vatican's "diplomatic" approach to issues in what he saw as its context, referring to its social conservatism, which conditioned its view of what was happening. Because in many academic quarters the contemporary usage of the term "conservative" is pejorative, Pawlikowski should have spelled out what he meant by the term and how it influenced Vatican policy. Related to that historical attitude he said that currently, "The tendency to view certain groups as 'unfortunate expendables' in the effort to guarantee the survival of the Catholic community is gradually receding," implying that the attitude was stronger and probably in full flood during the war. He echoed historian Nora Levin's earlier attribution of papal policy to the fear of Bolshevism, which she believed led Pius XII to view the Jews as "unfortunate expendables." In

3—The Vatican and the Pope

both cases mere assertions without evidence are used to support a most serious charge against the Church and the pope.

Professor Monty Penkower traced the efforts to at least restrain the German campaign against the European Jews. His extensive research documents how Jewish organizations in Allied countries and in occupied Europe tried to influence Allied governments to save Jews but met with little success. The result was *The Jews Were Expendable* (1983). Penkower believed that the leaders of the West who could have checked the "demonic reality that was Auschwitz-Birkenau ... misjudged its dimensions and denied that the Jews were an entity meriting distinct consideration." He included Pius XII "who never excommunicated Catholic murderers in Germany and Hungary." The leaders (including the pope) were linked in "the abdication of moral responsibility to defenseless human beings." Professor Penkower made his case systematically and in great detail, presenting the Allies as viewing the Jewish tragedy in terms of their wartime and postwar goals. Although he recognized the difficulty of reconciling those goals, and limited Allied resources with the plight of the Jews, he was adamant in faulting the Allies and the papacy for what he considered their failure to exert themselves to help the "expendables."

As did Professor Penkower, Eric Sterling criticized Pius, seeing him as an "indifferent accomplice" to the Holocaust. "One Christian who has received much criticism for his apathy toward Jewish suffering is Pope Pius XII. His refusal to chastise Hitler publically for the mass murders provided an indirect sanction of the genocide.... Because he coveted his role as political pawnbroker and despised communist Russia, he allowed Hitler to continue murdering innocent Jews." Leaving aside the question of "pawn brokering" when power brokering would be more apt, it is stretching the facts, and the truth, to suggest that Pius allowed Hitler to continue his evil work and indirectly sanctioned genocide. Regrettably, those opinions are so embedded in consensus history that although no facts can sustain them, neither will facts persuade the authors of those opinions of their falsity.

Pawlikowski's agreement with Nora Levin about Pius did not go as far as Richard Rubenstein, who asked if the pope regarded the elimination of Europe's Jews as a benefit for European Christendom. Both harsh speculations about the pope's attitude lack any historical basis but like other conspiratorial theories enjoy support from those who appreciate simple explanations of complex and confusing events. By endorsing Levin's theory of papal fear of Bolshevism, Rubenstein demonstrated that merely stating it as a fact was enough for him and many others to indict the Vatican for a preference for Germany and for ignoring "unfortunate expendables." Scholars with a pretense of objectivity would have to agree that the Vatican had good reason to be apprehensive about Soviet Communism as did many other religions and nations, with Finland a case in point. But while there is plenty of speculation, there is no evidence that prudent apprehension led to favoring Germany or treating Jews as expendable.

Pawlokowski also believed that Robert Graham was uncritically defensive of the pope, writing in a "polemical context" intended to "dilute" the accusation that Pius was silent about the Jews and always giving Pius the benefit of the doubt. The "polemical context" was not explained. Much of Graham's writing appeared in *La Civiltà Cattolica*, a Jesuit journal, and in other Catholic magazines. Were they, to put it delicately, the "polemical context" referred to by Pawlikowski? If the provenance of a writer's work is at issue, and at times it is fair to do so, for example, if someone wrote a story that appeared in *Pravda* in 1938, that should be made clear to the reader. If that was what Pawlikowski meant, he should have said so; otherwise the term is too vague to have other than an invidious meaning. To learn more about the journal, he could consult Roberto Sani's "Un laboratorio politico e culturale: *La Civiltà Cattolica*," which outlines the journal's background and approach. Readers might better understand Graham's position, to which Pawlikowski devotes considerable attention and takes strong exception, had he referred to more than one short publication, little more than a pamphlet, as representative of Graham's extensive writing. If being "polemical" consists of writings that are seen as defensive of the papacy, no matter how factual they are, then certainly accusing Pius of regarding Europe's Jews as unfortunate expendables, without evidence, surely qualifies as "polemical" with or without a context. In his general assessment of writings in this area, Pawlikowski argues his case more carefully although like many other writers he views what happened in the 1940s through the lens of the 1960s and 1970s.[15]

In 1942 a coalition of nations including Brazil, Britain, the United States and others condemned Nazi treatment of the Jews and asked the Vatican to join them. Cardinal Hinsley of Britain was a sponsor of the statement, which received popular support. The pope did not join the denunciation but in his Christmas message the pope referred to abuses of human rights in general terms, but as a matter of policy did not do so in specific terms. The Vatican's diplomatic stance was known by the Allies, and by the Germans. Many, including Pawlikowski, saw the Vatican's stance as inadequate and problematic and wished that the Vatican had joined the condemnation. Although he may have wished for a condemnation, it is surprising that a serious historian would have expected the neutral Vatican to have joined in an explicit condemnation of Germany. That would have been a major coup for the Allies and elicited a vicious response from Hitler.

Pawlikowski thought that although the diplomatic model followed by Pius XII still exists, "there are now clear signs that the Church is beginning to put it aside as it speaks in a manner that unquestionably carries some measure of risk for its institutional well being." The underlying utopian assumption of Pawlikowski, and he is not alone, is that the Church of the 1940s should have accepted greater risks, which discounts the very real possibility that the result would have been great harm, not only to the Church but to those the Church sought to serve and defend. The empirical test of what Pawlikowski hoped for the Church to put aside was hardly possible in a country like Poland. After the war it was an example of the high risk attached not only to protests but anything the regime defined as opposition. And that continued for decades after the war. Jozef Tischner documented a situation in which, for ordinary citizens, "risk was associated with every decision." That was because a previously largely Catholic nation was to be forcibly transformed into a Marxist nation through measures as rigorous as any Poland endured under Nazi occupation. Under the constraints of a police state, Catholic philosophers sought a dialogue with Marxism but Tischner showed that Marxism, "became a thought aimed at a single goal—the justification of the existing system and its flaws as objective necessities." Their effort was not all in vain because coupled with the population's passive resistance and the workers' movements, Poland slowly moved toward freedom. The genuine risks all elements of the opposition faced eventually were overcome, but Tischner's account reveals the naivete of Pawlikowski's assumption that what succeeded decades later would have been meaningful in the 1940s under the Germans or in the 1950s when the Soviets were unconcerned about where their tanks traveled. While Pawlikowski understands that the Church of his day can speak as it wishes with little risk of retaliation against those it defends, he ignored the vastly different situation in the 1940s. That he knows this, but evidently finds it hard to accept, is evident when he quotes Gunther Lewy that a "flaming protest" by Pius "almost certainly would have made no appreciable dent in final Jewish death figures, and might have made matters worse for both Catholics and Jews."[16]

* * *

What did Pius XII know and when, about the Via Rasella bombing that killed more than 30 German soldiers and led to the Ardeatine Caves massacre in March 23, 1944? In reprisal the Germans executed 335 Italians, 77 of whom were Jews. The pope is charged with knowingly refraining from intervening with the Germans to stop the reprisal. A similar charge was his supposed failure to stop the roundup of more than one thousand Jews on October 16, 1943, which eventually led to the title of Professor Susan Zuccotti's *Under His Very Windows*. Raul Hilberg quoted those words of Ambassador Weizsaker when he reported to Berlin after the deportation of the Jews. Overlooked was what the ambassador had added to what he said about the Vatican's windows, "as it were," a small but not insignificant change in its meaning. Some dramatic license must be allowed in book titles although the seizure of Rome's Jews occurred in the neighborhood known as the old ghetto, which is at some distance from the Vatican's windows.

Robert Katz said that he learned from SS Colonel Dollman that the pope knew what was about to happen to the hostages for the Via Rasella incident. Based on the Katz story, Ray Moseley claimed that Pius XII, "apparently more concerned about armed Communists in Rome than about German reprisals, did not intervene in the matter." He made that assumption because *L'Osservatore Romano*, the Vatican newspaper, cautioned against "ill-judged violence" on March 24, the day after the executions. The Partisans in Rome included more than Communists, and it was too early for the paper to know which group did the bombing and thus did not refer to any particular group. Moseley's suggestion that the pope knew on March 23 what would happen to hostages on the following day was sheer guesswork. As an experienced reporter he knew better than to present that guess as fact. The Germans moved quickly to conduct their reprisal on the afternoon of March 24, leaving no time for intervention even if there had been some non-specific foreknowledge that something would happen to the Jewish community. Furthermore, Mosely did not tell his readers that the newspaper was not alone in decrying the bombing, because Partisan leaders did the same, nor did he tell them that Robert Graham quoted Dollman as follows: "Mr. Katz, whom I know very well, badly misunderstood me. I only said that I did not know if the Pope knew ahead of time. I am absolutely sure that the Pope would have intervened as he did for events much less important, if he had been told ahead of time of the military's plans."

When preparing the list of hostages for the reprisal, ten more hostages were listed for execution than the authorized number. An Italian official was told to remove ten names from the list and he deleted the names of two men at random and the names of eight Jews. According to Giacomo DeBenedetti, that action was criticized by some writers as discriminatory because it treated Jews as different. Just as Jews were seen as different by the Nazis, removing the Jews from the death list, although some might consider that act compassionate, actually accepted the idea of Jewish difference. Unfortunately, although saved from the Ardeatine massacre, later the Germans sent the Jewish men to a death camp and none survived. There is no way to know why someone took eight Jewish names off the list, but is it unreasonable to suggest that it was because he felt Jews did not belong on it?[17]

Unlike Katz, John Cornwell did not suggest that the pope had foreknowledge of the reprisal, saying "it is unlikely that any initiative taken by Pacelli would have achieved an effect." Then he added, "But the Pontiff had sent a signal to the partisans, if signal they needed, that he had no sympathy with their methods." Cornwell did not add, but should have known, that if that was the pope's intent he was not alone. Instead of leaving the impression that the pope somehow was aligned with the Germans, he could have reported that Partisan authorities believed that a disproportionate price was paid for an action that they had not sanctioned. In addition, an early Italian military court did not condemn the reprisal per se, but its indiscriminate nature. The debate about the justification for the bombing continued for years until it was officially resolved as a legitimate act of war, in favor of those who carried out the bombing.

Citing an article by Robert Graham, Cornwell wrote, "Defenders of Pacelli *claim* [my italics] that the papal go-between with the Germans,

Father Pankratius Pfeiffer, also attempted to plead with the German commander." As intended, the word "claim" raises a doubt about Graham's report and is a slur on the reputation of a meticulous scholar. Graham could make no rebuttal because he died before Cornwell's book was published. In fact, there is ample evidence that a protest was made by Pfeiffer. Adroitly avoiding readily available evidence of what happened, James Carroll wrote that the pope's defenders said he worked behind the scenes to help Jews, "but for now, suffice it to say that such assertions remain in dispute." We were not told by whom they were disputed, but by the time his book was published in 2001, had he consulted accurate accounts of what happened in Rome in October 1943, it would have settled the question of whether the "assertions" were disputable. As a research associate at Harvard writing a purported history of the Catholic Church and the Jews, and with easy access to its vast library resources, it is strange that he failed to take that step.[18]

* * *

John Cornwell's *Hitler's Pope* was well received by the media after an extensive marketing strategy that began with a clever mendacious title and a 1927 picture of Pius XII being saluted by what seemed to be a German officer, who turned out to be a chauffeur. The deliberately provocative title guaranteed the book would receive wide attention regardless of its merits. Cornwell presented what purported to be a psychological interpretation of the actions of a key figure in the wartime drama, something that has become popular among political scientists and historians who seek to lend an interdisciplinary flavor to their work, assuming that thus they can "know" historical personalities from such "evidence." It is one thing when persons with credentials in both history and psychology or psychiatry engage in psycho-history, and even then it is highly speculative; it is another when done casually by historians without credentials in another discipline. Others have done the same, including Professor Jose Sanchez, who described Pius XII as "shy, aloof, obliging, obsessed with triviality, with a tendency to postpone decisions … just the type of person a strong figure such as Hitler could manipulate." Cardinal Domenico Tardini, who worked for Pius for years, would have agreed that the pope was concerned about details, although not "obsessed" with them, and that he had a tendency to postpone decisions. The postponement, according to Tardini, usually was overnight. Much closer to the pope, he saw him as a strong but private person and hardly one to be manipulated by Hitler or anyone else. A better insight to the pope's style came from what he told Tardini on November 5, 1944: "I do not want collaborators, but executives." That did not mean the pope was dictatorial, but since the buck stopped with him, on a much smaller scale, he emulated Harry Truman.

Cornwell interpreted the alleged "silence" of Pius in the face of German atrocities based on a psychological profile he created. His conclusion was that Pius was an anti–Semite: "We are obliged to conclude that his silence had more to do with a habitual fear and distrust of the Jews than a strategy of diplomacy or a commitment to impartiality." One need not be a defender of the pope to realize what was Cornwell's agenda. Beyond the title he included this discovery about the pope: "The poses he struck in prayer put one in mind of a saint in a stained glass window." When describing a person at prayer, or engaged in any other action, calling it a "pose" is a calculated way of demeaning the behavior. Cornwell got the fact right: The pope prayed. His interpretation was that the act lacked authenticity because it was a pose. Although some day we might find that Pius XII actually was both a hypocrite and anti–Semite, Cornwell provides nothing factual to substantiate his conclusion that Pius was hypocritical or the conclusion that he was anti–Semitic.

Nothing in Cornwell's book documents those conclusions, so how was the portrait of Pius XII created? Like an old-fashioned Freudian, Cornwell began with Pacelli's childhood and interpreted it and selected incidents in his early career as formative of his behavior during his pontificate. But Cornwell had none of the advantages of the psychoanalyst who personally studied a patient long enough to clarify what may have been a life's formative episodes. Instead the reader gets speculation and advocacy surrounded by extensive endnotes and references to archives, and in this aura of scholarship his diagnosis may sound persuasive unless one asks for the solid facts on which it is it based. Their lack keeps us from the truth, and the end result is the same as a deliberate lie.

Erik Erikson, who did as much as anyone to develop psycho-history, urged its use with caution. "I would not wish to associate myself with all that is done in the name of this term," he said. "To a psycho historian, for example, it might be unnecessary to define what history was and is. Before long, then, his work may fuse with trends that may just as well be called psycho journalism or psychopolitics — and this is one of the less savory connotations of those words." In practicing a craft that relies heavily on conjecture, Cornwell presents himself as an expert witness, although it is evident that he has no qualification for such analysis. He found it easy to place Pius on the analytic couch and substitute shallow speculation and pop psychology for serious historical analysis. The result is a well-written exercise in an unsavory psychojournalism. Cornwell and others would benefit from reviewing the so-called Goldwater Rule of the American Psychiatric Association, which told its members it is unethical for members to give a professional opinion unless they have conducted an examination and been authorized to make such a statement.

Cornwell's assessment of Pius XII was seconded by Professor Kevin Madigan when reviewing *Hitler's Pope*. He found that the pope "was the kind of Catholic who could blithely finger his rosary ... while the SS, who were all too real, were rounding up more than one thousand Roman Jews a few hundred yards away for deportation eastward. And he could do these things while still aspiring, and probably believing himself to be, 'saintly,' or at least not failing on his job." By insinuating that the pope knew about and ignored the deportation of Rome's Jews, Madigan went beyond Cornwell and as he did in other venues, in the face of clear evidence that the roundup was not known in advance, repeated the falsification of the historical record and impugned the pope's religiosity.[19]

The related issue of the pope's reputed disinterest in what happened to Rome's Jews led to a misrepresentation of the record by Anthony Read when he referred to the Nazi roundup of Roman Jews in October 1943: "Although he failed to speak out and condemn the action — which might have prevented it — the Pope had personally ordered his clergy to open the Church's sanctuaries to non–Aryans in need of refuge." Martin Gilbert reportedly was the source for the reference to opening shelters to non–Aryans, but Gilbert did not say that the pope failed to speak out or intimated that he might have prevented it. When referring to the events of October 16, 1943, Gilbert wrote, "A few days earlier Pius XII had personally ordered the Vatican clergy to open the sanctuaries of Vatican City to all non–Aryans in need of refuge." At best Read made an unfortunate error when combining his unsubstantiated opinion and a quote from Gilbert that misrepresented the facts.

Another who blamed Pius for not stopping the deportation of those

3—The Vatican and the Pope

taken by the Germans was Fabio Della Seta: because he "adopted a policy of extreme prudence. He was a politician ... influenced by political considerations rather than by humanitarian concerns. A clamorous gesture on his part in the days following the rounding up of the Rome Jews could very probably have avoided their deportation." A similar story was told by Stanislao Pugliese: "Pius XII, when informed of the impending massacre, decided neither to intervene nor protest an outrageous act planned and committed within his temporal and spiritual domain." His reference also was to Robert Katz whose account, although authoritatively contradicted, keeps being cited by writers either unaware or unconcerned about his disinformation.

Could the pope have done more? According historian Charles Delzell, "the historian today can hardly escape the conclusion that Pius almost certainly could have done more than he did for the people of Rome — as well as for people everywhere. At the very least, he could have spoken out in October 1943 when the Nazis rounded up Rome's Jews almost in front of the gates of St. Peter's and sent them to concentration and death camps, and in March 1944 when they massacred 337 Italians in the Ardeatine Caves." Despite ample evidence that the pope had no foreknowledge of what the Germans intended, this myth continues to be recycled. Unfortunately, it unwittingly supports what Josef Goebbels, the master Nazi propagandist, said about the bigger the lie, the greater its popular credibility.

When they described what happened at the October 16, 1943, roundup of Jewish residents of the Roman ghetto, Deborah Dwork and Robert Jan van Pelt compared the behavior of the Vatican and that of the local religious communities in Rome. "Nowhere is the discrepancy between la grande eglise and la petite eglise more obvious than in Rome. While the silence of Pope Pius XII glares bright as the canonical example of tacit collusion and collaboration, a number of monasteries and convents offered refuge after a sudden razzia in Rome's ancient ghetto." In an endnote the authors questioned Father Robert Leiber's claim in *La Civiltà Cattolica* that religious institutions sheltered some four thousand Jews during the German occupation. The authors referred to his numbers as "these distorted figures." Their claim was based on the fact that in 1974, Leiber's figures had been challenged by Sam Waagenaar, and they concluded, "On the basis of our research, we find Waagenaar's refutation convincing. Pope Pius XII did nothing."

Waagenaar challenged the numbers on a list prepared by a Swiss Jesuit and given to Leiber, who in turn, gave the list to the Italian historian Renzo DeFelice who quoted it in *Storia degli ebrei italiani sotto il fascismo*. Waagenaar said some figures on the list seemed highly inflated, basing that conclusion on two cases, one of the number of 400 persons sheltered in the Church of San Bartalomeo, and the other of the number sheltered in the Vatican. The church was said to be too small to hold 400 persons for months, and he suggested that the number at best referred to some 400 Jews passing through the church during the occupation. That did not take much research, nor did it contradict Leiber who explained that some numbers on the list might have been for a short time or even duplications as individuals moved from one place to another. Waagenaar went on to say that "after much research it has been possible to discover the trail of only one family of eleven Jews who found a four months' 'illegal' haven within the Vatican walls." By emphasizing "illegal" Waagenaar was not referring to their status under international law, but making a point about Vatican insensitivity. To confirm the exaggeration of the Vatican as a safe haven for Jews, Waagennar said a priest who lived in the Vatican during the war told him that approximately forty men lived in his building, and all were Italian officers. Another person who was in the Vatican at the time told him she never saw any Jews there, apparently not even the only family Waagenaar found. He failed to tell readers that the Vatican proper was a warren of buildings that effectively sheltered many refugees, for example, Allied military escapees and political figures during the war.

The mere fact that someone was unaware that "illegals," including escaped Allied POWs, were hidden in the Vatican proper proves nothing. In addition, the two cases mentioned hardly qualify as convincing "research" although Dwork and van Pelt found it convincing enough when combined with whatever was their own unreported research. Compare that with Leiber's assertion that the figures on his list had been confirmed by "una ricerca nelle singole case" or research in the individual houses, referring to the religious houses or places that provided shelter. For example, 2,775 persons were sheltered by nuns in 100 institutions and 992 persons were sheltered by parishes or other houses of religious orders. After more than half a century there probably is no way to check the research mentioned by Waagenaar and Leiber. Neither man had any known reason to concoct a plausible argument pro or con the question of numbers sheltered. On balance, however, and considering the number of Allied POWs aided by Allied agents in Rome during the occupation (some 4,000), Leiber's account of several thousand Jews being sheltered by religious houses, and the numbers checked after the war, is more credible. One is free to question the provenance of that story, which is *Civiltà Cattolica*, although that may imply a commitment to ideology since to date there is no evidence of documented mendacity on Leiber's part. Richard Lamb, who is quite knowledgeable about wartime Italy, having served there during the war, said that, "According to Michael Tagliacozzo, the acknowledged leading authority on the episode, many were sheltered within the Vatican and another 4,238 in the monasteries and convents of Rome."

Sam Waagenaar's *The Pope's Jews* is a very readable story of the vicissitudes of Italian Jews throughout the ages. His overall discussion of the German occupation of Rome and the deportation of the Jews corresponds closely to what is found in other books. However, when discussing SS Lt. Colonel Herbert Kappler's extortion of 50 kilos of gold from the Jewish community, Waagenaar managed to be skeptical of the Vatican's offer to provide additional gold if enough could not be raised by Kappler's deadline. "Although the coffers inside the German-surrounded walls were probably well stocked, there was no offer to help out with the full amount or weight (which of course had not been asked for either): but under the circumstances would have made things considerably easier for the hard-pressed Jews of Rome, and would have saved them many anxious hours."

Another more than skeptical innuendo about how the Vatican responded to the plight of the Jewish community is found in Uki Goni's *The Real ODESSA*: "An appeal for aid from the Vatican, however, brought forth only the half-hearted offer of a 'loan,' but Kappler's quota was finally met without dipping into the Vatican's coffers." Waagenaar went on to suggest that the Vatican's reluctance to criticize Germany was due to concern over the receipt of its share of religious taxes, which had continued during the war. "It would be difficult, if not impossible, to believe that financial considerations could have entered the mind of the Pope himself in deciding on matters of humanity. Yet in view of the huge amount of money involved ... the influence of this material dilemma might possibly have received a certain consideration in other Vatican circles." While the author said it was doubtful that the pope would be influenced by that money, on the other hand it was definitely implied that it could have influenced the pope's associates and thus the Vatican's alleged tilt toward Germany.

After contesting the number of Jews Robert Leiber said were sheltered by Vatican institutions during the occupation, Waagenaar continued, identifying Leiber and Monsignor Ludwig Hudal as German Jesuits. It may be a small point, but while Leiber was a Jesuit, Hudal was not, and his first name was Alois, not Ludwig, and he was a bishop, not a lower ranking monsignor. Although Waagenaar noted that Hudal wrote to the German general commanding Rome at the request of a "close collaborator of the Pope," he added, "If a simple monsignor could have obtained such results, how much more effective might have been words from the pope himself!" Because the background of this tragedy was well known soon after the war, Waagenaar should have known that Hudal's letter was not sent on his initiative or that of a "collaborator of the Pope," on the pope's initiative. Even Professor Susan Zuccotti, an ardent critic of Pius said the pope "permitted" Hudal to write a "mild letter" to the German general commanding in Rome. Both writers should have known that the initiative for Hudal's letter came from the pope, and in the interest of fairness that information should have been shared with their readers.

Dwork and van Pelt's extensively researched study of the Holocaust lacks balance when dealing with Pius XII. They relied only on books critical of Pius, overlooking or ignoring others like Carroll-Abbing's book published in 1965, thus available before Waagenaar's book that appeared in 1974, that supports Leiber's numbers. Ignoring or overlooking contrary evidence is tantamount to its suppression so far as authentic history is concerned. Italian and English language sources that have a different view of the actions of Pius during the tragedy of October 16, 1943, counter the authors' claim that Pius tacitly colluded and collaborated with the Nazis occupying Rome. Authentic history requires evidence to back up such claims. Quibbling about numbers sheltered does not advance our understanding of what happened that October in Rome. The exact number of persons sheltered can never be known because at the time it would have been folly to conduct a census, but reasonable estimates by reliable sources suggest that at least several thousand Jews were sheltered by religious institutions. Thanks to them and the many families and individuals who also offered shelter, most Roman Jews had a chance to survive the onslaught of the Nazis.[20]

3—The Vatican and the Pope

The German action to clear Rome's ghetto, which Hitler ordered, took place on the night between October 15 and 16. Of the 1259 persons arrested, many were women and children. When the Vatican learned of this on the morning of October 16, it protested to Ambassador Weizsacher, the German ambassador to the Vatican. As a result, the arrests ended, although those already imprisoned were sent to extermination camps. In its note the Vatican said that persons were made to suffer because they belonged to *una determinata stirpe*, which can be translated as "of a certain descent" (or race). Later when *L'Osservatore Romano* wrote about the incident, which Professor Zuccotti said unmistakably referred to seizing the Jews, she noted that the paper used the word *stirpe* instead of the word religion. For her this supposedly revealed the Vatican's questionable attitude toward the Jews. Andrea Grover referred to the "oft-cited message that Pius XII penned for the October 29, 1943 issue [of *L'Osservatore Romano*] in which — it is generally assumed — he referred obliquely to the Nazi round-up of one thousand Roman Jews." Professor Grover also cited the Italian text, which refers to *stirpe* and *di confessione religiosa* (of religious confession).

The implication is that *L'Osservatore* and the Vatican should have said that persons suffered because they were Jewish. The paper had used the word as the Vatican did earlier in its protest to Ambassador von Weizsacker, who clearly understood the message as specifically referring to Roman Jews and it helped reverse the decision to clear the remaining Jews from Rome. It should be recalled that the 1938 *Manifesto della razza* referred to race and not religion. In fact, in laws implementing anti–Jewish policies, Italians were told Jews belonged to a race and not to interfere with Jewish religious practice. Because Italians used the word *stirpe* to refer to race, it would be reasonable to have *L'Osservatore* do the same. That the Vatican was consistent in its use of the term is evident from a 1938 instruction by Pius XI to Catholic Universities and Seminaries. They were to refute "Ridiculous Dogmas," of Nazism and Fascism, one of which was that "human races are so different ... that the least of them differs more from the supreme race of men than from the highest species of animals." The original Latin begins *Stirpes humanae* (human races). The word was understood as it was intended by Ambassador Weizsacker and by readers of *L'Osservatore Romano*, if not by Zuccotti who misinterpreted its use decades later.[21]

Between 1952 and 1953, Antonio Spinosa wrote several articles in the journal *Il Ponte* that named writers and others who promoted the racial laws. He also was critical of the Church for its silence about the treatment of the Jews. However, in a 1994 book Spinosa reconsidered what he said earlier as well as the positions taken by Rolf Hochuth, and by Robert Katz who, in his *Death in Rome* reproached Pius XII for inaction at the time of the Ardeatine massacre. In Spinosa's 1994 introduction he said that the major accusation against the pope had been that knowing that the Germans intended a reprisal, the pope "refused to raise a finger." Spinosa said that, "In reality matters were very different. The German command carried out the reprisal in a very short time. The extreme rapidity of the action gave nobody time to intervene."

* * *

Thanks to the Center for Cryptologic History of the National Security Agency there now is a valuable guide to Western communications intelligence during the Holocaust. The author of *Eavesdropping on Hell*, Robert Hanyok, showed that early in the German occupation of Rome an intercepted message to Dublin by the Irish minister to Italy told of a German demand that Rome's Jewish community supply the Germans 50 kilos of gold. The message also said the "Vatican offered help" although no specific help from that source was mentioned. A further reference was made to the Vatican in this connection in Hanyok's note 34. "It is not clear what was the nature of the Vatican's aid, or from where the Vatican hierarchy (if from there at all) this offer originated." What this note meant by "if from there at all," is not clear without parsing it and asking the purpose of the parenthetical interpolation. We may wish that the Irish minister talked to his confreres in Dublin at greater length and gave more details about an alleged Vatican offer of help, but cryptologists know that such messages tend to convey meanings in a terse format. When the Irish minister merely referred to Vatican help, why did Hanyok wonder "if from there at all"? It is well to be skeptical, but is there any evidence that the Irish diplomat was repeating a mere rumor or what? That the minister did not specify the nature of the help did not need to pose a problem for Honyok because the context of the message allows a reasonable inference that the reference was to the extortion of gold from the Jewish community. Beyond that Hanyok easily could have discovered that, in

3—The Vatican and the Pope

well-authenticated fact, gold was offered by the Vatican but it was not needed. One of the many sources readily obtainable was a diary of the German occupation kept by Jane Scrivener who told how on September 28, 1943, Rome's Jews were told to deliver one million lire and fifty kilograms of gold to the Germans, otherwise some would be deported and others shot. Although she believed that the pope contributed gold to satisfy the extortion, that was not necessary. Fabio Della Seta is another who mentioned Vatican willingness to assist the Jewish community: "Jewish leaders received an offer whereby the Vatican proposed making a concrete contribution. The offer was turned down because the contribution proved to be unnecessary — but the moral value of the gesture remains." It is regrettable that Hanyok left dangling the implication that the Vatican was not involved in this matter. Another who failed to tell the complete story of Vatican involvement was Professor Andrea Grover: "The Gestapo gave the Roman Jews until September 28 to deliver a levy of fifty kilos of gold. As the deadline approached, Pius XII remained silent." Instead of a pointless protest that would be ignored by the Germans, the pope offered to assist the Jews who were raising the gold. It is strange that such a well-documented bit of history was overlooked by Grover and as a result casts a mistaken light on the episode.

Hanyok's note 34 went on: "The role of the Vatican during this roundup has been the subject of much controversy. A number of Catholic clergy and institutions, as well as many individual Italians, aided Jews by offering sanctuary or the means to escape the Nazi dragnet. These actions appear to have happened spontaneously, or at the least, without any explicit instructions from Vatican leadership. There is no evidence from the translations that any official policy of rescue originated in or was coordinated by the Papacy or its office even though it was informed of the impending German actions. See Susan Zuccotti, *Under His Very Windows: The Vatican and the Holocaust in Italy*. A more critical view of the Papacy's role during the roundup is offered by John Cornwell in *Hitler's Pope: The Secret History of Pius XII*.... The archived decrypts and translations contain no evidence that conclusively can resolve the controversy over the Vatican's official policy towards the Final Solution."

There are at least two contested issues here. One is whether the Vatican knew of the impending roundup of Rome's Jews and the other is whether thep ordered sanctuary to the Jews to prevent their capture. With regard to the latter issue, the reader is treated to the missing written order scenario of David Irving. The lack of a written order was urged by Professor Zuccotti as proof the pope did not lift a finger for Rome's Jews. Hanyok limited the lack of evidence of an order to decrypts of communications, but many readers could jump to the conclusion there simply was no evidence of an official policy of helping Rome's Jews. What competent historian would have expected to find such evidence in messages of the kind Hanyok was dealing with? Why would those messages refer to a verbal or written order from the Vatican? Hanyok probably was unaware of the testimony of Msgr. John Carroll-Abbing about the verbal order to help Jews that he received from the pope. Zuccotti knew of that claim but decided it was less than credible, but gave no reason for doing so. Whether considered credible or not by the two authors cited, a United States government document deemed authoritative by many readers should not deny them another side of the story from reputable sources.

Hanyok's claim that "the Papacy or its office ... was informed of the impending German action" starkly indicts the pope as knowing but failing to warn Rome's Jews about the impending disaster. We do know from Leonidas Hill that early in the occupation Weizsacker sent a message through an intermediary to leading members of the Jewish community alerting them that police measures against Jews would be carried out shortly after the occupation of Rome began. That also was mentioned by Robert Katz. However, the Germans waited for more than a month after the occupation began and started the roundup on October 16. Some who were warned went into hiding, others could not accept the story and some did not get the message. While someone in the Vatican may have been told about the Germans' plans, the timing of the action was not known. Now we know when and how preparations were made thanks to Robert Katz's story of the decoding of messages implementing the roundup. That knowledge came long after the event. Katz asked "Could the Allies have alerted the Roman Jews, without revealing their vital capability for interception? Would the Jews have believed them? The researcher is unlikely to find those answers in the CIA papers." He added, "In Rome and the Vatican — and now we know, in London and Washington as well — countless individuals in a position to lift their voice ... either in warning or protest, waited in silence ... but in the harsh reality were mute witnesses to a pre-announced journey to a gas chamber." Katz hammered home his point

3 — The Vatican and the Pope

that London, Washington and the Vatican "waited in silence" for what happened on October 15, implying that somehow they could have prevented the roundup. His readers will find him silent about what realistically could have been done.

As Katz and any other historian of World War II would know, the Allies often had to accept losses to prevent the compromise of the interception of ULTRA and MAGIC, an unfortunate but essential compromise if they were to continue their intercepts. As a long time student of the occupation of Rome, Katz teases with a rhetorical question, the answer to which he surely knows. Given the timing, the situation in Rome and other factors, including the risk of compromising vital intelligence gathering, the only answer could be no. His accusation that the Vatican, London and Washington were in a position to warn or protest misrepresents what was possible in Rome as well as in the Allied capitals. As a long time student of wartime Rome, he cannot fail to know the answer to his question and wishes had been otherwise. Instead he does not present the context for what happened and plays on the emotions of readers who depend on historians to level with them about the "harsh reality" of intervening far beyond enemy lines.

Hanyok might seem to be on firmer ground when he ended note 34 saying that the archived material cannot conclusively resolve the Vatican's policy. However, he referred not to supplying gold to Rome's Jewish community but instead to its policy toward the Final Solution. The latter is an entirely different matter that goes far beyond the tragic episode in Rome that cost so many lives. If reference to the roundup was intended, few historians would expect intercepts between Rome and Dublin or between Germans in Rome and in Germany to provide the full story of what happened. This decades old controversy was reanimated in the 1990s by Zuccotti and Cornwell. It is unfortunate that their tendentious books are the only ones that this government document refers to, presumably as knowledgeable and authoritative, about such a contested issue. It is even more difficult to understand the relevance of the reference to the Final Solution as if intercepts about what happened in October 1943 in Rome would shed light on Vatican policy relative to the murder of Europe's Jews. Readily available resources at the Library of Congress to the south of Fort Meade, the home of the National Security Agency, or at the National Archives at College Park just a few miles north of Fort Meade, could have clarified the situation for the Hanyok. What others have written about the tragedy should not be overlooked or ignored in an official government document that, by its very nature, will be accepted as authoritative by many readers.

With regard to the alleged foreknowledge of the roundup of the Jews, rebuttals of that story make no impression on those who repeat it. Professor Susan Zuccotti said, "evidence strongly suggests [*sic*] he [Pius XII] was aware of plans for a round up at least a week before it actually took place." Also, "In fact, the Pope *seems* to have learned about the impending roundup by at least October 9." If it seemed that he knew, why call it a fact? Continuing with her surmises, in another place Zuccotti said, "By the end of 1942 the Pope *almost certainly*" received reports of the gassings at Belzec. Berel Lang found almost inexplicable "the failure of the Vatican, which almost certainly knew of the impending roundup before it happened, to convey a warning to the Rome Jewish community — a warning that would have allowed them to go into hiding." Various sources suggest that a roundup was planned some time in the future, but there is nothing but an opinion "strongly suggesting" that the pope knew a week before the actual roundup. The same is true of the "almost certainly," used by Lang who referred to Ambassador Weizsacker's report to Berlin that the pope did not make any "demonstrative statements against deportation," as an indication of his less than positive attitude toward the Jews. True, no "demonstrative statements" were made, but Lang ignored the pope's intervention that spared the rest of Rome's Jews. One may speculate about why the Germans persisted in deporting the first group they captured, but surely the Vatican's intervention was worth more than a "demonstrative" statement. Knowing as we do that Weizsacker tended to put a positive spin on reports about Vatican/German relations, Lang might have been somewhat skeptical of what he told Berlin. About the same time as Lang, Kevin Madigan made the same reference to Weizsacker's report to Berlin about the deportation, adding "not a word of protest was heard." While it is true that nothing was said publicly, which would have been fruitless, Professor Madigan ignored the Vatican's intervention that meant the rest of Rome's Jews were not deported. Unfortunately his reliance on secondary sources, which either through ignorance or intention did not provide the full story of this tragic episode, also led him to tell his readers a partial and deceptive account of what happened. Professor Madigan went on to

3—The Vatican and the Pope

damn with faint praise: "Moreover, although he [Pius XII] never actively approved of Hitler and was far from being a philo–Semitic, he did do and say something (if not with vigor) on behalf of threatened Jews."

What about the ambassador's message to Berlin? According to Leonidas Hill, Pius knew that his "silence" in this matter would hurt him with the Allies. And despite Weizsacker's report that the story in *L'Osservatore Romano* was so "tortuous and obscure" that few would know it referred to the Jews, Hill said Weizsacker must have known that was untrue because he wrote that similar messages obviously referred to Germany. The Vatican's quid pro quo was "silence" for the lives of the remaining Jews in Rome.

The plight of Hungary's Jews gave *Eavesdropping* another opportunity to raise a question that has been disputed for years without an agreed upon resolution: whether only converted Jews were of concern to the Vatican. Rebuttals based on available evidence have been ignored or their authenticity questioned and the controversy continues. Thus, what follows is not directly but by implication related to the Vatican's policy. In September 1944 an effort was made to send Jewish children to hospitals in Sweden and Switzerland, but the Germans required that "the first train out of Budapest contained only 'Aryan' children (possibly a reference to baptized Jews)." In October despite the holdup of the train with Jewish children, the Swiss recommended to Bern that the train with the Christian children, of whom 40 percent were converts, be sent. "We recommend saving as many children as possible," the diplomats informed Bern. It is not known if this rescue effort was successful. Hanyok's interpolation of "possibly a reference to baptized Jews" may be explained by the reference to Christian children, of whom 40 percent were converts. But the reference to the "first train" mentioned only Aryan children, and the parenthetical, "possibly a reference to baptized Jews," was not in the original message. No reason was given for adding that gratuitous comment. Without any evidence to support it, and intentionally or not, it feeds the continuing controversy. What Hanyok did not acknowledge was that only the Germans controlled the fate of whoever these unfortunate children were.[22]

– 4 –
Papal "Silence" and "Fear of Communism"

> Could it be that Pius regarded the demographic elimination of Europe's Jews as a benefit for European Christendom?
> — Richard Rubenstein, 2002
>
> The pope abdicated his right as a leader of the Catholic church to make pronouncements based on moral principle.
> — Michael Phayer, 2000

In the preface to Antonio Spinosa's book about Mussolini as a reluctant racist, Francesco Prefetti said that Spinosa, "came to the conclusion that the image of Pius XII as the 'Pope of silence' is substantially unjust." Essentially the same conclusion was reached by Giorgio Angelozzi Gariboldi in a lengthy and detailed report on the Via Rasella incident and its aftermath. He showed that there was no time for papal intervention and that despite rumors, the pope did not learn of what happened until March 25, the day after the massacre. One of the best assessments of the Vatican's actions during the German occupation came from Meir Michaelis. Obviously wishing that Pius XII had done more, Michaelis nonetheless showed the dilemmas facing the pope and the unfairness of the criticisms leveled by Hochuth and others.

During the recent spate of books about the "silence" of Pius XII, Gary Wills returned to the fray with *Papal Sin,* in which he was blunt: "Pius never explained his silence on the Holocaust since he claimed there no silence to be accounted for." On August 3, 1946, for instance, Wills noted that the pope said, "We condemned on various occasions in the past the persecution of that fanatical anti–Semitism inflicted on the Hebrew people." Wills added, "That was a deliberate falsehood. He never mentioned the Holocaust." Wills is a masterful writer, but did he mean that Pius did not use the word Holocaust, or did he deny that Pius ever referred to the mass killing of Jews by the Nazis? The word "Holocaust" came into use after the war so it would not have been used earlier. Evidently Wills meant that Pius never referred to mass killings of Jews, and the pope's statement was a deliberate prevarication. Historians who know the pope's record, whether critical or not, would not go that far without evidence.[1]

If one assumed that Pius XII was aware of Auschwitz and what the Germans intended to do at the Ardeatine Caves, would his intervention, complaint or condemnation have made any difference to what happened? In Robert Katz's opinion, "Long ago, in the first storm over the silence, one of Pius's subtlest critics, historian Leon Poliakov — later to be joined by many Catholic writers — stated plainly that the Pope should have lifted his voice simply because it was the morally right thing to do, whatever the consequences. More than ever that appears to be the judgement of history." That opinion was shared by Deborah Lipstadt: "The effectiveness of a papal denunciation cannot be answered with absolute certitude. One thing is clear, however. By maintaining its thunderous silence and refusing to act, the Vatican bestowed a certain degree of legitimacy on Nazi atrocities."

Apart from Deborah Lipstadt's fatuous assertion about the Vatican bestowing legitimacy on Nazi atrocities, it is true that we do not know for certain what the result of a particular denunciation would have been. However, based on prior experience with the Germans, the only possible conclusion with 99.9 percent certainty, is that it would not positively influence German behavior. SS Colonel Eugen Dollman, who was not merely speculating, assures us that Hitler would have reacted violently. Of course not only the pope declined to speak about all he knew. In September 1942 there was a report that the Germans were using mobile gas chambers to kill Jews in Poland. Owen Chadwick explained that there was a proposal to air the fact in the House of Commons, but the Polish government in exile "preferred nothing be said in the House of Commons, lest it risk lives in Poland.... The British government, like the Pope, preferred silence for the sake of the Jews."

Richard Lamb described how Mussolini sent several protests to the German ambassador to the RSI because of the massacres of the populations of entire villages suspected of harboring partisans, including at least one occasion when he wrote directly to Hitler, but received no response. Lamb said, "Few historians give credit to Mussolini for his efforts to protest German atrocities.... It is true that he did not make outspoken denunciations of German behavior to Hitler.... Mussolini was realistic enough to know that ... shrill protests might have been counter-productive." Historians have not suggested any counterfactuals that even hint otherwise. Papal protests on the supposed moral high ground advocated by Poliakov would have made Cornwell, Katz, Lipstadt, and all the others feel good at a distance from the events of 1943–1944, without any responsibility for attempting to manage the risks to the lives of people in an occupied city and in occupied Europe.[2]

From the experience of World War II, the international community was supposed to have learned the need for early intervention to prevent the escalation of the abuse of human rights. Despite the harsh lessons of that war and international concern that such did not happen again, the international community dithered when genocide was rampant in Rwanda, Cambodia, the former Yugoslavia and the Sudan. Impassioned protests by the United Nations, human rights organizations and religious leaders denounced barbarous violations of human rights. The rhetoric was all that critics of the Red Cross and the Vatican would have wanted in World War II. The results were as obvious as the results of similar protests would have been if directed to Hitler in the 1940s.

* * *

Perhaps the most common theory explaining the pope's alleged "silence" in the face of Nazi atrocities is that he was more afraid of Soviet Communism than Nazism, and so ignored German outrages. Professsor Susan Zuccotti said that Pius XII was not an anti–Semite or personally afraid of the Nazi but he was "almost pathologically afraid of bolschevism." And according to Professor Michael Phayer, "Pius XII's failure to assist Jews during the war and to seek reconciliation with them afterward was his obsession with the threat of communism." Phayer continued that theme in another place, saying that, "The Second World War had begun with one great danger in Pius' eyes — Communism." He mentioned two incidents to support this assertion: the first was that the Vatican did not send a delegation to view the concentration camps after the pope was shown photographs of them; the other was a conversation between the pope and

General Eisenhower in which a new Hapsburg monarchy was mentioned by the pope as a bulwark in Central Europe. It is difficult to understand how a failure to send a delegation to view concentration camps represented a fear of Communism. It cannot be as clear to readers as it was to Phayer, because he failed to explain their relationship. Nor do we have any details about the pope's conversation with Eisenhower, but at best these "incidents" are very slender reeds to support Phayer's major theme.

If one assumed that the fear of Communism controlled papal behavior, one might expect a historian to explain why it played a dominant role in Vatican affairs during the war. That did not happen. The assumption may have been that Pius XII and his predecessor saw Roman Catholics in Russia, as well as all religions, threatened by godless Soviet Communism making inroads elsewhere. As a result, because the Nazi threat in Germany, which had a large Catholic population, was more recent, Pius XII decided not to antagonize Hitler, hoping for a modus vivendi. Thus, as the lesser of two evils, a conciliatory policy was adopted toward the Nazis. The specifics of the supposed conciliatory policy are not spelled out by critics beyond referring to the pope's "silence," or to the "incidents" Phayer alludes to. He would have benefited from what Professor Jose Sanchez found, that in 1943 the Spanish ambassador to the Vatican reported that Pius told him that Communism was not the only problem, and he spoke bluntly of the Nazi menace. Similar statements can be found during the period in question so it is hard to understand why they are they ignored by presumably serious historians when it comes to discussing the fear of Communism theory.

The history of the Soviet attack on religion was summarized by Richard Pipes: "In histories of the Russian Revolution, religion receives little if any attention.... Such lack of interest can only be explained by the secularism of modern historians." Whatever their reason for downplaying the importance of religion to the Vatican, fear of Communism theorists wonder why the Vatican would be so concerned about Communism. An example is provided in Professor R.J.B. Bosworth's *Mussolini's Italy*, which showed not only his knowledge of Italian life under Mussolini but also that he found it hard to understand the Vatican's stance toward Soviet Russia. "Pius XI's and Pius XII's Vatican became a more intransigent fount of hostility to the inter-war USSR than was the Fascist government," he said, and went on, "For all the normality of Fascist-Soviet diplomatic deals, a religious war smouldered not far below the surface of events in the east and was fueled in part by the Vatican." When making that comparison, it is surprising that a supposedly knowledgeable scholar of Italian history could overlook Communism's immediate and deadly threat to religious believers during the inter-war years. Soviet Communism posed no direct or immediate threat to Fascism, which meant business as usual continued between the USSR and Italy. Given what was happening in the USSR, would anyone, let alone a knowledgeable historian, be surprised that Vatican concerns "fueled" a smoldering religious war? Furthermore, the fire had been ignited by Lenin, not a pope, and the Vatican's efforts to dampen the fire had been rebuffed by the Soviets.

Bosworth may not have remembered that many European nations shared the Vatican's concern about the USSR. In the case of the Vatican, was it because it lacked a progressive attitude toward the social change promised by Communism? Could the closing of churches and religious institutions and executing and sending clergy to the gulag, all of which were well documented in the 1920s and 1930s, have anything to do with the Vatican's concern about Soviet Communism? For any doubters of the Soviet anti-religious campaign, Felix Corley provided an extensively documented account of religion under the Soviets. The Soviet anti-religious campaign was vicious and effective before World War II. Christopher Andrew and Vasili Mitrokhin described how it continued in postwar Eastern Europe, for example, with the repression of the Uniate Catholics (those related to the Vatican) in Ukraine.

A review of the relationship between the Soviet Union and the Vatican, beginning after the 1917 revolution, is found in *The Vatican and the Red Flag* by Jonathan Luxmoore and Jolanta Babiuch. This excellent book presents the Vatican's efforts in Eastern Europe before and after the war. They are candid about what they consider the Vatican's missteps in policy although they are well aware of the grave problems it faced. The Vatican was always concerned about the fate of Roman Catholics in the Soviet Union and with good reason, as documented in great detail by Christopher Zuggar, who showed what happened to its members after Lenin took power. What may not have been widely known abroad, thanks to sympathetic reporting by Western media, was known to the Vatican, giving it ample reason for concern. Whether that concern led it to compromises with Hitler is another matter to be addressed separately.[3]

John Loftus and Mark Aarons continued their pursuit of the Vatican's supposed complicity with Germany during the war and for assisting Nazi and satellite war criminals escape war crimes trials, in their *The Secret War Against the Jews*. Not only did Pacelli, as the Vatican's nuncio in Germany in the 1920s, provide funds to Hitler, in addition Pacelli supposedly persuaded the Vatican to invest millions of dollars in Germany before the war. Later, "The Vatican and the Dulles brothers had the same problem. Once their money was in Hitler's hands, how would they get it back?" That led to secret deals that allowed German industrialists to escape responsibility after the war. The book reeks of conspiracy, looted gold and scandalous financial maneuvering by corporations and public figures in Britain, America and Germany. In a book of 637 pages, 116 of which are endnotes, the reader receives an impression of serious scholarship. However, too many of the endnotes refer to "confidential interviews" and "sources" that cannot be verified. Chapter 1, for example, has 15 of 57 endnotes refer to "confidential interviews" or to "sources," none of which can be verified by another researcher. The same is true of chapter 9's 171 endnotes, in which 45, or 26.3 percent, are with confidential interviewees. Everything the book claims may be true, but writing in this mode, despite the extensive footnoting, how can one be sure? The authors recognized the problem saying: "We do not know for certain if our sources have told us the truth, only that they want us to believe it is the truth." In a courtroom or in assessing the efficacy of a drug, that criterion for accuracy would not be acceptable. Should it be acceptable in a supposedly serious book about history? The Loftus and Aarons book shares the structural appearance expected from serious works of history, except that it also shares the fatal flaw of lack of verifiable documentation and the authors' own admission that they could not vouch for the reliability of interviewees.

The story of Pacelli funding Hitler in the 1920s was based on Paul Murphy's *La Popessa*, a book about Sister Pasquilina, who was the housekeeper for Pacelli when he was a nuncio in Germany and remained with him when he became pope. Murphy has a detailed account of a supposed conversation between Pacelli and Hitler as reported many years later by Sister Pasquilina. She also said that Hitler received "a large cache of Church money" from the nuncio who told Hitler to "go quell the devil's works." The meeting between the two men did not surprise her, "in the light of Pacelli's hatred of the Reds." No date was given for this encounter, and

Murphy cites no corroboration for an alleged meeting in the 1920s. Murphy's book is an interesting journalistic account of episodes and people during an important time and place. Enough is known about people like Cardinal Spellman and persons in the Vatican who are mentioned in the book to lend an air of credibility to the undocumented parts of the book. Murphy was an experienced journalist who knew many players in the American Church and the Vatican. His sometimes unvarnished portrayal of them lends an aura of authenticity to the book that cannot overcome doubt about his reconstruction of the extensive dialogue and interaction between Sister Pasquilina and Pius that the reader is expected to accept as authentic. Murphy admitted that "the dialogue does not always represent the exact words of the characters," but that it, "does represent the best recollection of those whom we interviewed." This hearsay style makes for a more readable, faster paced book similar to other "new journalism" that followed Truman Capote's *In Cold Blood* of 1965. Described as creative nonfiction as well as a nonfiction novel, Capote's book fostered a more entertaining approach to telling stories about the past. However, it set a bad example for Murphy. His dubious reconstruction of a conversation that happened at least forty years earlier to portray Pius XII as an early supporter of Hitler is not credible history.[4]

* * *

Enough has been written about the theory of the pope's overwhelming fear of Communism to persuade many writers to accept it as a demonstrable fact. When Carlo D'Este reviewed *The Battle for Rome*, he found that Robert Katz believed "the Vatican was trying to bring the West and the Germans to terms to save the world from 'Communism.'" Katz persisted in that theory, claiming in another place that the peace strategy of Pius XII was "a general rapprochement between the western Allies and Germany to contain, if not to roll back, the fearsome advance of godless Communism." Why was it necessary for Carlo D'Este to place "Communism" in quotation marks as if it were a somewhat dubious reason for papal concern? From all that is known about the fate of Orthodox, Evangelicals and Roman Catholics as well as members of other religions, Communism was unalterably and implacably opposed to them and did everything possible to eradicate them. Could it surprise knowledgeable historians that the Vatican was concerned about such policies? For whatever reasons, obviously it did surprise them, and they continued to be surprised even after the fall of the Soviet Union.

Not everyone accepted Katz's facile explanation. In a critique of the wartime policy of Pius XII, Senator Giovanni Spadolini rejected the fear of Communism thesis. Instead, according to Robert Graham, he ascribed the pope's policy to his reliance on the concordat between Germany and the Vatican. A strong advocate of the rule of law, the pope saw it as providing a legal, if fragile, basis for German-Vatican relations. That reliance on the concordat is key to understanding much of the Vatican's policy toward Germany in the 1930s. Especially for a diplomat like Pacelli, the "rule of law" was paramount. He would have been comfortable at the League of Nations and later at the United Nations. Unfortunately, Hitler's only rule was winning by any means while the Vatican's attitude, for far too long, was based upon the illusion that they were dealing with someone who valued international law.

The pope's legalistic approach, and after all he had a law degree, was not exceptional, either in Italian society or in the Vatican. From the time of the Romans, the philosophy of law and its practice was at a level of abstraction foreign to Anglo-Saxon jurisprudence, and this characterized Italian and canon law that infused the attitudes of Vatican bureaucrats. Such background and attitudinal differences should not be overlooked when assessing their behavior. Summing it up, "To call Italian legal science abstract and conceptual is to state the obvious," according to Mauro Cappelletti, who added, "To a legal scientist the difference between Italian and American [legal] doctrine is not that the Italian is too conceptual but that the American is not conceptual enough." This more "sophisticated" Italian approach helped, at least from the mid-1930s, to mislead the Vatican about Germany's intentions, and for too long it hoped for the best. That was not unusual if one remembers how Neville Chamberlain sought peace in our time from Hitler and how President Roosevelt and Prime Minister Churchill were misled by Stalin, and also hoped for the best.

Robert Graham did not agree either with Spadolini or the fear of Communism thesis, but agreed with or not, Spadolini provided a plausible explanation of Vatican policy that deserves consideration when examining Vatican policy. The failure to explore such alternative explanations of papal policy is only one example of tenable explanations that escape exploration by English and American historians. Unfortunately although graduate students are taught the importance of keeping one's mind open to alternate theories, no matter how contrary to the current consensus, actually doing so is not easy to get past the editors of consensus oriented professional journals.[5]

How Pius XII was driven by the fear of Communism was explained by Richard Rubenstein. Few writers about the period go as far as he did to explain the "silence" of Pius XII when he asked, "Could it be that Pius regarded the demographic elimination of Europe's Jews as a benefit for European Christendom? Put differently, did the Pope recognize any moral obligation whatsoever to rescue Jews?" Rubenstein went on: "It is my conviction that the pontiff recognized no such obligation and that he did regard the demographic removal of Europe's Jews as a benefit for European Christendom." As evidence he cited the pope's family background, his childhood, education, service as nuncio in Germany, and most important, the pope's fear of Bolshevism. In addition he believed, "In effect the Nazis were implementing a long cherished Vatican goal, the disenfranchisement of non-believing Jews in Christian Europe and their ultimate return to the ghetto." The mixture of Hochuth and Cornwell makes for high drama, with Rubenstein portraying a duplicitous, satanic Machiavellian pope whose goals far exceeded those found in *Hitler's Pope* or *The Deputy*. As long as presumed scholars persist in believing conspiracy theories of this ilk, no evidence will persuade them otherwise. Regrettably, the same holds true for flat earth and UFO enthusiasts.[6]

John Pawlikowski joined the revisionists when he emphasized the Vatican's defense of the social order of Europe from the threat of communism. This "muted" its criticism of Nazism, which, despite its abuses, was considered a bulwark against Bolshevism. Judging from the Nazis' reaction to *Mit Brennender Sorge* and other papal pronouncements about Nazi abuses, they were seen as far from "muted" by the Nazis and evoked strong retaliation, of which Pawlikowski seemed strangely unaware. It also is difficult to understand his criticism of the Vatican's supposed defense of the social order of Europe without any specification of the elements of that social order that were being defended. Pawlikowski contended that the Church's policy changed in the 1960s with Vatican II, which is true in some matters, for example the liturgy, but he ignored the far from conservative critiques of the existing socioeconomic order in Europe by *Rerum*

Novarum (The Rights and Duties of Capital and Labor), historic "social encyclical" of Leo XIII in May 1891, and another by Pius XI in *Quadragesimo Anno* (On Reconstruction of the Social Order) in May 1931, to mention only two. The Vatican harshly criticized the excesses of capitalism and advocated the concept of subsidiarity, a form of popular democracy embraced by Western Europeans well before anyone thought of liberation theology. Surely Pawlikowski's scholarly research made him aware of these long ago currents in Church policy that argued against the status quo but why he failed to consider them in the context of wartime papal policy is puzzling.

For a different but critical view of the Vatican's relationship with Hitler and Mussolini, one must turn to an older book by Anthony Rhodes. He had a balanced survey of what happened in Vichy and turned a cold eye on the activities of Croatia during the war while noting the Vatican's repeated protests of the behavior of the Ustachi. In Rhodes opinion, the Pope's reliance on the concordat in dealing with Germany was a serious mistake, a misjudgment of Hitler's policies whose attitude toward the Church was already on record. Although other Western nations feared Communism the Vatican had reason: "Yet it became so obsessed with the anti-religious nature of Communism as to have no balanced view of it politically." Beyond stating that opinion he sought reasons and believed he found them in Vatican structure. Between 1922 and 1945, "the Vatican possessed a Secretariat of State of a most antediluvian model." That was because it was part of a small, in-grown Italian bureaucracy. After World War I its size and composition was not adequate for the management of a worldwide institution, much less one in the midst of a worldwide crisis. Whether one agreed with his opinion about the fear of Communism (how else might one expect a threatened religious institution to react?), he is balanced in his analysis, especially when compared to later critics like Cornwell and Phayer. Rhodes differed with them because his approach was more analytical; he realized that the structure of the Vatican's policymaking was important in explaining limitations of its policy. Ways that served for centuries could no longer cope with the changes after World War I. His approach to the institutional Vatican was something he shared with Ambassador d'Arcy Osborne, Britain's envoy in the Vatican during the war.

The Vatican's reaction to Communism continues to puzzle many writers about its policies before, during and after World War II. James

4 — Papal "Silence" and "Fear of Communism"

McMillan described a Pius XI whose "growing anti–Communism after 1936 has often been noted, if only to put it down to papal dotage or to changes in his entourage." This was compared to his willingness "to collude with dictatorships of the extreme Right, as his conclusion of agreements with Mussolini in 1929 and Hitler in 1933 had shown." Professor McMillan went on to suggest that Pius XI conspired with Hitler and Mussolini, but leaving the conspiracy falsehood aside, why did Miller ignore the context of what was not happening at the time? The German concordat was signed before the Nazis began attacking the churches. In Italy although there were tensions between the Fascists and the Vatican, the government was not overtly anti-religious when the Lateran Pact was signed. In the view of Richard Wolff, studies that focused exclusively on the relationship between Mussolini's government and the Vatican did no justice to the complexity of Catholicism or the confusing nature of Fascism. It is true that the Vatican had relations with two extreme right regimes, as did the United States, Britain and most other nations, and like many other nations the Vatican made overtures to the extreme left Soviet regime in the early 1920s but was rebuffed. From a religious perspective the situation in Russia had deteriorated ever since. One would not have known that from the accounts of the progressive Fabians Sidney and Beatrice Webb or the correspondent of the *New York Times* as they traveled to Potemkin collective farms while real peasants died by the millions.

Whatever Rhodes, McMillan and others believed about the inordinate fear of Communism that drove Vatican policy, an arch foe of the Vatican and all religion saw matters from a different perspective: "The Pope has made a speech to a large crowd in St. Peter's Square. Significantly he said not a word against bolshevism but inveighed against the false doctrines of nationalism, race and blood. Clearly the Pope is shutting his eyes to the rise of bolshevism all over Europe." That was the opinion of Joseph Goebbels in March 1945.[7]

* * *

Similar to the criticisms leveled at the Allies and the Vatican for not behaving in ways deemed more appropriate by latter day critics is Jean-Claude Favez's critique of the wartime International Red Cross. In a thorough and generally balanced account of the role of the Red Cross during World War II, he described what the Red Cross did to assist not only

POWs, which was its primary function, but also civilians and concentration camp victims, unfortunately with little effect on the conditions for the latter groups. Believing itself bound by its charter to assist POWs, and aware of probable German reaction to efforts the Nazis would consider political, it was reluctant to jeopardize that basic function, although it was aware of what was happening to Jews and others in the concentration camps. Finally, however, Favez concluded, "Even the material aid it was able to deliver has not succeeded in convincing the world that it had given sufficient proof in this instance of it effectiveness, all the more so because it did not make the supreme risk of throwing the full weight of its moral authority into the scales on behalf of these particular victims." Calling its hesitation mistaken, he continued, "We have no choice but to recognize that it really should have spoken out." Favez provided no evidence of any instance in which an appeal to moral authority caused Hitler to change his mind. To argue that the Red Cross should have risked the tenuous hold it had on German cooperation for a foredoomed appeal to Hitler's moral sense not only contradicts the reality of what the author himself found that the Red Cross faced during the war, it can best be described as although well intentioned, both surprising and fatuous.

Walter Laquer was another who said that the Red Cross was well aware of what was happening to the Jews and yet felt constrained not to speak out. As a result it might not have done all it could within the difficult conditions it faced but, "it was also true that keeping silent in these circumstances was tantamount to abetting the 'final solution.'" That harsh judgment for not broadcasting its revulsion over what was happening could have had an outcome of which Laquer was well aware. Years later he was willing to bravely take that risk for those who were living under Nazi domination.

What Favez wrote replicated the conclusions reached much earlier by Nora Levin who believed the Red Cross failed to stand up to Germany. Levin was critical of the inability of the Allies and the Red Cross to have the Jews designated as prisoners of war and the failure of the Red Cross to distribute relief parcels to concentration camps. "Had the reclassification of Jews been firmly ordered in 1942, their fate might have been different." She also was dismissive of explanations by the Red Cross that it was unable to send parcels to the camps because it could jeopardize services to POWs and civilian internees. Levin's opinion might be summed up by her conclusion, "During the war the rescue of Jews interfered with the principle of victory." Put that bluntly, one could consider the military insensitive, or worse, to the fate of the Jews. Her concern for the victims comes through clearly in a well-researched book, but like many others, she failed to place what happened in the contextual reality that existed during the war when decisions had to be made without thought of the critics of another generation.

Allied pressure on the Red Cross to denounce German atrocities was similar to that facing the Vatican. Robert Graham explained how an explicit protest would be viewed by the Germans with the almost certain result that it would not only be rejected but could endanger the basic function of the Red Cross, which was to aid POWs. The Red Cross knew that Germany had toyed with renouncing the Geneva Convention and had refused access to civilian internees. It also refused access to 700,000 Italian soldiers it called military internees and treated them so harshly that one in ten did not survive. The Geneva Convention and the Red Cross provided at least minimal protection for POWs. If the Red Cross had forfeited its role, Allied POWs would have been left at the mercy of the Nazis. Russia was not a party to the Geneva Convention and according to Raul Hilberg, 40 percent of the 5,700,000 Soviet POWs died while in German captivity.

The critics of the International Committee of the Red Cross (ICRC) display remarkable ignorance of the wartime reality that faced that institution as well as the conditions confronting POWs. Both lived with a real-life crisis, not some long after the fact counterfactuals. Critics would benefit from learning from Vasilis Vourkoutiotis, who described in detail what the ICRC did in Germany to insure that prisoners were treated with at least minimal decency. Anxious to see that Germans in Allied custody received similar treatment, the ICRC inspectors were allowed to visit Allied camps and report their findings, thus insuring reciprocity. Loss of ICRC access would have been fatal for many Allied POWs, a price not to be taken lightly. For those engaged in humanitarian activity, results were more important than public indignation that would not have any real effect and could worsen the situation of those needing help.[8]

* * *

Claims that the Vatican and the Red Cross failed to denounce German atrocities may seem plausible indictments of two presumably eminently respectable institutions. Michael Phayer was blunt: "The pope abdicated his right as leader of the Catholic church to make pronouncements based on moral principle." The "silence" of the pope, and of the Red Cross, which knew what was happening in the concentration camps, is inexplicable to critics who contend that each had a moral obligation to put a denunciation on the record at that time. They ignore that bishops and clergy protested atrocities as did the pope on many occasions, albeit in diplomatic language that was well understood by the Nazis and the Allies. However, as Camille Cianfarra saw many years before, "The innate prudence and reticence of the clergy, trained all their lives to be discreet, create a mental habit which is often puzzling to the layman." Perhaps nowhere is that more apparent than when the layman happens to be writing history. Perhaps because he did not understand the formality involved in diplomacy, John Roth believed that the pope's words were not understood: "The preponderance of the evidence clearly gives Cornwell's hand the greater strength at this point. How Pius XII could have thought, as he apparently did, that his words were clear and crisp in their meaning seems to be a comment more about his self-deception than his self-estimation." It is doubtful that Pius ever thought his words were clear and crisp, and Roth leaves us in the dark about an unexplained "preponderance of evidence" or any evidence that allowed Cornwell to trump the pope. But he also failed to reveal how he arrived at the opinion of papal self-deception.[9]

The pope was harshly criticized for what happened at Belzec, which became an extermination camp for about 600,000 Jews. According to Carol Rittner and John Roth, if Christians, including the pope, avoided abstractions and spoke out "loud and clear" in favor of those who are most in need, "Belzec would not have existed." That anyone would make such an extravagant and emotional claim in a supposedly serious book is unusual. Their counterfactual completely ignored the genesis of the war and the fact that the party that began the fighting was ruthlessly anti-religious and refused to listen to appeals by Christians and anyone else. Had they known of a Vatican request in late 1944 on behalf of Polish Jews in Belsen Bergen with South American passports to receive relief packages, Rittner and Roth might have been less sanguine about their counterfactual. According to Aryeh Kubovy, in effect the German reply was: "Pope, what business is it of yours? This rude reply was given less than five months before the German surrender." Sadly, in the year Rittner and Roth published their book, religious leaders, the United Nations, the European Union and others spoke "loudly and clearly" to stop genocide in Sudan, but to no avail. That was only one of many empirical tests of their hypothesis that showed its fatuity and futility.

A letter written by Cardinal Boetto, the archbishop of Genoa, illustrates why communications to those in power were couched in diplomatic language. The Cardinal wrote to the Italian provincial governor in an effort to free Rabbi Pacifici, who had been arrested with his congregation. The Cardinal's secretary, Don Repetto said: "The letter is without humanitarian appeal or indignant protest. When the ecclesiastical authorities find themselves in front of hostile civil authorities they must use cautious and conciliatory language." Msgr. John Carroll-Abbing, who was a bureaucrat in the Roman Curia for many years, added another dimension to the use of curial language: "Papal pronouncements were reverently received, commented on by the studious, skimmed over by many, and generally watered down to fit in with a conscientious but not always sufficiently enlightened view of local needs." He added that because of the nature of its structure, the Roman Curia's "tendency to calm deliberation, so admirable under many aspects, would inevitably lead to excessive caution." He might have added that the habits of Curia-trained generations were not easy to change, largely because they had served so well in the past.

What Vatican critics really fault is what they see as a failure in rhetoric. Ringing denunciations would make today's judges of past events feel good, but they refuse to acknowledge that serious historians agree that denunciations at the time would have been meaningless and, based on experience, most probably would have made matters worse. If the Pope did not publicly denounce Hitler, it is also true that Roosevelt and Churchill remained silent about atrocities. They knew about Stalin's ordering the Katyn massacre of Polish military and political figures but said nothing and pressed the Polish government in exile to do the same. Historians writing about that episode have no problem explaining why Allied leaders refrained from criticizing Stalin. Gabriel Kolko's heavily documented apologia for an act that led "toward implementing a social revolution in Poland" revealed both the complex reasons the Americans and British had for abstaining from denouncing the massacre and why the

Soviets took advantage of the opportunity to eliminate future potential opponents. At a safe distance critics pillory the pope for his "silence" as if Hitler had been amenable to reason and would have been responsive to pleas to stop. Knowing Hitler's record, one must ask what the pope could have done that would have altered the course of a tragic history.

Allied "silence" about the Soviet massacre of Polish officers at Katyn was understandable at the time although in retrospect it may not appear admirable, but at the time the Allies had other priorities. Another lesser example of remaining "silent" happened when the novelist Evelyn Waugh was a member of a British liaison team with Tito's partisans. Waugh prepared a lengthy report about partisan activity including the fact they were executing Catholic clergy and suppressing religion. Naively, Waugh expected the British government to protest what was happening. However, British policy was to foster stability in the region and support Tito. While aware of what was happening, the Foreign Office said it had "no grounds at all for intervening.... That would be gross interference with the internal affairs of the Yugoslav state." Waugh was threatened with court martial if he released his report.[10]

An example of what happened when non-diplomatic language was used was recounted by Frans Josef van Beek. As a young altar boy in February 1942 during the German occupation, "at the 7 a.m. Mass, our feisty pastor had surprised us. Emerging from the sacristy after the Gospel, he emphatically read a pastoral letter from the Dutch bishops: any Catholic directly or indirectly engaged in identifying Jewish citizens to the occupying German authorities was excommunicated. He repeated his performance at four more Masses; I went every time. Later I heard he had done so to prevent his assistants from being arrested. One result of the Dutch bishops' letter was retribution. Within weeks, SS troops were rounding up Jews who were Catholic converts or associated with Catholics; Jews associated with Protestants were mostly left alone. Nine months later, I found my violin teacher's apartment sealed — his wife was Catholic; two weeks later, he was killed in Auschwitz."

When Ronald Rychalak's *Hitler, the War and the Pope* made basically the same argument as Van Beek, Goldhagen accused him of the misleading use of evidence, explaining the high death rate of Dutch Jews as due to "well-documented factors (length of occupation, geographic density of the country), concentration of Jews, lack of safe refuge within the

4—Papal "Silence" and "Fear of Communism"

country) ... that produced this high death rate. Had Dutch churches not intervened, the Germans and their Dutch helpers would have killed as many Jews." Anyone who carefully reads Rychalak will not find any misleading evidence. He merely quoted the angry German response to the bishops' protest that related the deportations to the protest. And, unfortunately, Goldhagen does not mention where he found the "well-documented factors" that explained the high death rate. That makes it impossible to verify his assertion. However, he made it clear that his book was not a "historiographic exercise" so presumably he was not to be held to the usual canons of writing history.

Of the back and forth on this issue there is little chance of a resolution in favor of either side. Perhaps the consensus view of the problem was stated best by Professor Frank Coppa in his review of Margherita Marchione's *Pius XII: Architect for Peace*. "Her assertion that a more forthright and forceful condemnation of Nazi antisemitism would have made things worse is no more credible than the counter claim that it would have helped.... She cannot understand the position of those who later found his diplomatic stance weak in the face of the subsequent disclosures of the horrors of the Holocaust." This argument seems supported by Professor Jose Sanchez who asked, "Would he [Pius XII] save more by protesting or by not protesting? The question can never be answered, because we do not know what would have happened if a strong protest had been made." Whether Marchione's position about the futility of "forceful condemnation" would have been effective is one issue; whether she could understand those who found Pius weak is another matter. On the first issue it is surprising that two professors who have written on the subject of Pius XII during the war obviously ignored testimony about what happened in Holland, and that of the pope himself, that contradicts their position. In the face of all that is known about Nazi reactions to protests, it is fatuous for Professor Coppa to assert that "the accommodating strategy diplomatic finesse and 'silence' of Pius XII, which may have saved many lives, compromised the moral stature of the Holy See." Because it is known that papal strategy saved many lives, even if one assumed that it was an "accommodating strategy," it would be interesting to learn from Coppa how that compromised any moral or ethical code.

Instead of dismissing Marchione's credibility, Professor Coppa might have examined the abundant credible evidence that protests rarely if ever had a positive outcome with the Germans. He mentioned no credible or other evidence that protests could or did change German behavior. To mention only one example: Hitler's long time friend Benito Mussolini telephoned him to complain about what happened on September 29, 1944, when two regiments of the Adolph Hitler SS surrounded Marzabotto and in two days massacred 1,830 men, women and children. Only the scale of the massacre was somewhat unusual. Hitler ignored the protest, and Il Duce gave up the idea of any more protests to Hitler. When Hitler paid no attention to protests from his friend and ally, how much attention would he have paid to Pius XII?

The same lack of evidence undercuts Professor Sanchez because we do know what happened when strong protests were made. The available evidence clearly favors Marchione, but it could not influence Professor Coppa's opinion, and it would have even less success with Cornwell and others. Professor Coppa ignored that Marchione talked about wartime Europe, not about the criticism of Pius's diplomatic stance subsequent to disclosure of the horrors of the Holocaust. Obviously, critics can write whatever they want, disregarding context and facts, but they do so only much later under vastly changed circumstances. Unconcerned about the facts, the pope's critics probably will remain firm in their opinions regardless of incidents such as that reported by von Beek.

When discussing the tenure of Pius XII, Professor Coppa emphasized his long experience as a diplomat and service as secretary of state for Pius XI. He went on to recount the pope's efforts to influence events before the war as tension grew between Germany and Poland. On August 31, 1939, "Pius begged the governments of Germany and Poland to avoid all incidents, refraining from any action that would aggravate the existing situation. His effort failed.... Still preserving his impartiality, Pius failed to raise his voice to condemn the aggression." Coppa went on to say, "From the first the papal failure to condemn the aggression provoked criticism." He did not add that most of it, as would be expected, came from the Allies.

In the context of what happened, Coppa's first use of the word "failed," as in "tried but failed" seems appropriate. The second and third use of the word are pejorative judgments with which most historians in this area would agree. However, in view of Pius's background, as described by Coppa and others, there is another way of viewing the pope's alleged "failure to act" and that is to assess what happened as a diplomat's "refusal" or

4—Papal "Silence" and "Fear of Communism"

"reluctance" to abandon a policy of above the fray neutrality that often was successful in the past. Whether Pius's diplomatic decision was wise and reasonable at the time, is a matter of opinion. And while it may be true that we do not know for certain what would have happened had Pius made a "flaming protest," we do know what he believed would happen. Considering the situation in Europe in the 1940s, is it fair to call his belief unreasonable? Coppa and Sanchez could have considered that context. To ignore or deny it is not leveling with the reader.[11]

* * *

Most serious historians of World War II understand what Dean Acheson meant when he said that war time "was one of great obscurity to those who lived through it. Not only was the future clouded, a common enough situation, but the present was equally clouded. The significance of events was shrouded in ambiguity. We groped after interpretations of them, sometimes reversed lines of actions based on earlier views, and hesitated long before grasping what now seems obvious." A similar suggestion to understand the context of war time decisions came from George Kennan: "The decisions taken throughout the remainder of the war years were those of harried, overworked men, operating in the vortex of a series of tremendous pressures, military and otherwise, which we today find it difficult to remember or to imagine. I think that some injustice is being done to ... the cause of historical understanding by the latter-day interpretations which regard specific decisions of the wartime years as the source of all our present difficulties." So based on what was known at the time, and not what critics thought half a century later, for better or worse decision makers in Washington, London and Vatican City acted on their best judgment of available intelligence. Faulting them for acting in good faith based on what they knew then clearly implies that had today's omniscient historians, with a more developed sense of morality, been available, matters would have ended differently.[12]

* * *

During the war, persons in the Vatican, with or without official sanction, aided Allied fliers, Jews and others who were wanted by the Germans. Many dramatic stories tell about ordinary people who helped hundreds of Allied fliers return to their lines. Hugh O'Flaherty, an Irish priest in the

Vatican, is known to have created what could be called a "rat line" in Rome that helped several thousand Allied POWs and fliers (some estimates suggest 4,000) escape from the Germans. After the war, aid to escapees continued, only this time for Germans and others who wanted to escape the Allies. Perhaps the best known, or notorious, person to help fleeing Germans was Bishop Alois Hudal, an Austrian who served in the Vatican. He was the rector of the Collegio Teutonico di Santa Maria dell Anima in Rome, which was not a college in the British or American sense but a residence where German priests lived while attending papal universities. The church to which the Collegio was attached was the German national church in Rome serving the German speaking colony and visitors. Bishop Hudal had been a theologian, a fervent German nationalist and early supporter of the social policies of the Nazi party. His support of Nazism led to him being called the "Brown Bishop." After the war he was involved in what Allied intelligence called a "rat line" to South America, aiding those wanted as war criminals. Stories about Hudal's aid to SS and other fugitives leave the impression that he helped hundreds of war criminals to leave Europe. There is no way to know what the number might have been, but one fugitive he did help was Franz Stangel, who commanded the camps at Treblinka and Sobibor. Sereny did an excellent study of Stangel after his extradition from Brazil and conviction by a German court. While very critical of the pope and the Vatican, the book has a balance not found in most later books dealing with the wartime Vatican. Although Hudal was suspected of aiding Adolph Eichmann, Stangel may be the only individual actually identified as aided by Hudal, who admitted to helping forty Germans in an article published in 1961.

According to Inga Clendinnen, Hudal "was protected in his turn by Pope Pius XII himself." Clendinnen presented no evidence for that claim. In any event Hudal and others had a rationale for helping fugitives. The age-old tradition of sanctuary was an element in the decision to help Allied personnel or former SS officers. David Alvarez and Robert Graham believed that Hudal rationalized his helping Nazi fugitives as inspired by the same charitable motives that led him to help some Jews during the war. One can understand, if not agree, with the stance of clergy who, like physicians treating patients regardless of their background, believed that they must do the same. That defied civil and military authority on both sides during the war. It made sense to Anglo-American writers when Allied personnel were helped; it was dismissed when German SS members and others were helped to escape to South America. Escapees on both sides were not asked to submit resumes before being helped, which undoubtedly meant that men later identified as notorious war criminals escaped justice. An ironic coda to the subject of aiding combatants is found in the experience of Father Hugh O'Flaherty the "Irish Pimpernel," who, after escaping being killed by the notorious SS Colonel Herbert Kappler, who was responsible for carrying out the Ardeatine massacre, helped Kappler's wife and children flee to Switzerland and escape the vengeance of the partisans after the Allies entered Rome. O'Flaherty later baptized Kappler, who was serving a life sentence in an Italian prison.

Former SS Captain Erich Priepke, who participated in the Ardeatine Caves massacre, was one who fled to South America. After he was extradited from Argentina in 1995, he claimed that Father Pancrazio Pfeiffer helped him escape. Robert Graham found that would have been difficult because Pfeiffer was hit by a truck on March 12, 1945, and died of his injuries on May 19, 1945. However Priepke's claim continues to support the story of Vatican involvement in the "rat line." Priebke was convicted by an Italian court and sentenced to life in prison. He died in Italy in 2004.[13]

According to Peter Godman, Bishop Hudal helped Adolph Eichman travel to South America. His authorities for this story were John Loftus and Mark Aarons. In *Unholy Alliance: The Vatican, the Nazis and the Swiss Banks* (1998), *Unholy Trinity* (1991) and *Ratlines* (1991) they wrote that Bishop Siri of Genoa was "allegedly Walter Rauff's contact in setting up Bishop Hudal's escape network to smuggle wanted Germans out of Europe ... including Adolph Eichmann." Those books were followed by *The Secret War Against the Jews* (1994) claiming that in 1947 the Vatican "Ratline," as it was called by U.S. intelligence, was the single largest smuggling route for Nazi war criminals. Nearly all the major war criminals, from Adolf Eichmann to Pavelic, ended up following Dulles's money route from the Vatican to Argentina." As with much in their apparently heavily documented work, too many of their claims are based on "allegedly." However, knowing about Hudal's background it would not be surprising if the allegation was confirmable. Unfortunately, it is not. It should be noted that Godman, who delved into Hudal's background at length, concluded that his help to escapees "has been taken as proof that Pius XII wished to assist ex–Nazis by allowing Hudal to "be in touch" with them. The Pope allowed nothing of the kind."

When a paper is presented at a professional academic conference, the presenter has somewhat more latitude with opinions than in a peer reviewed article. In a paper he presented at a conference on Holocaust education, Professor Henry Huttenback, a prominent figure in Jewish-Catholic dialogue, took advantage of that leeway when he affirmed that Christianity came out of the war with blood on its hands because of Christian participation, "with various degrees of conviction," in the Final Solution. Furthermore, "The Vatican, with the covert assistence of thousands of clergy, organized a mass escape route for Catholic Nazi criminals to Latin America. Symptomatically worse, not a single Catholic Nazi was expelled from the Church. Both Goebbels and Hitler, the former a practicing Catholic and the latter a nominal Catholic were not excommunicated and died, therefore, with the congregation of the faithful." The thrust of Professor Huttenback's paper was on Jewish-Christian relations, so it was unfortunate that he was mistaken about the two men dying in the "congregation of the faithful." More important from a factual viewpoint is that he seems to have relied on John Loftus and Mark Aarons, who make the same argument about the "Vatican rat lines" to South America. Their sensationalist work about the mass exodus of Nazis thanks to clerical help sells well but does not qualify as authentic history. And about all that can be said about excommunicating Goebbels and Hitler is that they obviously defected from the Church of their youth and their behavior caused automatic excommunication without the need for any formalities. Goebbels died after killing his entire family and Hitler committed suicide. If their prior behavior was not enough to consider them outside the Church, their last acts would more than qualify to do so.

A letter from Don Luigi Sturzo to Aryeh Kubovy in May of 1943, noted that the last "nominal excommunication was that of Napoleon. Before that we must go back to Elizabeth of England. Neither Napoleon nor Elizabeth, after the excommunication, changed their policy." Sturzo believed that Hitler's reaction to the threat of excommunication would be to "execute as many Jewish persons as possible and nobody could prevent it." With regard to the excommunication of Hitler, it is well to recall what happened when, as noted earlier, Ambassador Bullitt suggested to Cardinal Maglione that the pope consider excommunicating Mussolini if he

4 — Papal "Silence" and "Fear of Communism"

dragged Italy into war. The cardinal said the pope should not be asked to do something that modern progress has ridiculed for more than a century. Had there been a public excommunication at the time, it would be hailed half a century later, but the cardinal was not thinking in terms of a public relations coup.

Beginning in 1936, the British Minister to the Vatican, d'Arcy Godolphin Osborne, spent ten years in Rome, including four years inside the Vatican during the war. By all accounts he can be considered an astute observer of life in the Vatican. On March 4, 1947, he wrote the following about the pope: "Papal charity aspires to being absolute and universal. I have often discussed this at the Vatican and pointed out the dangers of such an aspiration. It goes back, I suppose, to the medieval right of sanctuary. During the German occupation of Rome the Vatican and the extraterritorial Vatican premises in Rome were full of fugitives and refugees from Nazi and Fascist persecution, including Alcide de Gasperi who later became prime minister, the socialist leader Pietro Nenni, and other leading anti–Fascist politicians. It may be, and I think it likely, that some Fascist refugees were also helped and hidden when their time came to hide and be helped, but these would be exceptions; nothing like the wholesale protection of the victims of Fascism. And the Pope is on record that the authors of war crimes should pay for their evil-doing." According to Chadwick, Osborne confessed that the pope's neutrality was "meticulous and seemingly pusillanimous.... There was no line indicating reprobation by name, or cursing by bell book and candle."[14]

* * *

Unfortunately for those favoring the fear of Communism theory, and a resultant tilt toward Germany, and Inga Clendinnen's notion that Bishop Hudal was close to the pope, Hudal denied having seen the pope more than once in the 1930s, so the record fails to support that conspiracy theory. Contrary to the notion that he was close to Pius XII, Hudal wrote that he never had a private meeting with the pope. Clendinnen seemed unaware of Robert Graham's article about a peace effort in 1943 that Josef Goebbels mentioned in his diary. The presence of this reference in the diary would seem to confirm secret arrangements between the Nazis and Vatican. However, Graham tracked down some principals in the peace effort, and his article about this episode places both the theory and Hudal's place in the Vatican in perspective. On their own initiative Bishop Hudal and a group in Germany sought a rapprochement between the Vatican and the Reich in 1943. It was based on requiring political changes in Germany including freeing all clergy from concentration camps and stopping the campaign against the Jews. In return the Vatican would work to have the Allies join Germany in war against the Soviets. Initially the proposal received some attention from Goebbels, but since it was so contrary to German policy, it soon was disregarded. Bishop Hudal's proposal received no attention in the Vatican. According to Graham, Hudal was not in the inner circles of the Vatican and was known as a Nazi sympathizer. His effort to broker an agreement may have been sincere but his fantasy was destined to fail because in principle neither side could negotiate the conditions for such an agreement.

More evidence of Hudal's marginality in the Vatican came from an incident in December 1942 when there was a furor in Berlin because of an article by Professor Francesco Orestano in *Gerarchia*, an official Fascist publication founded by Mussolini. Orestrano was very critical of the Nazi attitude toward religion, and Bishop Hudal wrote a reply to Orestrano. In an article about the meaning of the debate, Robert Graham sketched Hudal's background. An early advocate of Anschluss, Hudal saw himself as a bridge builder between National Socialism and the Catholic Church. Although the party now was dominated by a radical left group, he believed that the basic tenets of the party were sound, and he supported an older, more conservative wing of the party. His favoring this kind of Nazi found no resonance among his fellow German and Austrian clergy in Rome.

Responding to Orestrano, Hudal outlined how the Church and Nazism could be reconciled if the latter abandoned its racism and radical socialism. In a memoir published after his death, Hudal admitted that his ideas received no attention in the Vatican. Father Robert Leiber, who advised the pope on German matters, told Hudal of his disagreement with his ideas. And a Swiss Jesuit journal called his optimistic ideas about a modus vivendi between the Church and Nazism "infantile."

As an indication of how Hudal's ideas about a possible modus vivendi between the Church and Nazism were received, a book on that theme that he wrote in 1936, *The Foundations of National Socialism*, was seen as so alien to Catholic principles that it was considered for the Index by Pius XI. Because Hudal was a bishop, the then secretary of state, Cardinal

4—Papal "Silence" and "Fear of Communism"

Pacelli, negotiated a stern public criticism in *L'Osservatore Romano*, the Vatican paper. As a fervent German nationalist he was used on the pope's initiative to send a letter of protest to General Rainer Stahel the German commander in Rome, requesting that the roundup of the Jews cease immediately if a protest by the pope was to be avoided. The intervention succeeded because on Himmler's orders the deportation operation, which was to take 8,000 Jews, was stopped at 1,259. According to Godman, Hudal had no further dealings with the pope. When Hudal retired he wrote his memoirs, "providing Rolf Hochuth with material for *The Deputy*, so formative of Pius XII's negative image."

In view of Hudal's background Raul Hilberg evidently did not approve having him contact General Stahel. After describing the bishop's background, Hilberg said, "Yet it is to Hudal that a nephew of the Pope, Carlo Pacelli, went one morning in October 1943 to inform him that arrests of Italian Jews had just begun in Rome. Hudal immediately wrote to the German army commander of the city, General Rainer Stahel, beseeching him to order the immediate cessation of this roundup, lest the Pope intervene publically, bringing harm to Germany." Hilberg did not add that the intervention by the pope, through the "brown bishop" and what better interlocutor than a German sympathizer, helped to save several thousand lives. Certainly, in such a case the end justified using what later seemed distasteful means.[15]

Why a rapprochement between the Vatican and Germany was improbable is evident when one considers that the Vatican was well aware of Hitler's attitude toward religion and the persecution of religion in Germany. But the pope also knew how far the Nazis planned to go because of the evidence of the extreme anti-religious measures they applied in Poland. The Nazis were Utopian planners dedicated to using eugenics to create a new, virile race to populate the Thousand Year Reich. Before the war the SS encouraged the breeding of young Aryans, while the mentally ill, retarded and other "misfits" were euthanized. Then, in 1940 the occupation of Poland provided the opportunity to expand their planning for the future. A large area in western Poland with a population of about 4,500,000, and with Poznan one of its largest cities, became their laboratory. The Germans named the region "Warthegau" and planned to develop and test the policies that would be enforced in Europe after German victory. One such policy with long-range demographic implications, forbade

Polish men to marry before the age of 28 and Polish women before the age of 25. Over time this would reduce the Polish birth rate, thus easing control over a subject population. Education for Poles was severely limited to insure they would be a lumpen proletariat.

In this mostly Polish and Catholic area, many Poles were expelled and replaced by Volksdeutsch. Catholic and Protestant churches were severely controlled, and Germans and Poles were prohibited from using the same clergy and churches, baptisms were forbidden, religious institutions closed and contacts with outside church authorities forbidden. Not all these restrictions were applied elsewhere in Poland with the force they were in Warthegau, although throughout Poland there was widespread killing of clergy, and many others were sent to concentration camps. Although the Vatican complained to the Germans about what was happening in the Warthegau, a public condemnation was rejected. However, in his Christmas message of 1941 the pope made an obvious reference to Warthegau's demographic policies: "There is no place for open or occult oppression of the cultural and linguistic characteristics of national minorities, for the hindrance or restriction of their economic resources, or for the limitation or abolition of their national fertility." The Vatican went no farther because, according to Cardinal Tardini, "in the present circumstances a public condemnation by the Holy See will be widely exploited for political purposes by one side in the conflict, In addition, the German Government, feeling that it is struck at, would, without doubt, do two things: it would persecute in still more exasperating manner Catholicism in Poland and it would prevent the Holy See from having any kind of contact with the Polish hierarchy and from carrying on its charitable work, which it can presently, although in a restricted manner." With the Vatican aware of German behavior as early as 1940, and unable to change it, it is difficult to believe that the Vatican could negotiate an accommodation with Hitler.

Another example of an erroneous claim about efforts by the Vatican to interact with the Soviets came from Mark Aarons and John Loftus who said that an OSS report from 1942 told of an agreement between the Vatican and Hitler to send a Vatican emissary to the Ukraine to explore the possibility of a union of Rome with the Ukrainian Orthodox Church. The British minister in the Vatican reported that the alleged agreement was false. Robert Graham, an expert in such matters, knew that Hitler's hostility to the Church rendered such an agreement improbable, but also knew that there was no basis in fact for the story. However, it made a dramatic story and was included in their book.[16]

The British complained that the Vatican's condemnation of the bombing of cities, and especially seeking protection for Rome as an open city, played into the hands of the Germans. After the Armistice of September 8, 1943, the plea to respect Rome was considered self-serving and favoring the German occupation of the Eternal City. Later, some argued that the pope was more concerned with protecting Rome than he was in protecting Rome's Jews. The Vatican noted that it had successfully urged Germany not to bomb Athens and Cairo because of their historic importance and believed that Rome was no less an historic site deserving protection. For a time some consideration was given to this plea and Rome never was treated like Berlin, but elsewhere the Allies, like the Germans, eventually adopted a no holds barred approach to the bombing campaign in Europe.

The British strongly objected to the pope's Christmas message of 1943 that condemned British-style bombing in diplomatic language, although not explicitly. They ignored what he said about Germany, again in diplomatic language, although also not explicitly. Although the British readily understood the pope's diplomatic language because they used their own variant of it, did they believe that the Germans were any less adept at decoding diplomatic language? Writing to his Foreign Ministry, the German ambassador to the Vatican, Ernest von Weizsacker, referred to "the Vatican typical style that is contorted and cloudy." Despite that, he clearly understood the message. As practitioners of the same language the British understood only too well but wanted Pius to breach Vatican neutrality. Students of those times should realize that Allied criticism of Vatican neutrality was highly pragmatic and self serving, and could hardly be otherwise, and was not rooted in a higher moral sense than the pope's. Understanding the pope's messages was not a problem for the Germans, with the pope's 1942 Christmas message a case in point. Anthony Rhodes said that the Christmas message was criticized by some nations, including Britain, because it did not mention Germany by name. However, according to Rhodes, "Heydrich's R.S.H.A. had no doubt about the Christmas address which it analyzed most carefully.... In a manner never known before the Pope has repudiated the National Socialist European Order.... It is true, the Pope does not refer to the National Socialists in Germany by name, but his speech is one long attack on everything we stand for.... Here he is clearly speaking of the Jews. ... he is virtually accusing the German people of injustice toward the Jews."[17]

Michael Phayer showed the involvement of Croatian Catholics, including clergy, in the persecution of Jews. He tells about the same happening elsewhere, and the cumulative effect is a powerful indictment of Catholics whose faith was subverted by nationalist politics and age-old hatreds. As part of the historical record of the Catholic Church, such matters deserve documentation and reflection. At times, however, Professor Phayer fails to place matters in context. One such case is his mention of a German priest who justified euthanasia, with the author's obvious implication that it showed German Catholic support for the program to kill the mentally ill and mentally defective. Somehow that solitary example was to balance the protests of the bishops and the Vatican that before the war at least temporarily stopped the program. In any balanced historical prosecution, and Professor Phayer is an excellent prosecutor, the historian also should reveal the defense so the reader learns both sides of the story. Phayer does this on occasion; typically, however, the other side is unrealistically incomplete, and that unfairly tilts his case.

With regard to Croatia, Professor Phayer could have followed Carlo Falconi, who was very critical of the pope's "silence" but tried to place it in the context of the times and the delicate situations confronting the Vatican. That is illustrated in his description of the conflicting currents of opinion within the bureaucracy about Vatican policy toward the new puppet state of Croatia. It showed that no matter how top down most writers view the Vatican, the roles of subordinates must be given serious consideration. Formal Vatican policy toward Croatia was reserved because official ties continued with the royal Yugoslav government in exile. Yet it was important for the Vatican to have a relationship with a country that was largely Catholic, so there were constant contacts between the Vatican and Croatia. The Croatians desperately wanted Vatican recognition, and Falconi relates their lobbying efforts with various Vatican functionaries who might influence Vatican policy. Most proved unfriendly, probably because they knew the horrors perpetrated by the Ustashe. The Vatican intervened with Italy to press for Croatian restraint but did so in a manner that would not end whatever influence it might have with the Croats. Many would consider that by keeping any ties to Croatia, the Vatican made a bargain with the devil. The hundreds of thousands of Serbs and

4 — Papal "Silence" and "Fear of Communism"

thousands of Jews who were its beneficiaries, at least for a time, might disagree.[18]

As the Vatican tacked between the demands of the Axis and the Allies, its neutrality policy evoked strong criticism from both sides. In June 1941, for example, both the Germans and the British complained about Vatican Radio broadcasts that were critical of their behavior. The Vatican's reply rebuffed both complaints, telling the British that the Vatican had no agreement with any of the powers about its broadcasts and that "the Holy See intended to maintain in every circumstance its full independence and absolute impartiality."

There was more about Vatican and Church neutrality when in June 1941, Myron Taylor, the president's representative to the Vatican, complained to the papal nuncio in Washington that some bishops were supporting the isolationist America First Committee. Cicognani assured him that this was not so, pointing out that the Committee misrepresented a statement by the bishops. Although he acknowledged that some bishops were against entering the war, he said this was not due to their support of Germany. He pointed to the many critical comments about Nazism made by bishops like Archbishop Francis Spellman of New York. When ending his conversation with Taylor he assured him "of the solicitude of the Holy See and the bishops in teaching and promulgating those moral principles of dignity and human liberty, also with practical application in the events of our time." That delicate diplomatic language could not have done other than reassure Taylor of the Vatican's attitude. Archbishop Spellman served in the Vatican for several years and knew it from the inside. He also was a patriotic American who was close to Washington and wanted an Allied victory and who could be expected to deal candidly with the Vatican. His opinions, including political ones, were frank, and sometimes too much so for the comfort of both Catholics and others.

Although Spellman was not the only Catholic prelate to support the British, he was one of the few who ventured boldly into the political arena. Another outspoken bishop, and perhaps the most outspoken American Catholic bishop against anti–Semitism in that time, was Bishop Bernard Sheil of Chicago, a strong critic of Father Charles Coughlin, the "radio priest" who in the years before the war not only preached an old-fashioned progressive social gospel but was an ardent anti–Semite who promoted the Protocols of the Elders of Zion. The bishop's attack on anti–Semitism "endeared him to Chicago's Jewish community," according to Steven Avella, "who took up a large collection for Pope Pius XI in 1939 and handed it to Sheil to personally deliver to the pontiff. Bishop Sheil was one of the few American bishops to speak out against the destruction of European Jewry during the war." A progressive of the old school who supported the New Deal, the bishop was well known in Washington. In a conversation between Ambassador Myron Taylor and the Vatican secretary of state on February 27, 1940, the ambassador said that with the possibility of appointing a new bishop in Washington, the president mentioned that "Msgr. Sheil, Assistant in Chicago, would be welcome in Washington circles." The Vatican's answer was non-committal but in fact the president's comment ended the matter. Bishop Sheil remained in Chicago.[19]

It can be argued that individual bishops and clergy very often voiced strong criticism of what was happening in Axis nations, and thus the institutional church acted to counter the persecution of Jews and others victims of Nazi oppression. However, such principled action by Church members tended to be restrained for all too human reasons, and when they happened, often created a vicious backlash that led to further restraint. Not many clergy were eager to embrace martyrdom. In Holland the condemnation of Nazi treatment of the Jews led to an even more draconian treatment that decimated the Jewish community. The lesson was not lost elsewhere, but in many places such efforts continued, often at a high cost.

When the puppet Slovak government issued a Jewish Code on September 9, 1941, the Vatican secretariat of state sent the government a note that read in part, "With the deepest sorrow the Holy See has learned that also in Slovakia, a country whose population almost totally honors the best Catholic tradition, a 'Government Ordinance' issued on September 9 establishing special 'racial legislation' and containing various regulations in open contrast with Catholic principles." "In fact the Church, universal by the will of her divine Founder, welcomes to her bosom people of all races, and views all mankind with a maternal solicitude for the purpose of creating and developing among all men feelings of brotherhood and love, in accordance with the explicit and categoric teaching of the Gospel." The language was diplomatic, but its intent was clear.

Even before that, in August the Slovak bishops sent a protest note to Jozef Tiso, the president of the puppet state: "It does not escape the attention of the careful examiner that the philosophical conception on the basis

of which the present ordinance has been drawn up is the racist ideology....
We do not intend to enumerate here all the dangerous errors that this doctrine conceals in itself. ... the materialistic theory of racism is in direct contradiction with the teaching of the Catholic Church on the common origin of all men from a single Creator and Father, on the substantial equality of men before God stressed especially by the Apostle of the peoples, on the Common supernatural destiny of men in consequence of the universal redemption work of Christ... The so-called Jewish Code violates natural law and the freedom of individual conscience."

Fiorello Cavalli traced how, over the next few years the Vatican protested vigorously against the treatment of the Jews, but to little avail. Although at times the Vatican and local bishops distinguished between baptized Jews and others in their dealings with the government, all clearly condemned the treatment of any Jews. In dealing with the Slovaks, Cavalli noted that, "while publically the Pope had to abstain, as he himself said, from saying what would end doing more harm than good, he could assume a very different tone in his diplomatic activity." Unfortunately, neither approach to the government had a positive outcome. Ultimately the Germans occupied the country and proved more zealous in the deportation campaign.[20]

* * *

By defying "international efforts to bring Holocaust perpetrators to judicial accountability, the Vatican allowed fascist war criminals and fugitives from justice to become engaged in the postwar struggle against communism. The ethical credibility of the papacy fell to its lowest level in modern times." That was Professor Phayer's conclusion about Pius XII, and he also believed, "The pope was also anxious to see that convicted war criminals be given clemency, and in all likelihood he opposed the Nuremberg Trials." That opinion contradicted British Ambassador to the Vatican d'Arcy Osborne's statement that "the Pope is on record that the authors of war crimes should pay for their evil-doing." Perhaps Professor Phayer, who was teaching at a Catholic university, was unaware that in modern times the Vatican has questioned the death penalty. It is not alone among religious groups in seeking clemency, although not pardons, even for perpetrators of heinous crimes. To imply a cynical motive behind such appeals, which did not question guilt but the death penalty, ignores or shows an unfortunate lack of knowledge of certain basic tenets of Christian theology. If Pius opposed the Nuremberg Trials, Professor Phayer should have known that he would not have been alone. Those interested can find legal and political briefs contesting "victors' justice." In their book about the trials of war criminals, Aaron Freiwald and Martin Mendelsohn found that American backing for the trials of Nazis was vulnerable because "many prominent American lawyers and jurists, even some of those very much in favor of prosecuting Nazis, were uncomfortable with the absence of any appeal mechanism in the Allied Nazi trials." Although Phayer might be willing to overlook such legal niceties, Pius was not alone in showing concern about them. Phayer's accusation is his opinion, but it is without evidence and is not the stuff of scholarly history.

Although Bishop Hudal and others aided men wanted as war criminals, there is no evidence that it was a "Vatican" program. Much went on in the Vatican, just as much went on in Washington and London that had no official or unofficial sanction, of which Churchill and Roosevelt had no knowledge. Professor Phayer also might have explained why, after faulting the Vatican for aiding wanted criminals, he did not do the same for leaders of the international community in Paris, London and Washington who knowingly did so as they sought allies in the postwar struggle against a genuine Soviet threat. His answer might be that the Vatican should be held to a higher standard. That might be fair if he had proven that the Vatican as such did the same as the United States, Britain and France as a matter of policy. Despite the sensational claims of Mark Aarons and John Loftus, there is no evidence of tacit or otherwise papal or top level Vatican involvement in establishing an escape line for Nazis on the run from justice. Frustrating as it may be for conspiracy theorists, unless and until the Vatican's or other archives reveal a "smoking gun," it is best for historians to temper their conclusions about a presumed loss of Vatican and papal credibility.

Professor Phayer's indictment of Pius XII included his efforts to relieve the suffering of the Germans after the war. Although former President Herbert Hoover, who headed relief efforts in Europe, praised the Vatican for its efforts, Professor Phayer saw that effort as questionable in view of the punitive attitude toward Germany taken by the Allies. American occupation authorities were against fraternization, but they opposed the Soviet expropriation of industry in its occupation zone and, unlike the French and Soviets, hastened to provide food for the population in the American zone even when the shipping of relief supplies to Europe delayed the return home of American troops. There were untold thousands of Germans who had enthusiastically supported Hitler and might be considered unworthy of American concern, but there also were millions of others, including children, who would have been victims of mass starvation had the stern resolve of Professor Phayer and others carried the day.

When Professor Phayer criticized Pius's failure to press for German restitution of Jewish assets and property, the reason was because on one occasion Pius did not discuss restitution with the Vatican envoy to Germany. Phayer saw the Allies' charge of collective German guilt much as did Daniel Goldhagen and questioned papal opposition to it. Both authors followed the philosophy of the abortive Morgenthau Plan that would have reduced Germany to an agricultural economy, a policy that was strongly opposed by the American military for very practical reasons. Had Professor Phayer remembered the debate about Goldhagen's thesis some years before his own book was published, he might have understood why the idea of collective guilt was considered unjust, as well as juridically and religiously questionable. Pius's rejection of collective guilt could just as well be seen not as a political move to enhance the position of the German Church, but because it was of dubious morality.[21]

* * *

Daniel Goldhagen's first book gave the reason why the Germans treated the Jews so barbarously, because of an "eliminationist antisemitism" that made German society a willing participation in the Holocaust. He ascribed much of the responsibility for that attitude to the traditional teaching of the Catholic Church. That thesis was echoed by James Carroll whose *Constantine's Sword* is a lengthy indictment of the Catholic Church for its anti–Semitism. Elsewhere he said he wanted to show "how this primordial sin of the Church prepared the ground out of which grew the Nazi program to eliminate the Jewish people." Goldhagen rejected what he called conventional explanations suggesting that other people operating in the place of the Germans, and under the same conditions, could have behaved in similar fashion. "Since the conventional explanations ignore the identity of the perpetrators, they assert additionally, by implication, that had the Italian government ordered such a genocide ...

ordinary Italians would have slaughtered and brutalized Jewish men, women and children more or less as the Germans did. This fanciful notion is falsified by the actual historical record. Italians, even the Italian military, by and large disobeyed Mussolini's orders for the deportation of Jews to what they knew would be death at German hands." *Hitler's Willing Executioners* was a media sensation in Europe, and Goldhagen was lionized at speaking engagements there. The attention he received from a sensationalist book that had scarcely been reviewed in other than television sound bites and articles in the popular press revealed the intense interest in the subject by certain sectors of the public.

Despite the positive note about the Italians there are reasons for reservations about Goldhagen's thesis about the Germans. One example of a severe criticism of Goldhagen's scholarship and conclusions came from Norman Finkelstein and Ruth Birn who found, "As it stands, this book only caters to those who want simplistic answers to difficult questions, to those who want the security of prejudices." Finkelstein and Birn were harshly criticized for questioning Goldhagen's thesis, almost as if their book was Holocaust revisionism, which it definitely was not. Instead they were in the company of many scholars who found Goldhagen's work fatally flawed. One was Claudio Pavone who criticized those who circulated an ancient anti–German propaganda: "There are documents ... in which the Germans are seen as the eternal 'Teutons,' the eternal 'barbarians,' a kind of eternal damnation of the German people a priori and forever. That is a slippery slope that can lead to a racism for which a people who have given civilization so many high contributions are reduced to only an instrument of a horrible tyranny." Explaining a complicated socio-political process as the result of a corrupted national character is very attractive in a dynamic, readable book like Goldhagen's, but it is too simplistic to carry weight as a credible analysis of a terrible episode in human history. Although often cited by writers critical of the Church, serious historians of the period tend to give Goldhagen the scant attention his work deserves as history. The reasons for disparaging Goldhagen's scholarship are rather gently outlined in Geoff Eley's *The "Goldhagen Effect,"* which recounts how slipshod the research for this pot-boiler was.[22]

In contrast to Goldhagen, Christopher Browning and Jurgen Matthaus have a masterly study, *The Origins of the Final Solution*, in which they present a complex and nuanced explanation of why anti–Semitism took root

4—Papal "Silence" and "Fear of Communism"

and flourished in Germany. Whether one agrees with all its elements, it represents an effort to acknowledge the influence of the socioeconomic, the political and the religious background that created the climate for the Final Solution. Unfortunately, it does not receive the attention of Goldhagen's book. Its scholarly complexity and detail does not lend it to talk shows, sound bites and the kind of publicity campaign that popularized Goldhagen's book in Europe and the United States.[23]

Professor Goldhagen believed that he could go beyond description to explain differences in the behaviors of people. But significant differences are hard to explain, although we believe we know a lot about national characteristics. Why did so many Italians help Jews while their northern neighbors, the Austrians, harassed them almost to extinction? These are surface differences between the two societies: one orderly and well organized, the other tolerant of disorder and disorganization; one relishing beer, the other wine; the fact that Austrians do not cross a street against a traffic light, while Italians accept the challenge. The striking differences between Italian opera and Austrian opera add only a few of the many ways that distinguish people who share a continent. However, they do not explain why these neighbors differed in their treatment of fellow citizens.

Generalizing from such behaviors or any others and going beyond describing them is an attractive but slippery slope. Having said that, and also having expressed disagreement with Goldhagen's theory about why the "Final Solution" occurred in Germany, I agree him that it is hard to imagine many Italians playing a Germanic role in the Holocaust. After living in Italy for several years, I can describe how most Italians seem different from most Germans. Why they are different is another matter. Although Luigi Barzini's insights in *The Italians* are useful descriptions of how they differ, one must be cautious about extrapolating to the why. One might as well compare the average precipitation in each country as a clue to the social psychology of these neighbors. Pushing the case of national characteristics beyond description, on the theory that psychological insights about a complex society are meaningful, can lead to interesting psychobabble, but it seldom adds to historical analysis and understanding.

* * *

As new facts trickle out, the assessments of major figures in the wartime drama can tend to shift pro or con, often depending more on the inclination of the writer than on the new material itself. Because villains are more interesting, as Hochhuth, Cornwell and others have found to their profit, the pursuit of the pope's reputation will continue. In an era of historical deconstruction that decries "objectivity," nothing less should be expected. That makes it difficult for readers to obtain a fair assessment of the enigmatic Pius XII. A very private person who had a brilliant diplomatic career, he became pope during a global crisis when diplomacy's traditional role counted for little. The time was long past when Pope Gregory VII in 1076 could bring a ruler like Henry IV to Canossa, which is what Pius XII's critics, ignoring the times, seem quick to demand. Despite the reality confronting him, in the opinion of some historians, Pius XII did not rise to the occasion as a moral leader. Exactly what he should have done is often unstated, but presumably he should have denounced the evil doers more vehemently. Professor Zuccotti made her position clear, contending that if Pius XII had publicly condemned the roundup of Roman Jews in October 1944, it "probably would not have forestalled the roundup, but it certainly placed the Pope on sounder moral ground." That his private, diplomatic communication stopped the roundup and saved thousands of lives paled in comparison to the rhetorical advantage he might have gained with latter day critics. Zuccotti's preference could have severed what few lines of communication with German-occupied Europe, something any diplomat would resist, especially in the absence of meaningful alternatives. Unfortunately, according to Luxmoore and Babiuch, "For all the deftness and perseverance, there was no real evidence that the era of diplomacy produced dependable results." That became clear, but only in retrospect. Without other resources to pit against Hitler, it is understandable why Pius continued the diplomatic game, with some marginal success as in Hungary. Today that can seem insignificant when measured against what is now known about Nazi ferocity, but at the time it meant life for at least some people.

When discussing the controversy over Hannah Arendt's criticism of the cooperation of Jewish leaders with the Germans in the ghettos during the Holocaust, Peter Novick said something applicable in other situations: "One good reason for avoiding sweeping judgments is that distinctions, exceptions, qualifications, and nuances get away. Those intent on making what they think is an important theoretical point are likely to ignore this, as Arendt did, and as others did for other purposes. Another good reason for at least being very cautious about judging moral choices made under totalitarian terror is that in such circumstances choices are terribly constrained — they hardly seem to the actors like choices at all. No one knew this better Hannah Arendt, but Arendt the stern moralist triumphed over the sophisticated analyst."[24]

Owen Chadwick's *Britain and the Vatican* helps one understand the context of Vatican policy during the war. It is more than an account of the interplay of the Holy See and the British government and shows the behind the scenes activities of major players and their sometimes all too human reactions as they made policy. The Vatican was, after all, also a human institution, something to be considered when studying what happened during the war. This was the context for what happened in the wartime Vatican so aptly described by Chadwick: "Not only is the atmosphere of the Vatican supranational and universal, at any rate to an extent sufficient to affect political judgement and decision, but is also fourth-dimensional and, so to speak outside of time.... They reckon in centuries and plan for eternity and this inevitably renders their policy inscrutable, confusing and on occasion reprehensible to practical and time-conditioned minds."[25]

There was another firsthand witness to events in the wartime Vatican, Harold Tittmann, the assistant to Myron Taylor, Roosevelt's emissary to the pope. During the war Tittmann spent two and a half years in the Vatican representing American interests during Taylor's absence. Although often disagreeing with Vatican policy, as might be expected, he represented it fairly to Washington. In a report to Ambassador Taylor on June 4, 1945, Tittmann told him of a conversation with Dr. Josef Mueller, a Bavarian Catholic lawyer who had been a leading figure in the anti–Nazi German underground movement and was its liaison between the movement and the Holy See. "Dr. Mueller told me last night that contrary to what I had heard, he had no part in drafting any part of the Pope's speech, but that he had furnished the Holy Father with the information on which certain passages were based. Dr. Mueller said that during the war his anti–Nazi organization in Germany had always been very insistent that the Pope should refrain from making any public statement singling out the Nazis and specifically condemning them and had recommended that the Pope's remarks should be confined to generalities only. Dr. Mueller said that he was obliged to give this advice, since, if the Pope had been specific,

Germans would have accused him of yielding to the prompting of foreign powers and this would have made the German Catholics even more suspected than they were and would have greatly restricted their freedom of action in their work of resistance to the Nazis. Dr. Mueller said that the policy of the Catholic resistance in Germany was that the Pope should stand aside while the German hierarchy carried out the struggle against the Nazis inside Germany, without outside influence being brought to bear. Dr. Mueller said that the Pope had followed this advice throughout the war."

In October 1942, in a message to the State Department quoted by Raul Hilberg, Tittman commented on the Vatican's neutrality as stemming from "many years of 'conditioning' in Germany." Years later, however, Tittman referred to the pope's "silence" saying, "Personally, I cannot help but feel that the Holy Father chose the better path by not speaking out and thereby saved many lives." Clear examples of papal practice in this regard is found in the response of Pius XI to the killing of priests in the Spanish Civil War and Pius XII to the Katyn massacre. The popes made no specific mention of such atrocities. Maintaining a policy of strict neutrality the Vatican issued well-understood protests in general terms against the bombing of civilians and other atrocities, not citing British, American, German or Soviet examples by name. Those protests were clearly understood not only by diplomats but by the media and government officials on both sides and obviously were ignored.

Robert Graham's explanation of why there was not wholesale condemnation of Germany is well to have on the record. (The following is a paraphrase of the Italian text.) "To use the spiritual arm in a military war against an entire people opens deep wounds. Today the Germans, the Japanese, and the Italians are among the best friends and allies of the United Nations and now silence can cover what was said in the United Nations about the Germans, the Japanese and the Italians during the war. Politics is politics. But even after centuries a nation or a people cannot forget a spiritual wound inflicted by its Pope in moments of grave crisis. That is why historians ought not expect the Holy See to conduct itself in a manner that serves only in the world of politics." What Tittman and Graham had to say about papal "silence" may not satisfy today's critics, but they are disingenuous to suggest that the "silence" was the product of anti-Semitism or favoritism to Germany.[26]

4 — Papal "Silence" and "Fear of Communism"

Long after the war, Cornwell and others argued that Pius XII was anti–Semitic. Those who believed otherwise were apt to be dismissed as partisan defenders of the papacy. What could the critics say about one of the pope's powerful enemies during the war? While the war still raged, Roberto Farinacci, the anti–Semitic editor of *Il Regine Fascista* in the puppet Salo government, wrote in January 1945, "Pope Pius XII has fully espoused the Jewish cause to the point of offending the sensibilities of his flock.... We never imagined that our Pastor, the Vicar of Christ, the Head of our Church could one day be regarded as the most influential defender of the interests of the Jewish people." After the Armistice on September 8th, Farinacci had become increasingly hostile to the Vatican, which, along with Spain, refused to recognize Mussolini's puppet government. An article he wrote in February 1944 claimed that Fascism's effort to reach an accommodation with the Church was met with contempt, the rejection of Fascism and an attitude of distrust in the Vatican that existed for years. To counter the Church in Salo's territory, he fostered an effort by a small group of priests who supported Fascism to develop a national Catholic church. Certainly no partisans of Pius XII, if critics believed that history deals factually with the real world, at the very least they could listen to Roberto Farinacci and Joseph Goebbels, and then ask if Pius XII was an anti–Semitic "Hitler's Pope."[27]

– 5 –
Afterword

> By condemning those who did not live up to what we would like to think we would have done.
> — Michael Marrus, 2002

> To smuggle in elements of a later knowledge when describing the mental patterns of people in an earlier period is a common temptation to writers, which should be resisted.
> — Arthur Koestler, 1941

This work cannot resolve some of the contentious issues that surfaced after the war and continue to bedevil both historians and the general reader. They may, however, suggest other approaches to such questions as: was the pope really "silent," did the Vatican cozy up to Hitler because of the fear of Communism and did Italians measure up to Goldhagen's impression of them in relation to the Jews. In the case of the pope's "silence" and the Vatican and Hitler, revisionist writers have shifted the story from what it actually was during and after the war, essentially reversing the story of what happened. They did so by interpreting what happened years earlier in the fashionable manner that characterized a newer generation of historians. One example may suffice to illustrate this approach. According to historian James Miller, "History is not immutable but constantly reinterpreted to fit society's requirements." If those "requirements" meant adapting the language of the past by changing archaic spelling or because new material became available, it would be unexceptional. But what Miller said means tailoring the past to meet today's fashion in history. What is in the history books and history journals is not immutable, but should it be tailored the way Soviet professors produced looseleaf history to fit Stalin's requirements? Unlike their American colleague they could argue that they could do nothing else.

Studies of the events of World War II that involved the Vatican, including this one, should be viewed as interim reports subject to change without notice, when there is actual evidence to do so. Critics of Pius's "silence," who far outnumber his defenders since the 1960s, have mined the historical record for evidence to support their claim that at best through mistaken prudence, or at worst because of anti–Semitism and secret support of Hitler, Pius XII failed to denounce the atrocities that happened during World War II. On the other side, Pius XII is often defended by what amounts to hagiography, which serves neither the man or history. On both sides, unfortunately, ideology too often trumps the facts.

Determining what happened in World War II and why presents a host of problems, some of which are beyond the historian's control. Many of the principals during the war died before they could be interviewed or write their memoirs, and almost all of their contemporaries also have died. They can no longer clarify accounts that beg for an explanation. Furthermore, the existing archival sources that ought to be examined are so numerous that they defy the solitary researcher, or even a well-financed team. Unfortunately, much important archival material remains dispersed and unavailable for reasons that frustrate historians. Experience with the Russian archives reveals that they can be restricted for political reasons. That is more than implied about the Vatican's reluctance to allow unimpeded access to its archives. Of course, if candid with their readers, Vatican critics might mention that even in the United States not everything in the National Archives is on an open shelf and that most of the British intelligence records of the war have yet to be released.

Not everything that transpired found its way to paper. That suggests scholarly caution in believing that documents always tell the whole story of what people on any side were thinking at a given time. Significant conversations at meals or during casual meetings were not always recorded by the parties involved, and if they were recorded it usually is in a one-sided report. We know much more about the inner thoughts of Richard Nixon and Lyndon Johnson because of their tapes than we could get from their memoirs or from documents in their libraries or the speculation of historians. But during the war Vatican City was not alone in lacking tape recorders.

Even when sources about World War II are available, few of us have mastered the languages needed to approach events from a rounded

5—Afterword

perspective that would enrich our understanding of the past. Why this happens is illustrated by a remark by historian Gerhard Weinberg, who wrote the excellent *World at Arms*. He acknowledged that Italian histories of the war "often are not likely to be of interest or easy access to American and British readers." In too many cases the same is true of the interest of American and British historians. An example of top-heavy reliance on English language materials is found in an excellent book on the Italian Campaign. The bibliography lists more than one hundred books, three of which are in French and none in Italian although one book was translated from Italian. Another example is the fact that the widespread atrocities committed by the Germans in Italy have received little attention compared to what happened elsewhere. Because a bibliographer can list only reports that are available, Norman Tutorow could list 2045 books and articles on European war crimes, war criminals and the Holocaust, but only 20 of them referred to what happened in Italy.[1]

It is unfortunate that most historians who are interested in this niche area do not read Italian and thus cannot have access to the many Italian books and articles that deal with the role of the Vatican and Pius XII in World War II. Some Italian writers recall a long standing anti-clerical tradition in Italian historiography; others are like Giovanni Miccoli, who was by no means always favorable to Pius XII, but placed him in the context of his tradition and the time. Miccoli argued that the age-old approach of the Vatican to diplomacy was ill-adapted to react to what happened in the 1940s. Not anti–Semitism or favoritism toward Germany but what turned out to be an outmoded concept of the role of the Vatican led to the pope's reticence in the name of neutrality. Whether pro or con the popes and/or the Vatican, Italian writers are more aware of the background of the politics of the Vatican and of the often subtle relationships between the church and the state institutions of Italy, which enables them to knowledgeably either damn or praise what happened during the war.

The chapters in Andrea Riccardi's *Pio XII* by Italian historians who wrote about Pius XII's tenure are examples of approaches that differ from those found in most books about him in English. Among other matters, they are concerned about the internal politics of the Italian Church during the war. An example is the manner in which the Vatican anticipated the war in April 1940, telling the Italian bishops that if war began, their clergy were to conduct themselves, while patriotic, with prudence and be strictly religious in regard to political matters related to the war. Understandably this was seen by the authorities as hostile to Fascism and Nazism.

The manner in which the Vatican handled relations with the Soviet Union during the war, according to Riccardi, showed a contrast between the unbending attitude of Pius XI and that of his successor. While elements in the Vatican concerned about doctrine were hard liners, the diplomats did not exclude the possibility of establishing formal relations with the Soviets. During the 1920s and 1930s the Vatican had very limited success in dealing with them, mainly in obtaining the release of some clerics and other persons. An example of Vatican diplomatic sophistication was that although fully aware of the Soviet attitude toward religion, it told the American bishops that the encyclical *Divini Redemptoris* did not require opposing aid to the USSR. It took what Riccardi called "a pause to reflect" about the relationship to the USSR, and as the war progressed it quietly reviewed its limited options in dealing with Stalin, but did not close the door to possible future relations. Stalin firmly closed the door. Although English language writers may refer to this episode, Riccardi placed it in its proper perspective, but only in Italian.[2]

* * *

Caution and skepticism suggests that the existence of a document need not be convincing. Documents can be authentic but their contents mistaken or false. Documents of the German foreign ministry revealed that the German ambassador to the Vatican often sent cables to Berlin touting the positive attitude of the Vatican toward Germany. Some historians accept them as proof of Pius XII's tilt toward Germany during the war. Placed in context, however, those messages must be carefully weighed because the German ambassador was known to place a positive spin on Vatican opinion. The same caution should be observed if judging the cables sent to Washington by Joseph Kennedy, the ambassador to the Court of St. James, who early in the war predicted British defeat.

To further confuse matters, the absence of a paper trail, which David Irving insisted showed Hitler did not initiate the Final Solution, proves nothing. However, Professor Zuccotti argued that the absence of documentary evidence showed that Pius XII did nothing to help Rome's Jews at the time of the October 1943 round up of Rome's Jews. Even assuming a lack of documentation, which is debatable because there are

5—Afterword

credible accounts that the pope initiated Vatican protests at the time, Professor Susan Zuccotti should have known that other means of communication existed. When OSS records covering Allied intercepts during the occupation of Rome were released, Richard Breitman and Timothy Naftali found that "the SS and the police conveyed some information through other means such as personal visits, couriers, and telephone calls." Did Professor Zuccotti imagine that the Germans were the only ones to use couriers and verbal communication?

An example of a nondocumented order of Hitler came from a deposition in 1972 by former SS General Karl Otto Wolff, who commanded SS forces in Italy during the war. When Hitler intended to occupy the Vatican and deport the pope, "There were no written instructions for this absolutely secret order of Hitler." Other sources have confirmed Wolff's account of a plan by Hitler that was superseded by events. Should lack of a paper trail render his testimony irrelevant historically? That plans were made without documentation was true of all the principals in the events of the day, including the Vatican, for reasons that should be obvious to any historian. Closer to home in the spring of 1940 President Roosevelt contacted Mussolini in an effort to keep Italy out of war. A thinly veiled threat of American intervention was involved so the American ambassador to Italy was to present the message orally, not in writing. While there is an American record of the unsuccessful contact with Mussolini, searching Italian archives would not produce the kind of evidence Zuccotti deems essential.

Those who insist on paper trails (which are highly desirable) might be interested in a exchange between General Dwight Eisenhower and the historian Douglas Freeman. Professor Freeman had suggested the desirability of documenting the General's decisions, to which Eisenhower tactfully replied: "I am unable to say whether or not the records of my office are sufficiently explicit to establish in every case, reasons for decisions taken. Since some of these decisions are made under circumstances where no secretaries are present, preliminary discussions do not find their way to paper." It requires no great leap of faith or understanding for historians to realize that the same can occur in other venues.

Assuming evidence is gathered, what Harold Mattingly said about studying Imperial Rome becomes no less true when studying what happened in World War II. "The evidence is often broken up into minute fragments, hard to assemble, hard to handle when assembled." At one time the handling meant being objective about the evidence, something too often lost in translation by revisionists. Despite their contempt for "objectivity," treating the past insofar as possible as it was, and not as the writer would have preferred, has merit. Students of history should realize that they are not seeing events as they were experienced by those who were condemned to live through them. The same holds for those who write about the past. They can legitimately engage in interpretation of past events, but the facts and their context must be presented to readers, else how are they to fairly judge the past?[3]

* * *

Two books published in 1999 and 2000 present widely divergent views of the papacy during World War II. John Cornwell's *Hitler's Pope* is a searing indictment of Pius XII. Ronald Rychlak's *Hitler, the War and the Pope* can be considered a defense of Pius XII. Both books are well written and extensively documented. In June 2004, the World Catalog, a data base of books held by libraries, listed 1912 libraries with Cornwell's book. Rychlak's book was listed in 421 libraries. These figures do not reflect the number of copies sold to the public. One might assume, however, that Cornwell's prestigious New York publisher invested more in marketing than the religious and smaller regional publisher that issued Rychlak's book.

Many books in this niche subject are written by and for academics so it is interesting to see how libraries made books available to students who may be assigned papers about the period and for faculty who teach the courses on World War II commonly taught in most colleges and universities. Libraries have their own collection policies and cannot purchase every book on every subject so their policies reflect the interests of the faculty. The fact that a library does not have a book in its collection does not mean it is not accessible to students and faculty through interlibrary loan. Still it is interesting to know that Harvard University is not the only major research university with history professors who write and teach about the Holocaust and other aspects of World War II, that has Cornwell's book in the library; however, Rychlak's book is available only on interlibrary loan. The same happens to be true of Margherita Marchione's 2002 book *Consensus and Controversy: Defending Pope Pius XII*, which is a scholarly, unabashed defense of the pope held by 137 libraries. However, Ralph McInerney's *The Defamation of Pius II*, also a vigorous defense of the pope, is found at Harvard and in 487 other libraries. Unlike Marchione and Rychalak, Michael Phayer's indictment of the Vatican in his book on the Catholic Church and the Holocaust, which is in 959 libraries, is in Harvard's library. Susan Zuccottti's *Under His Very Windows* is in 1183 libraries including Harvard's. Her *The Italians and the Holocaust: Persecution, Rescue and Survival* is at Harvard and 1128 other libraries.

Harvard University is not alone in having preferences in forming its collection of books in this niche area. Another university that teaches many Holocaust related courses is the University of Wisconsin–Madison. The University has a wonderful library (one that I learned to appreciate when teaching there) with the usual complement of books by John Cornwell, Susan Zuccotti, Daniel Goldhagen, Michael Phayer, et al. Although it has books by Margherita Marchione and *The Pius Wars* by Joseph Bottom, it does not have those of Ralph McInerney and Roland Rychalak.

All the books should be where they are and held by even more libraries because the debates about Pius will not disappear. At the very least, however, the distribution of some recent pro and con books about Pius XII in libraries shows that the latter are of more interest to academic libraries. That may reflect popular interest in such books, as well as the interest of faculty members, but it does not speak well for an evenhanded management of information by libraries. They purport to support a scholarly approach to disputed matters in history, even if the revisionist consensus seems to be that the question of papal "silence" is settled. Not every library needs to acquire every book on a subject, but some libraries do have that charge, or at least claim they do. They should not scorn to acquire even obscure, off-the-wall books, whether they are pro or con. Some libraries collect comic books for research purposes, others make space for racist tracts no matter how odious and regardless of their provenance. Research libraries should shelve the necessary resources for the faculty and students who are expected to winnow the "truth," wherever it may be found.

As the Internet increasingly becomes a resource for students, another dimension is added to ensure an evenhanded approach to issues explored by students and scholars. This was evident in a University of Washington Web site for History 498, "Pius XII and the Holocaust," that suggested readings for the course. It also introduced several Web sites identified as

"Catholic" cautioning readers: "These web sites are just a few that have popped up to debate Cornwell's contentions or to defend Pius XII. When using these web sites keep in mind possible biases." As a gatekeeper to knowledge, one might expect the library to explain why that caution was limited to only "Catholic" sites. In the scholarly community a request for information about such a practice usually elicits a response; however, repeated requests to the university librarian and then to the university's provost were not answered. After months, a final appeal to the university's president brought a response, but not an answer, from the dean of libraries. The dean explained that the intent was to alert students that Web sites on controversial issues can have "a particular viewpoint (or bias)." Although the words "viewpoint" and "bias," have different meanings, that eluded the dean. More important, why should a university library identify only so-called Catholic resources as possibly biased, something that can have a chilling effect for students as well as scholars.[4]

Not only university Web sites and libraries have their preferences for what information is shared with the public. The National Archives Web site has a finding aid dealing with information about Swiss gold and Holocaust assets that includes this brief statement about Pius XII:

> 22. Born, Eugenio Pacelli, Pius II [sic] was elected Pope in March 1939, having previously served as papal nuncio in Germany from 1917 to 1930 and as Vatican secretary of state from 1930. Researchers may find useful Saul Friedlander, *Pius XII and the Third Reich* [New York: Octagon, 1986]; Carlo Falconi, *The Silence of Pius XII* [London: Faber & Faber, 1970]; Nazareno Padallaro, *Portrait of Pius XII* [London: J. M. Dent, 1956]; Alexander Ramati, *While the Pope Kept Silent* [London: Allen & Unwin, 1978]; John Pollard, *The Vatican and Italian Fascism* [Cambridge: Cambridge University Press, 1988]; Mark Aarons and John Loftus, *Unholy Trinity: The Vatican, the Nazis, and Soviet Intelligence* [New York: St. Martin's Press, 1991]; Mark Aarons and John Loftus, *Unholy Trinity: The Vatican, the Nazis, and Swiss Banks*, new and rev. ed. [New York: St. Martin's Griffin, 1998]; David Alvarez and Robert A. Graham, S.J., *Nothing Sacred: Nazi Espionage Against the Vatican 1939–1945* [London and Portland, Oregon: Frank Cass, 1997].

The pope's association with Swiss gold was not spelled out, but obviously his presence on the Web site does more than imply that there is an association between Pius and "Swiss gold." That "fact" is boldly asserted by Aarons and Loftus who the NARA suggested may be helpful to researchers. Whether the imbalance in the list of suggested resources was

5—Afterword

intentional or by happenstance, it is impressive and highly questionable, especially in a government document.

Of course, the pope was not the only subject of lurid speculation about gold the Germans took from the banks of the nations they invaded and from victims of Nazi persecution. Switzerland handled much of it and became the prime target of criticism for accepting gold that helped finance German war production, and for failing to restore the assets in dormant bank accounts to survivors or their heirs. According to Jean Ziegler, "But for the effective gold laundering services provided by the Swiss National Bank, and but for Swiss arms deliveries and loans to Berlin, the war would have ended earlier—probably in 1944. Swiss bankers, in particular, were responsible for millions of deaths." Ziegler added, "The horrifying theory that Switzerland prolonged the war has just received additional support from Stuart E. Eizenstat, U.S. Department of Commerce undersecretary, and William Z. Slany, the State Department's Chief Historian."

That Switzerland prolonged the war is based on Slany's assertion: "Beginning in mid-1943 with the Allied invasion of Italy, the D-Day invasion in June, 1944, and the diversion of German forces to halt the Soviet Army's advance, the Nazi occupation of Europe was rolled back and the threat of the neutrals greatly diminishes, although there were still fears of other forms of reprisal.... The neutrals continued to profit from their trading links with Germany and thus contributed to prolonging one of the bloodiest conflicts in history. During this period, the Allies suffered hundreds of thousands of casualties and millions of innocent citizens were killed."

If Slany was correct that the neutrals, and especially Switzerland, were responsible for the deaths of millions of innocent citizens after September 1943, then major revision of the historiography of World War II is needed. That serious charge appeared in an official U.S. government publication, which gives it credibility that undocumented conclusions otherwise would not enjoy. How many term papers have accepted that as gospel? Itmar Levin, a severe critic of the Swiss financial dealings with Germany and its failure to restore funds to wartime depositors, admitted that "it is impossible to make an unequivocal determination, as Eizenstat did, that Switzerland prolonged the war. Bern correctly states that there is no proof of this in the report, and therefore it is a political and not a historical conclusion." But readers will not find Levin mentioned by the Web site. They will discover that the Vatican and the Swiss were somehow associated, not only in laundering Nazi gold, but in thereby prolonging the war and responsible for millions of deaths.

The Swiss government formed the independent Bergier Commssion in 1996 to examine questions raised by the United States and others about its wartime neutrality and the "Swiss gold" controversy. Composed of five Swiss and three outside experts, its conclusions were critical of many aspects of what happened there during the war. On the matter of prolonging the war, however, despite such matters as allowing transit to German trains and exporting war materials until late in the war, "The Commission found no evidence of such an impact. Though access to Swiss resources could not be said to have been of no significance, it also was clear that given the reserves in the Germany economy and Germany's determination to continue to fight, the absence of Swiss cooperation could not have shortened the war in any material way."

The 1998 Eizenstat report was not the only official government document that implicitly questioned the role of the Vatican during the war. There is an "Appendix O" in the *Proceedings of the 1998 Conference on Holocaust Assets* hosted by the U.S. State Department. That appendix is about the multivolume *Actes et documents du Saint-Siège* that contains Vatican archival material about World War II. Because the conference was focused on the financial holdings and art confiscated by the Nazis during the war, Appendix O seemed out of place in the massive volume reporting the conference proceedings. However, why it is there becomes clearer if one notes the reference to archival material on page 916 of the *Proceedings*: "Archives in many countries continue to hamper and restrict research efforts by being inaccessible, maintaining prohibitive classification systems or by using local privacy laws as the basis for blocking out references to specific individuals." Then on page 917: "The most often repeated theme was that researchers should have free access to relevant archives worldwide." Those comments can be said about several countries, including those in Western Europe. The public has not heard about them, but it has heard much about the Vatican's not opening its archives. To assume that there was a connection between those references and the "balance" provided by Appendix O should not be surprising.

The conference agenda included discussions of some archives that had documents relating to the confiscation of specific art works, but apart

5—Afterword

from allegations that the Vatican received Croatian gold, there is little reason to believe that its archives contained the kind of documentation of primary interest to the conference. Given the rampant innuendo about the *Actes*, however, the inclusion of Appendix O could be seen as an effort to "balance" what knowledgeable conference participants would understand was intended by the above remarks and allegations about the supposed "selectivity" of documents by the *Actes* editors as well as the closure of most of the Vatican's archives for the war years.

In a speech to investigative reporters by Greg Bradsher of the National Archives staff, there was this reference to Croatian or Ustashi Gold: "Researchers, especially journalists, began focusing on the roles of the Vatican and the Croatian Utashi and their dealings with Jewish assets." His message was that the Vatican somehow had dealt with Jewish assets, and he delivered the same message in a later speech to fellow archivists at the annual meeting of the Society of American Archivists. Archivists usually do not jump to conclusions before there is evidence, but in this case Bradsher was not alone. Stuart Eizenstat, who headed the American research into what happened to Holocaust assets, had referred to the Vatican-Croatian connection in a 1998 briefing on "Nazi Gold." According to Eizenstat, "We came across the issue of Ustasha gold. This therefore raises, in this chapter, questions about aspects of the Vatican's record during and after the war to which answers may only exist in Vatican and Croatian and Serbian archives." He went on to say that the pontifical college of San Girolamo was "most likely funded, at least in part, by the remnants of the Ustasha treasury ... and may have operated, at least with the tacit acquiesence of some Vatican officials." His statement about the relationship of the Vatican to the Croatians closely resembled what Aarons and Loftus have speculated about this subject. A full accounting of what happened, Eizenstat said, depended on the opening of the archives in Croatia, Serbia and the Vatican. Although not accusing the Vatican directly of complicity in dealing with the Ustashi, its linkage to those war criminals is clearly implied, based on the "informed" speculation of Eizenstat and the Archives staff.[5]

* * *

The identification of writers as Catholic when they write about the Vatican and the Pope is counter to the general practice among historians not to identify individuals by their religion unless it is an important identifier. Pius XII and John F. Kennedy, for example, can reasonably be named as Catholics. John Morley, a severe critic of Pius XII is invariably identified as a Catholic priest, perhaps because it is assumed to be unusual for Catholic priests to be critical of the pope. Some may have noticed that while to be identified as a Catholic enhances the credibility of papal critics, it has the opposite effect for Catholics who are seen as "defensive" of the papacy. Although it is not general practice to identify writers by their religious belief or non-belief when writing in this area, is this exception for writers who are Catholic a subtle way to alert readers to their possible bias? It may seem unduly provocative to ask whether, in the interest of transparency, the religious background, or lack thereof, of all who venture to write in this realm be revealed to readers.

Both Margarita Marchione and Ralph McInerney write about or "defend" Pius XII from an overt Catholic perspective, which does not sit well with most of those who write in this niche area of history. They are seen as writing for members of a choir that is usually ignored by academicians. Apart from McInerney's sometimes apologetic pages, it would be unwise to dismiss out-of-hand the cogent arguments he makes in Pius's defense. Although his book has been in the market since 2001, by 2005 it was reviewed by only one scholarly journal, and that one Catholic, and by a Catholic journal of opinion. Marchione and Rychalak share the same obscurity in the history journals. They were joined by an excellent 2002 book by Professor Jose Sanchez of St. Louis University, whose *Pius XII and the Holocaust: Understanding the Controversy* received two reviews, but not by history journals. This short book has an evenhanded presentation of both sides of the controversy and is the best current account both for the scholar and general reader. It can be found in Harvard's library and 714 others.

When introducing *Pius XII and the Holocaust*, the editors, Carol Rittner and John Roth, told of convening a group of scholars to assess the state of scholarship about Pius XII during the Holocaust, "without the hype that surrounded John Cornwell's intentionally provocative *Hitler's Pope* or the polemical defenses of Pius that are illustrated by Dalin's journalism." Unfortunately, they began by marginalizing someone who obviously is the other side of the debate about Pius XII. Their polite invective was only the first step in their approach because among "scholars"

5 — Afterword

labeling someone a "journalist" often is an epithet. The intrusion of the "non-credentialed" is resisted by status-conscious historians. Adding to their put-down of David Dalin, we are told that he wrote in a "conservative" journal, the *Weekly Standard*. Why the editors thought that description necessary is strange because other publications mentioned in the book do not carry a descriptor such as "liberal" or "neutral."

David Dalin continued to be the editors' bête noir as they accused him of unspecified "simplistically polemical descriptions" of some critics of Pius XII whom he suggested use criticism of Pius as a surrogate for their desire to force change in today's Church. Doubting that was the case, the editors found it strange that he had in mind writers Gary Wills, James Carroll and John Cornwell. Evidently the editors paid little or no attention to blunt assertions by those men that such change was indeed on their agenda. In his *Toward a New Catholic Church* Carroll said that the world desperately needed a Catholicism "profoundly reformed." In the early 1970s Gary Wills wrote *Bare-Ruined Choirs,* which outlined his view of the Church's defects and need for radical change. If Rittner and Roth needed further evidence of the agendas of these men, they could have read that or Wills' later *Papal Sin*, while Cornwell's *Breaking Faith* hardly could be considered a neutral tract about the Church. Books by Wills and Carroll were published before Rittner and Roth published their book and were available for review during their research. Whether Dalin's inference from what they say about the Church directly relates to their characterization of the pope is another matter, but mentioning their agenda for the benefit of his readers was descriptive and hardly "polemical."

Dalin also allegedly made dubious, sweeping claims that the editors assert are not "scholarly strategies but political and journalistic ones that aim to silence opposition because they cannot refute it empirically." It would help readers if that broad brush description of allegedly dubious claims was spelled out, but not one example was given. Although Rittner and Roth agreed that Dalin had a point when he recalled the many Jews who praised Pius after the war, they disputed his calling Pius XII a "righteous gentile," saying that title is usually reserved for non–Jews who risked their lives to personally rescue Jews. Because they recognized that there were exceptions when awarding that recognition, their objection is petty, but understandable in the context of their book. What might have been a genuine contribution to the understanding of Pius XII and

Jewish-Catholic relations by Roth and Rittner was marred by setting up David Dalin as a straw man at the very beginning of their proclaimed effort to increase understanding of Pius XII. Their book is in the Harvard University collection and in 307 other libraries, and ought to be in many more as an example of how research can be tainted by dismissing evidence to which the reader is entitled.[6]

In another counter to Dalin, and without any confirming evidence, Professor Zuccotti gave several reasons why Jews thanked the pope after the war. Some did so because they were misinformed, others for personal reasons, still more in the mistaken impression that their shelter was the result of his direct order, and more did so because they wanted Vatican help. After half a century as Professor Zuccotti viewed those statements of gratitude, the reasons she ascribed to those who were there became increasingly tawdry. Unfortunately, in the interim between the war and when she wrote, those who made the statements had died and could not explain them or have anyone directly assess their credibility. If Professor Zuccotti did not find their written accounts credible, would she have believed them in person? We are not told what distinguished these witnesses from those she did believe, if any. Without providing some evidence, internal or otherwise, of a witness statement that confirms that it lacks validity, must we assume that she reached her conclusion intuitively? However she reached it, her depreciation of those witnesses who praised the pope was seconded by Daniel Goldhagen who reported that Pius "received considerable praise, even from Jews who were more concerned with contemporary politics, with inhibiting the expression of more antisemitism, and with trying, in vain to get the powerful Church to take a more favorable position on Israel." Golda Meir certainly was concerned about contemporary politics. Was her praise of the pope effectively a lie in order to have him take a more favorable position toward Israel? Would it be reasonable also to question the integrity of a group that Aryth Kubovy met with in Rome in September 1945? They were members of the Union of Italian Communities, individuals who had endured the horrors of war in their country. Kubovy told them that he had good prospects of having a personal interview with the pope and they "insisted that I should also represent the Union of Italian Communities to convey its thanks for the Pope's activities on behalf of the Jews." What reason is there to doubt their sincerity, unless predisposed to do so? If both professors followed an age-old principle known as

5—Afterword

Occam's Razor, which recommends explaining matters parsimoniously, and dropped their dubious psychologizing about the memories of long-dead witnesses, history would be better served. Instead they have contributed to a long-running but unprovable counterfactual.

Professor Zuccotti is in good company when alerting readers to the fallibility of memories that can be partial, embellished or mistaken, and that desirably need confirmation. The importance of assessing the accounts of survivors is highlighted by articles in the scholarly journal *History and Memory*, which is dedicated to an in-depth analysis of the role of memories in episodes such as the Holocaust. Peter Novick claimed that survivor memories "are not a very useful historical source," adding, "Or, rather, some may be, but we don't know which ones." Both were gross overstatements. If some stories told by survivors can be questioned, it is the properly skeptical historian's task to avoid the trap of assuming all of them lack authenticity. More to the point about memories was D.D. Guttenplan: "The struggle to find the right way to describe the destruction of European Jewry is sometimes depicted as a contest between history and memory. And as we have now all been taught, memory is a very unreliable guide to ... how it really was.... Yet without witnesses, without human voices to put flesh on the facts, we have something that while it may pass muster as history, can never tell the truth." The historian's task is to avoid an either or approach to memories and instead interpret them in context. Used properly, memories are not myths but can be as genuine as anything found in the archives that has been tested for authenticity.

Although the sincerely held memories of many survivors may have been affected by subsequent experiences and events, as well as by the aging process, there are ways to identify memories that are valid recollections of past experiences. What the larger meaning of memories were for the individual's identity and future life is important, but recollected experience per se can be as significant a bit of data for the historian as anything found in an archive. To ignore or depreciate a survivor's recalled experience, especially when effectively corroborated, would leave us relying only on sterile written records. Although important, written records can be enriched when related to the experiences of those like Primo Levi and Anne Frank who told us what it meant to endure the past: otherwise, how are we, at some level of understanding, to comprehend what happened there? In the introduction to *If This Is a Man*, Primo Levi wrote, "The need to tell our story to 'the rest,' to make 'the rest' participate in it, had taken on for us before our liberation and after, the character of an immediate and violent impulse, to the point of competing with our other elementary needs. The book has been written to satisfy this need." He went on to say, "It seems to me unnecessary to add that none of the facts are invented." Those survivors who praised Pius may not have had the talent of Primo Levi. Is that what made their stories less credible for Professor Zuccotti? What would be the outcome of applying Professor Zuccotti's credibility test, whatever it might be, to Primo Levi's work?[7]

More questioning of memory arose when Professor Zuccotti asked about the credibility of what Msgr. John Carroll-Abbing (1912–2001) allegedly told William Doino. Carroll-Abbing said that he received direct orders from Pius XII to hide and protect Jews during the war. Unfortunately, he did not ask the pope to put the order in writing. A member of the Vatican's diplomatic service, Carroll-Abbing worked with refugees during the occupation and was a Vatican liaison with the Allies. After the war he became known internationally for his work with abandoned children whose plight was documented in classic postwar Italian films like *Shoeshine* and *Bicycle Thief*. He created the still existing Italian Boys Towns and Girls Towns for children.

How did Professor Zuccotti assess the credibility of his testimony? Would it be more or less credible than that of a Jewish survivor who said the pope saved Jews? She found that Carroll-Abbing mentioned that a convent was permitted to shelter men and said, "The Vatican may well have given explicit permission, as Carroll-Abbing said. But it took no initiative in rescuing Jews, and issued no directive before or after the fact." She thus effectively discounted Carroll-Abbing's statement about a verbal papal "directive" he was given to help Jews. What might this imply for William Doino's recollection of the (alleged?) conversation with Carroll-Abbing in which he referred to the pope's directive? With the source dead, how could Zuccotti authenticate Doino's story? During the German occupation it is well authenticated that Father Hugh O'Flaherty was responsible for operating a "rat line" for several thousand Allied personnel in Rome. He did this under the noses of diligent Nazis like Herbert Kappler. Why should it be hard for Zuccotti to believe that at the same time and place Carroll-Abbing helped to save Jews at the pope's direction? As

5—Afterword

one learns more about this man of initiative, he probably would have done so with or without orders.

An experienced scholar, Professor Zuccotti sometimes falters in her interpretation and conclusions when the data lack necessary context. This appeared in her article on the lack of the written papal directive to help Jews. Professor Zuccotti expressed concern that Carroll-Abbing rarely mentioned Jews in two of his books and never said that he took personal initiative to hide Jews. She wrote admiringly of his work during the German occupation of Rome but downplayed what he was supposedly told by Pius XII. She found his story questionable because it did not surface until the 1980s when there was a spate of similar stories defending the pope, noting that the defense really began with Rolf Hochuth's play in 1963 that savaged the reputation of Pius XII.

Carroll-Abbing wrote his books after the war when Pius XII needed no defense, especially when he was praised by icons like Golda Meir who became Israel's prime minister. Instead of Professor Zuccotti's interpretation, is it unreasonable to conclude that in that earlier time Carroll-Abbing saw no need to mention Jews in his books, if indeed he did not? However, he did mention Jews on page 7 of his *But for the Grace of God* (1965) as well as on page 33, and on page 34, when he was alerted by a German diplomat and went to a friend's house "to warn them to transfer elsewhere the Jewish lady whom they were hiding." Did that qualify as showing some initiative in helping Jews? Then on page 45 he said that he and a colleague were "becoming increasingly involved in the problems of the hideaways.... Soon we were in touch with many of the more than 150 religious institutions that were sheltering the Jews." After September 1943 until June 1944 he must have been in contact with at least scores or hundreds of Jews who were hidden in Catholic institutions. Under those circumstances could that be considered "personal initiative?" Does history require him to have touched every base that Professor Zuccotti much later considered essential in order to prove his credibility? It is well for historians to be skeptical, but there are limits, and one is excessive reliance on the lack of a paper trail when credible sources affirm that only verbal orders were given. In the case of Pius XII such insistence recalls David Irving's discredited claim that the lack of a paper trail means that Germany's leader did not know about the Holocaust.[8]

Based on Professor Zuccotti's claim that there were no written orders to help Jews, Professor Daniel Goldhagen took the matter a step further, "Susan Zuccotti, for example, has recently exposed a central exculpating myth — in her view consciously fabricated or encouraged by the Pope and others, and sustained by Jews who themselves were misled or wanted to placate the powerful Church — that the Pope gave orders for the Italian Church officials to hide Jews in churches and monasteries." Those who helped save Jews were heroic, "but there is no evidence of the Pope's guiding hand." Goldhagen's conclusion was: "Based on extensive, painstaking research into one locale after another, she [Zuccotti] methodically debunks claims that Pius XII was active of behalf of the Jews. These findings have devastated Pius XII's reputation." Accepting Zuccotti's "exculpating myth" early in his book, Goldhagen reached the book's conclusion early but took 242 more pages to wrap up Pius's devastated reputation. He managed to do that without reference to the work of any of those Zuccotti called "supporters" of the pope who happened to differ with his, and her, preordained conclusion about the pope's alleged fabrication. Accusing anyone of consciously fabricating or encouraging a "myth" of helping Jews is serious business that usually is accompanied by more than the mere assertion of an unsubstantiated opinion.[9]

Whether selectively or inadvertently, Professor Goldhagen missed sources other than Professor Zuccotti. He could have referred to her partial list of "supporters" of Pius XII that included Rychalak, Graham, McInerny and others. Books by Carroll, Cornwell, Goldhagen and others were called "critical" of Pius. One does not have to be hypersensitive to nuance in this field to find that the distinction between the description of the two camps is interesting. The word "supporters" implies fans of the pope, although some "supporters" also are "critical" of aspects of Pius's tenure in the sense the word is typically used by historians. On the other hand, the latter group is merely "critical," a much more neutral term. Among the "critical" authors are writers like Gary Wills and James Carroll who by common consent go well beyond being "critical," and instead can be fairly described as "attacking" Pius XII and his Church. Attack merely describes their work; it does not necessarily mean that they are wrong, but to blandly describe them and others as only "critical" is misleading.

To sum up the issue of trusting the witness, it is useful to note Saul Friedlander's comment that, "In many works the implicit assumptions

5—Afterword

regarding the victims ... have turned them into a static and abstract element of the historical background." He added, "Indeed their voices are essential if we are to attain an understanding of this past. For it is their voices that reveal what was known and what could be known." And while historian Gerda Lerner, who escaped from Europe in 1939 and lost relatives in the Holocaust, considered it extremely painful to think about that time, "If we don't, then the eyewitness primary account is lost, and the only people who will interpret this period are people who don't have a clue. They weren't there." If there is validity to social history, or history from the bottom up, to understand the American labor movement as seen through the lives of New England textile workers, then it is no less important to understand what happened during the war through the memories of people who endured it. A clue Professor Zuccotti missed was a fair and open test of the credibility of the witnesses. Surely the reader should know the criteria a writer used to make a judgment about a witness instead of dismissing their testimony out of hand because it did not agree with a preferred conclusion. With access to that criteria, I might have assessed the veracity of the elderly Roman Jew, who sat at his kitchen table telling me of wearing a cassock for six months in a monastery during the German occupation of Rome.[10]

* * *

Before World War II, according to Professor Zuccotti, the Vatican newspaper *L'Osservatore Romano* was more articulate in its condemnation of racism and the treatment of the Jews than seems to have been the case after the war began. Apparently it was more than reticent about what was happening to Jews: "*L'Osservatorio Romano's* comments on racism, welcome as they may have been, had some limitations. Like so many of the newspaper's editorials, they were often obscure, pedantic. and unintelligible — characteristics that must have limited their readership. Much more important, however, at a time when Jews were being rounded up, deported. and murdered, the denunciations of racism remained abstract and never directly mentioned them. Contemporary readers of goodwill made the association, but it is unlikely that those less favorably inclined toward Jews were provoked into rethinking their attitudes." Whether it was obscure and pedantic, Professor Zuccotti might be surprised to learn that the paper had enjoyed a circulation of 150,000 before its widespread distribution was forbidden by the Italian government. Apparently its many readers, and the censors, were quite capable of understanding its contents.

Summing up her study, Professor Zuccotti concluded that the paper could have "with impunity" published more articles about racism and the treatment of Jews throughout Europe. However, "It never tested the limits." She added that in June 1944, a papal speech appealing for compassion and charity for the Jews could have made a difference and saved lives, but the pope did not provide that leadership. Professor Zuccotti engaged in wishful thinking because there is literally no evidence that such appeals influenced German behavior. Along with many others she would have applauded a gesture not only doomed to failure but one that evoked brutal retaliation against those such a protest sought to defend.

There is an overlooked context for both the content and the "obscure" writing style of *L'Osservatore* that Professor Zuccotti complained about. First, the style of that newspaper was and continues to be arcane, especially when compared to articles in the *New York Times* or *Boston Globe*, and they probably were much more so in the 1930s and 1940s. Americans reading Rome's *Il Messaggero* or Milan's *Corriere della Sera* of any era also will find them "different" from what we expect in our home papers. That articles in *L'Osservatore* could be hard for the uninitiated to follow would not surprise anyone who also plowed through the often dense prose of *L'Unita*, the vehicle of the Italian Communist Party. Stylistically the prose of the two papers sometimes was almost a mirror image in denseness. Such different styles of communication are problematic for those accustomed to the more direct, terse styles of writing of American papers. On the whole, however, the Italian papers did and do manage to communicate effectively with readers who even today often must decode the meaning of a story. The historian may not appreciate the way *L'Osservatore* or any other newspaper approached its sociopolitical environment but should be aware of who the paper considered its public, the times and the situations it faced. During the war the Vatican paper often was under actual constraints and Zuccotti's claim that it could act "with impunity" ignores the reality of wartime Italy. When the Vatican paper carried the pope's message of sympathy to Holland, Belgium and Denmark when they were invaded by Germany, the Italian government harassed its readers, confiscated copies and effectively suppressed its distribution outside of Rome. Evidently the paper could not say anything it wanted with the

5—Afterword

"impunity" Professor Zuccotti imagined. Historians may regret that the newspaper of a neutral state followed a cautious path during a time of crisis, but should help their readers understand why that was so.[11]

* * *

Status-conscious, credentialed historians tend to depreciate the work of non-members of their guild who venture to write history without having doctorates in history. The in-group wields its doctorates against intrusions by outsiders, much as unions do for similar and understandable economic reasons. The late Daniel Boorstein suffered a bit from such criticism because of his education in the law, but he still managed to make some contribution to American historiography. Along such lines, a classic example of appealing to the authority of the guild, which is much criticized when used by ecclesiastics, is found in a forum in the *U.S. Catholic Historian*. Authors who wrote about the Holocaust and the Vatican included Susan Zuccotti, John Morley, Michael Phayer John K. Roth, Joseph Chinnici and John Justus Lawler. Each critiqued the work of other authors. Michael Phayer, for example, was severe in his criticism of Margarita Marchione, Ralph McEnerney and Roland Rychalak, noting that the last was an attorney. Specific errors they supposedly made were not mentioned, and the substance of their work mattered less than guild credentials. Apparently their style of overt and sometimes brusque defense of the pope was taboo, unlike the brusque criticism and attacks on the Vatican and Pius XII by non-guild as well as guild members.[12]

* * *

There is an interesting symmetry in the manner the Red Cross and the Vatican are treated for their alleged failure to protest Nazi atrocities. Most often by implication, their behavior was attributable to a lack of concern for the fate of Jews, if not to anti–Semitism. Whatever the reason for their "silence," they were not alone in being accused of moral failure. The Allies also have been accused of failing to do all they could militarily to stop the death camps, and the implication is clear that basically it happened for the same reasons as it did with the Vatican and Red Cross. According to Robert Weisbord and Wallace Sillanpoa, "The moral failure of Roosevelt and Churchill to bomb Auschwitz or the rail lines leading to it has been repeatedly highlighted by historians." Among them was Walter Laquer who thought, "Many Jews could certainly have been saved in 1944 by bombing the railway lines leading to the extermination centres, and of course, the centres themselves." David Wyman also made a detailed argument for bombing the rail lines, while Larry Ceplair contended, "A much more horrifying, and destructive, example of the moral shallowness of the war against Fascism was provided by the Allied governments, who made only token efforts to save the lives of the Jewish people of Europe.... During the war American and British leaders refused to countenance substantive rescue or refugee operations or military measures against the death camps."[13]

The debate over the non-bombing of Auschwitz received renewed impetus when Michael Beschloss wrote *The Conquerors* about Roosevelt and Truman. According to Beschloss, "With more than a half-century of hindsight, it is clearer now than in 1944 that the sound of bombs exploding at Auschwitz would have constituted a moral statement for all time that the British and Americans understood the historical gravity of the Holocaust." Later, in words reminiscent of those used about Pius XII, "by tacitly suggesting that the United States did not know about the genocide or care enough to issue a specific protest, Roosevelt's silence may have emboldened Nazis to pursue the Jews of Europe with greater vigor, presuming that they would have to pay no special postwar penalty for their offense in case the Allies won." That is an astonishing sentence from a presumably serious historian. But Bechloss has an entertaining narrative style that obscures the fatuity of that statement. Has anyone ever intimated that the Nazis needed encouragement from FDR or anyone else to reach their goal of exterminating the Jews? Nor were they worried about losing the war until the very end, indeed up to their last Götterdämmerung moment they continued to kill. While *The Conquerors* was written in his role as a historian, in a speech he summarized his thoughts about Roosevelt's attitude toward the Jews. They resembled those of critics of Pius XII's "silence" and echoed Kevin Madigan's style, which described Pius fingering his rosary while Jews were deported and John Cornwell's having Pius posing in prayer instead of denouncing the Nazis.

Bechloss argued, "There was a side of Roosevelt that I think is not so great. In 1942 he began getting pretty specific information about the Holocaust — which is a word that we now know, but that was not used at the time — that Hitler was trying to do something unprecedented: remove an

5—Afterword

entire people, the Jewish people, from the face of the earth. And through 1942 and 1943 and into 1944, people would come to him, Jewish leaders and others, and say, Mr. President, reveal what you know, give a speech saying, 'This is what we Allies are fighting against Germany to eliminate, and when we win the war the first people to be punished in post-war Germany are going to be the Nazis who are involved in this monstrous crime'— with the idea that might deter them and stop some of the killing. There were other pleas to bomb the death camps and rail lines. Roosevelt refused, refused to relax immigration quotas, to admit Jewish refugees, to seriously entertain using our military to try to stop the killing directly. In 1944, when there were a lot of suggestions to stop the killing by bombing the death camps and/or the rail lines, it was something that he sort of flicked from his lapel like a fly. It was not important to him and he didn't give it the kind of consideration a president should for a matter that grave and decision that important."

Most serious scholars of that time know that the German government did not need to hear official statements by Roosevelt, which it would ignore or rebuff as interference in that nation's domestic affairs, to know that he was concerned about Nazi anti–Semitism. The President took the same reserved stance toward public condemnation of Germany that he did toward the atrocities that the then Mexican government was committing against Catholics. At the same time, according to historian Severin Hochberg, a diary entry as early as April 1933 by James G. McDonald revealed that Roosevelt was greatly concerned about the treatment of Germany's Jews and was far from indifferent to their fate. McDonald was the League of Nations high commissioner for refugees at the time and later became the first U.S. Ambassador to Israel. Is Beschloss allowed to forgo nuance and careful distinctions about such an important matter as claiming Roosevelt flicked aside the Jewish tragedy? Of course. Historians need not always wear cap and gown and are free to provide an interesting sound bite by going beyond the record in characterizing Roosevelt as dismissing the Jewish tragedy. That it ill serves history and the public is another matter.[14]

* * *

According to Robert Dallek, the bombing of Pearl Harbor, Yalta and not doing more to save the Jews were the issues that raised the sharpest questions about President Franklin Roosevelt's tenure in the White House. With respect to the Holocaust, "In recent years the most damaging attack on Roosevelt's war-time leadership has come from journalists and historians decrying his failure to make a greater effort to save Europe's Jews from Hitler's extermination camps." After presenting the case for bombing the camps and other more aggressive action, Dallek believed more was not done both for pragmatic military reasons and because the Holocaust was not fully comprehended until late in the war. Yes, "Roosevelt knew as early as November 1942 that the Nazis were systematically killing Jews, but neither he nor anyone around him conceived of the magnitude of the killing." Dallek ended, "Since David Ben-Gurion and Chaim Weizmann, German Jews and future leaders of Israel, did not see the Holocaust at the time for what it was, why single out FDR for such bitter criticism.... The blame for the Holocaust is best put where it belongs: on the Nazis and their local collaborators who facilitated the extermination of their Jewish countrymen."

Much has been written in recent years about what critics see as the "failure" to bomb Auschwitz, a place that symbolizes all the death camps, and the rail lines leading to them. Pro and con arguments can be found in *The Bombing of Auschwitz* by Michael Neufeld and Michael Berenbaum, although because most of the discussion was by writers who favored the bombing, the book is unavoidably weighted in that direction. In his introduction Neufeld fairly concluded that Auschwitz could have been bombed but that its effectiveness is open to question, while railroad bombing "was likely to be a failure under any circumstances."

Historian John Keegan saw the controversy in terms of an overwhelming emotional argument for bombing, but added: "Emotion, of course, is misleading. Bombing Auschwitz would simply have assisted the Nazi work of massacre; one of the greatest horrors of the Second World War is that bombing — in both Germany and Japan — did kill thousands of innocents confined in camps near other targets. Choosing Auschwitz as a target would have added to that toll. Why then, the more sophisticated argument runs, did the Allies not bomb the railways that fed Auschwitz? The rail network to Auschwitz-Birkenau, the chief killing place, is extensive; I have walked over its rusting tracks. That failure is more difficult to explain away. Bombing the railways would certainly have interrupted the massacre. It would, however, only have interrupted it. The damage would have been repaired,

5—Afterword

perhaps using the labour of those inside the camp awaiting their death. Repetition of the damage would have been repaired by the same means. The irony is ghastly. Auschwitz had the capacity to be a self-sustaining killing machine, until the site itself was captured by Allied forces, as it was by the Russians in January 1945."

In the harsh environment of war the Allies had other priorities than attacking Auschwitz. After almost five years of war the British believed the best way to stop the killing was to end the war, and the Americans agreed. That some in both governments may have had biased reasons for not acting is unfortunate and irrelevant. The basic rationale by top commanders on the scene for not bombing Auschwitz was military operational considerations. Because a war plant next to the camp was bombed, it is obvious that the camp itself could be bombed. However, in late 1944 and early 1945 when Jewish organizations and others suggested bombing the camp, there were no precision "smart" or laser guided bombs that could be used against specific targets. At that time the chances of hitting a specific target such as a crematorium were uncertain at best, and a bomb was as apt to hit barracks as anything else. Whether the decision not to bomb was made by Roosevelt, as Beschloss contended on scant if not dubious evidence, the ultimate final decision was left to the military. Did an element of anti–Semitism influence their decision? Although unstated, it is a reasonable inference from the tenor of Beschloss' remarks and those of other critics. Insofar as that implication hovers over the reputations of commanders like Omar Bradley, Dwight Eisenhower and George Marshal, their reputations and those of their colleagues will not rest in peace.

A perhaps less popular but more scholarly student of Roosevelt's policies had a different opinion of FDR's attitude toward the Jews. Professor Robert Dallek reviewed the president's activities on this issue with attention to the various groups that influenced his policies, ranging from Zionists to anti–Zionists, the Arabs, the British who wanted Palestine left alone, the French and Portuguese who wanted their colonies exempt from refugees, and Latin American nations, some of which had a positive response to accepting refugees while others were obdurate in their rejection of refugees. In the context of what was happening at the time, it is understandable that Dallek concluded, "Roosevelt was not indifferent to the plight of the Jews. On the contrary, Nazi crimes profoundly disturbed him, and he looked forward to the day when Nazi leaders would face the consequences of their actions. Yet at the same time, he saw no effective way to rescue great numbers of Jews from Hitler's Europe while the war continued."

What is left out of the equation by critics of the Allied decision is that the record is clear that extreme efforts were made to interdict Axis rail transportation in France, Germany and Italy at a high cost to aircraft crews, but with uncertain results until very late in the war. By that time most of the camps were closed by the Germans as they retreated westward. Despite Operation STRANGLE, the Allied effort to cut transportation routes in the summer of 1944, somehow the Germans continued to maintain their rail transportation network almost to the very end.

After the hostilities the staff of the German Headquarters in Italy evaluated the campaign from their perspective. In the section on supplying the German forces, one finds their opinion: "The most important rail traffic could actually be kept up almost until the capitulation, and the number of supply trains for the Italian theater of war had not to be drastically curtailed." Despite the intensity of Allied bombing, stopping rail traffic was not an easy matter with damage repaired and traffic restored in a short time. Furthermore, had a train en route to Auschwitz been halted at a destroyed bridge, based on prior German behavior, the victims probably would have been left to die in locked cattle cars. And if Auschwitz had been bombed, the "collateral" damage caused by bombing would have left many prisoners as victims. Then what would the hue and cry have been?

Because of its emotional impact, the controversy over the bombing continues to resonate in academia and among the public and probably will do so indefinitely. What is to be avoided, according to Deborah Lipstadt, is "moralistic condemnations that attempt to resolve contemporary issues by using a historical period that was dramatically different from today." Ironically, in view of his belief about Belzec, after reading an article by Gerald Fleming, John Roth said, "As Fleming's 'Engineers of Death' suggests, short of Germany's military defeat by the Allies, no other constraints, social or political, moral or religious — were sufficient to stop the Final Solution." Fleming's article in the *New York Times* described how engineers designed the killing buildings at several camps. The Institute for Historical Review took issue with Fleming because he was able to mention only four German engineers who had worked on death camp

5—Afterword

crematoria and who were interrogated by the Soviets after the war. They had described knowing about the killing of innocent victims, but it was not sufficient for revisionists who persisted in denying that there were extermination facilities in the camps.

Academic historians have long debated the use of counterfactuals, or the "what ifs" of past events. In most histories some "what ifs" creep in quietly and may not deflect the narrative from reality. A typical example of a "what if" was the claim by Rittner and Roth that if Christians, including the pope, avoided abstractions and spoke out "loud and clear" in favor of those who were most in need, "Belzec would not have existed." More examples can be found, some of which are mentioned in passing by an author as an interesting sidelight on history, but others, like that of Rittner and Roth, are emphatically stated as realistic alternatives to what actually happened. Another example is the assertion that the Allies could have saved Jewish lives by bombing railroads to the death camps. Steven Paskuly made that point: "For it is well documented that the Allies and the Christian churches, especially Rome, did not speak out strongly enough to stop the horrors, nor did the Allies take the proper action to halt the trains that led to Auschwitz." We might fervently wish that was the case but the contrary evidence disabuses us.

A lengthy essay in the *American Historical Review* by Martin Bunzl showed how counterfactuals have entered into much of history and made a case for their use to expand our understanding and interpretation of history. On the contrary, the temptation is to present a counterfactual as a realistic possible outcome of an event or situation at a given time. However, the total dynamics involved make that an impossibility, no matter how attractive it appears on a page. One can hope that Bunzl and other advocates of "what ifs" encourage their use only with a caveat, and as tantalizing alternative scenarios that fascinate writers and readers and make narratives more entertaining, but otherwise abjure their use except in fiction, gaming and dramas with axes to grind and unconcerned with reality. History is hard enough to understand without adding the burden of having a credentialed historian's guesswork, no matter how seemingly plausible, further complicate our understanding of the past.

* * *

The Roman Catholic Church is invariably portrayed as a monolithic, authoritarian institution in which its members and national churches march in lock step. Discussing the role of the churches during the war, Raul Hilberg asked, "What about 'monolithic' Catholicism? ... That there should have been no single manifest Catholic message is a consequence in large part of the attitude of Pope Pius XII." Hilberg shared a common opinion about the Catholic Church's "monolithic" nature. Although doctrinally centralized, in many ways the Vatican, and the pope, in fact, preside over a congeries of churches. They can have very different traditions and a sense of autonomy that has to be recognized by Rome. Sensitive to this fact, Peter Kent stated, "An understanding of the complexity of the situation facing individual Roman Catholic churches in Europe during the Second World War, coupled with an appreciation of the perspective of the church in the United States, is essential to a comprehension of the role played by the papacy." He added that the Vatican found it was necessary "to accept the accommodations which churches had to make with the circumstances in which they found themselves." On the other hand, Kent regretted the pope's rigidity in regard to what was happening in Eastern Europe and suggested that he might have been a more effective leader in helping his flock in coping with an impossible situation after the war.

What shaped the national churches can be seen by examining the differences between them described by Richard Wolff and Jorg Hoensch in papers dealing with the relation of Catholics to the governments of European nations between the wars. The contributors related the historical background, sometimes reaching back centuries, of the political situations as well as the internal politics of Catholic groups in the several countries. Tensions between liberals and conservatives, urban and rural groups, linguistic and ethnic differences and other factors existed that should disabuse any serious student of the notion of a monolithic church within these nations as well as in relation to other "Catholic" nations. The life of one individual illustrates the effect of such a sociopolitical environment in Poland: Karol Wojtyla, the future Pope John Paul II. He first experienced life in Poland under the Nazis. Later, according to Luxmore and Babiuch, he gained firsthand knowledge of the competition between more "liberal" and "conservative" elements in the Church, in the context of opposition from secular and radical, pro-communist elements in the country. The experience of the Church in Czechoslovakia was as complicated as in Poland because of an aggressively secular and anti–Catholic government. Add to the religious and social currents that mixed in such

5—Afterword

countries with an often excessive nationalism and the sometimes questionable behavior of churchmen during the war, who after all were part of that society, and the often delicate path the Vatican considered necessary in dealing with them becomes more understandable if sometimes less acceptable many years later. The Vatican did not always accommodate to the national churches, as in the case of Austria before the Anschluss. The Austrian bishops, acting on their own, and probably based on nationalistic feelings as well as promises that Hitler made to Cardinal Innitzer to respect Catholic education, youth organizations, and so forth, urged a vote in favor of union with Germany. Pius XI told Cardinal Innitzer to issue a statement repudiating the earlier one and reaffirming the rights of the Church. Hitler's promises vanished after the Anschluss, as Pius XI knew they would.

Different responses to crisis by national churches after the war paralleled those that happened before and during the war. Under Soviet domination the Czechoslovakian government began imposing restrictions upon the Catholic Church despite the fact that Archbishop Beran was accommodating in his dealings with the government and advocated Catholic-Communist collaboration. His attitude was very different from that of Cardinal Mindszenty of Hungary, where the church was virtually suppressed. Soon, however, Prague's Communist government upped its demands on the church, and the Czech situation became almost as it was in Hungary.

It is unfortunate that few historians in this niche field have acknowledged the complexity of religious institutions and their national character. As mentioned earlier, Richard Pipes alluded to this when he noted that histories of the Russian Revolution paid scant attention to religion. The importance of the Russian Orthodox Church in Russian history and society is evident when one considers the stern measures adopted by Lenin to eliminate its influence. As a case study it merits more than casual mention, and the same is true of the differential roles of other religious institutions in national societies. A more nuanced interpretation of the behavior of churches in the Axis orbit vis-à-vis the Vatican would be possible if attention was paid to the fact that although historically the churches in France, Germany, Poland and elsewhere were not freestanding, each had a definite identity that had to be recognized by the Vatican. Historians should factor that into their analysis of the differential responses to crisis by religious institutions and their members.

With regard to the relationship between the Vatican and the national churches, it is instructive to consider the not always even tenor of the relationship between Rome and the Irish hierarchy. Although the "isle of saints and scholars" was renowned for its Catholicism, Dermot Keogh found relations were often strained when the Irish bishops or the Irish government opposed various Vatican initiatives. The bishops' policy was based partly on the belief that the British wielded too much influence with the Vatican, and their belief that they knew best how to deal with church-state issues in Ireland. Tensions did not develop into public brawls, but disagreements over whether Rome should send a nuncio to Dublin, and who it should be, illustrate that Roman wishes were not always received graciously by the Irish hierarchy.

It should not be surprising that the same could be true in the United States. After the war the Vatican wanted to formalize the status of Ambassador Myron Taylor, but understandable Protestant opposition stalled the process. That was not the only group reluctant to have official diplomatic representation at the Vatican. Archbishop Karl Alter who chaired the administrative board of the National Catholic Welfare Conference, the organization of the American bishops, "confided that he and most other members of hierarchy opposed the establishment of diplomatic relations because they believed that, if the Holy See and the United States government wished to communicate with one another, they could do so through a bishop, an American citizen." That was only one issue among many that gave rise to tensions both within the American Church and between the American Church and the Vatican.

In addition to all the above differences there often was a lack of unanimity about policies within the Vatican, within the Italian Church and between the Italian Church and the Vatican. This is not the place to elaborate on those tensions, but one example had a surprising resolution, Don Luigi Sturzo, who founded the Catholic Popular Party, was a "liberal" in the context of the 1920s and 1930s. As an anti–Fascist his ideas were not always welcomed by more conservative churchmen and politicians. His career in Italy ended with the Lateran Pact and he moved to the United States, but his influence continued in the Federazione Universitaria Cattolica Italiana (FUCI), a liberal organization of Catholic university students who opposed the Lateran Pact and Fascism. During the war many of them were active in the

5 — Afterword

Resistenza and would become notable in the postwar Christian Democratic Party, whose policies often were opposed by the Vatican. For a time FUCI's religious advisor was Giovanni Battista Montini, who was an implacable foe of Fascism. For internal political reasons he was reassigned and ended with a job in the Vatican. Eventually he became a close aide to Pius XII, and later became Pope Paul VI. When he was with FUCI, who would have imagined his future career.

A writer who did not factor national considerations into his analysis was Daniel Goldhagen who believed, "In many ways, Catholic bishops and priests across Europe supported political transgressions ... the destruction of democracy and the establishment of persecutionist [sic] dictatorships, which they continued to support as they watched the persecution." He believed that there is "every reason to believe that the desire for democracy's destruction ... was not confined to a scattered few clergy." He added, "We do not know exactly how widespread such broad support was, but all those who did support these political transgressions are morally blameworthy. Pius XII ... bears such moral and political blame." What the "every reason to believe" was, was not explained. Of course there is ample evidence that some clergy, numbers unknown, supported their government right or wrong and perhaps because of what they saw as a threat from Bolshevism. That does not explain how any could support the destruction of democracy in the 1930s in the countries he talks about where there was no "democracy." Goldhagen's royal "we" relieved him of the need to specify how "many" may have supported the vague "transgressions" he mentioned, and where they occurred, or why Pius XII "bears such moral and political blame" for such an undefined fault. Goldhagen's rhetoric may be stirring; his reasoning was puerile.

Professor Goldhagen said that Professor Gordon Zahn found that German Catholics who looked for spiritual guidance to their superiors regarding service in Hitler's wars received virtually the same answers they would have received from Hitler. What those answers were was unstated but the coincidence of clergy and even Hitler referring to "Render unto Caesar" seems plausible. We know that the same advice might have been given in many other countries. Goldhagen did not mention that Zahn also wrote about a Catholic Austrian peasant who refused to serve in the German army and as a result was beheaded. Unlike Goldhagen, and although critical of the Church's role in Germany during the war, Zahn was sensitive to the dilemma of church members, as well as of the Church itself when confronted with an evil such as Nazism. It is clear where his sympathies and preference lay, but as a sociologist he recognized that the Church as an institution finds it difficult to be what he called a "divisive force" in protesting state actions. "To require, or even suggest, that the Catholic Church could have assumed such a posture vis-à-vis the Nazi State may be a sociological impossibility." While it was true that Bishop Galen and some other spokesmen of the Catholic Church offered strong protests, that was an institutional form of protest and only incidentally related to individual behavior. "This religious community did face a peculiar challenge to recognize and develop its potential as a source of dissent and deviance at that more significant level of the individual and his actions." Zahn's nuanced interpretation of the situation in Germany showed that unlike Professor Goldhagen, he understood the genuine problems that faced his co-religionists in the everyday world of the 1930s and 1940s.

Reviewing the issues surrounding the Vatican's role in the war, Jacques Nobecourt lamented, "So many hypotheses without proof, so many questions left unanswered. These proceed from a great ignorance as to the functioning of the institutional Church and from a stereotyped vision of the historical reality in which Pius XII lived and acted. The press has ensconced these latter incertitudes in the public opinion." Nobecourt's intention was not to excuse the pope but to remind us of the complexity of what has become a historical cause célèbre.[15]

Another important caveat came from historian Michael Marrus, who noted that because of the Holocaust we "now value 'speaking out' as a measure of historical rectitude and a goal for all responsible agencies. We continue to look back upon the massacre of European Jewry to understand the consequences of inaction or failing to live up to our ideals. We draw these lessons from the historical record — but this does not mean that in doing so, we are always fair to those whose actions we implicitly or explicitly criticize for their inadequacy. To some degree, I believe, we seek vicarious involvement in these events of World War II ... by condemning those who did not live up to what we would like to think we would have done. But is this a way to write or assess history? You will appreciate that I have my doubts." That echoed what Arthur Koestler said many years before: "To smuggle in elements of a later knowledge when describing the

5—Afterword

mental patterns of people in an earlier period is a common temptation to writers, which should be resisted." Koestler's injunction makes sense as one who was there, but it continues to be ignored by historians who should know better.[16]

* * *

It should be no surprise that the strategies of the Vatican and of the Allies had goals both for the war and afterwards. The Allied leaders agreed on the defeat of the Axis but they differed, sometimes bitterly, on how it was to be accomplished. Furthermore, although under strong leadership, Britain and the United States experienced serious internal differences about the management of the war. We may know less about the Vatican, which also had a strong leader, but what is known suggests the same happened within its precincts, and like Roosevelt and Churchill, the final decisions were the pope's. Although the Vatican's apparent stance was to be above the fray, it was deeply involved in reaching certain goals, not the least of which was its survival. It was not an inert observer of what was happening, although it had limited resources to affect the outcome of the war. Many assume that the pope could bring significant and effective moral influence to bear on the behavior of belligerents, and did not do so. In fact, however, papal influence of the kind critics desired was illusory, although it would have been useful for propaganda purposes if it could be enlisted by one side or the other.

Like the Allies the Vatican made mistakes, sometimes for the same reasons that generals and politicians made mistakes. Why that happens, according to Kenneth Macksey in his account of military errors in the war, is because, "In a life and death struggle, reactions tend to be instinctive, although a modicum of foresight in visualizing and making provision for certain instantaneous contingencies prior to close combat may be possible." But misinformation, disinformation, and the misinterpretation of information or obstinacy in sticking to a misconceived plan and a host of other reasons, all can conspire to defeat even the best laid plans. Fortunately for the world, the Axis was more prone to such mistakes than the Allies. The Vatican was no less immune to such realities than the military.

Some of what seem in hindsight as serious mistakes followed from the lack of good intelligence. Despite having what most historians believe is an excellent intelligence service, soon after the Nazis took power the

Vatican received disinformation that misled its policy vis-à-vis the German government, and then it persisted in relying on the concordat to manage relations with Hitler. Misled by Vichy, which was afflicted with too many ultraright bishops, the Vatican failed to accept the extent of Vichy's corrupt collaboration with Germany or how its apparent tolerance of episcopal collaborators would affect its future relations with both the faithful and the postwar French government.

The Vatican's effort to straddle the gap between the Croatia of Ante Paavelic and the government in exile satisfied neither and laid it open to legitimate criticism for tolerating ties to a ruthless puppet of Hitler. The Vatican's rationale for this policy was theologically complicated and differed from the rationale of Churchill and Roosevelt in kindred cases, but most commentators hold the pope to a "higher standard." His policy was based on an overriding pastoral responsibility to Croatia's ordinary Catholics. Although the presumably Catholic leaders of Croatia ignored its pleas, the Vatican's concern for those in the pews was a reason not to be lightly considered by the papacy. The result, however, has been seen as more than a public relations disaster.

There also were what today would be considered management failures. For years the Vatican was poorly served by what amounted to sometimes unwitting misinformation received from Cesare Orsenigo, its nuncio in Berlin. Like too many generals, he may have been kept in place too long. As did his counterpart, the German ambassador to the Vatican, at times he seems to have massaged information to give the least negative impression about his host's policies and behaviors. Robert Graham considered Orsenigo's mission to Berlin a failure, but that it was not his fault. "He was criticized by the German bishops for having a weak and defensive attitude. It is said that he did not report some important events on the grounds that the Pope would only order him to make the usual protest — which he knew for certain would be rejected." Perhaps he was not recalled because of fear that a replacement would not have been accepted by Hitler, and having some representation in Berlin was better than none. In fairness to the man, it is clear from messages to Rome that he was well aware of what was happening in Germany, reporting the futility of protesting the treatment of Jews, including converted Jews. His response to one request from Rome to intervene on behalf of Jews was, "I must add that these interventions are not only useless but they are even

5—Afterword

badly received; as a result the authorities show themselves unfavorable to other and even less serious cases." Orsenigo's assignment may have exceeded his talents, but it is hard to imagine that under the circumstances in Berlin, any replacement could have done better.[17]

The Nazi sympathies of Alois Hudal, the "Brown Bishop," were notorious in Rome. Institutional tradition protected his embarrassing political behavior because the Vatican sought to avoid the scandal of a public rebuke or dismissal. The Vatican was not alone in tolerating egregious misbehavior for an apparent "greater good"—it happens often in governments and public life—but if the Vatican avoided a scandal at the time, as it had earlier when Pacelli kept Hudal's book off of the Index, the ultimate public price was the claims of Aarons and Loftus and others who inflated Hudal's supposed influence and activity beyond all reason. Because the Vatican is a fallible human institution, such lapses are not surprising, but given the nature of the institution, they are difficult to accept. Timely corrective action did not occur, and the problem festered and caused unnecessary damage to the Holy See.

* * *

References to "moral shallowness" or "moral failure" are common in critiques of Pius XII. The many references to morality in these essays reveal the importance historians seem to attach to morality, although few bother to define it. Daniel Goldhagen's accusation that Pius XII bears moral blame for his failures was mentioned earlier. Frank Coppa contended that "the accommodating strategy, diplomatic finesse, and 'silence' of Pius XII, which may have saved many lives, compromised the moral stature of the Holy See." Michael Phayer claimed, "The pope abdicated his right as leader of the Catholic church to make pronouncements based on moral principle." That was only one of his strictures against Pius but perhaps the capstone of his criticism, and revealed his core complaint not only about Pius XII but the Roman Church. According to Phayer, Pius's own moral code required him to vigorously denounce Nazi depravity regardless of the consequences for the Vatican, Rome, or the Jews. The pope's own statements show that Pius was not concerned about his future, but he did worry about his church, Rome and the Jews, although his concern did not end there. He made prudential judgments that can be debated, but for Phayer to fault him on moral grounds, leaving those grounds unspecified, perhaps assuming that his readers understood whatever moral principles he referred to, is a questionable practice for historians.

John Keegan also questioned the pope's morality, saying, "A good man but weak Pope, [he] declined to confront his worldwide flock with a denunciation of Hitler's crimes lest he provoke the German occupiers of Italy into violating the Vatican's immunity. His decision to stand above the great moral issues of the Second World War compromised papal authority for much of the postwar period." That reason for "silence" is specious. A masterful military historian, Keegan is usually balanced in his assessments of complex matters and rarely suggests simplistic explanations. Thus, it is surprising that he accepted a simplistic explanation for so-called papal silence based on the undocumented opinions of other historians highly critical of the pope.

Concluding *Unholy Trinity*, Aarons and Loftus wrote, "Before his death Pius XI had already published one Encyclical condemning Nazi teachings. The Church did not suffer: in fact, its status was enhanced. At death's door, he had prepared another denunciation of the Nazis' anti–Christian doctrines. His successor, Pius XII, quietly buried it. Therein, we submit, lies his guilt: from the moment he assumed St. Peter's mantle he chose diplomacy over truth, his temporal power over truth, his temporal powers over his moral duty." Those outside the cockpit of Europe in the late 1930s applauded Pius XI for his condemnation of Nazism. But how could Aarons and Loftus claim that the Church did not suffer in consequence? Considering their experience in researching the events of the war, that is something against all the evidence. The encyclical certainly was not applauded in Germany, where an effort was made to suppress it, and it led to dire consequences for many clergy and laity as well as the church.[18]

By introducing the concept of morality into the debate over Pius's "silence," it began to resemble the continuing debate over whether it was immoral to use the atomic bomb to end World War II. Theologians and philosophers, especially those in the Western Judeo-Christian tradition of the just war such as Professor Gertrude Anscombe, soon after the war condemned its use as immoral in specific terms. So did philosopher John Rawls, who called his untraditional approach secular and based on democratic principles. These writers had specific reasons for calling the A-bomb immoral, unlike Pius's critics who use the word "moral" as if everyone knew and agreed on what "moral" meant. Whether there can be

5—Afterword

any agreement on principles of morality has been questionable for many years, even apart from Robert Orsi's contention that, "just as post colonial intellectual culture calls into question central tenets of Western thought, so a new kind of moral inquiry must be open to construals of the 'ethical' profoundly at variance with Christian ideals and formulations." If this is the case, then dealing with moral issues becomes much more problematic. The mere assertion that a moral issue exists provides no foundation for a meaningful discussion of the "morality" of the A-bomb, carpet bombing, or the "silence" of Pius, among countless other contentious issues.

Reliance on the idea of common values is flimsy, according to Richard Posner when confronted with the harsh reality of multiculturalism. "That the Germans killed millions of defenseless citizens is a fact; its truth is independent of what anyone believes. That the Nazis' actions were morally wrong is a value judgement: it depends on beliefs that cannot be proved true or false." Long before postmodern Western thought, morality became a pragmatic matter of multicultural opinion, although that term was not used until later. The American evidence for this is how certain major "moral" issues—abortion, the death penalty, and euthanasia—are contested on "moral" grounds. Those grounds differ, and proponents and opponents lack agreement on common principles that are needed to profitably discuss such issues.

This was illustrated by how C. David Heymann, the biographer of the anti–Semitic poet Ezra Pound, discussed whether Pound should receive a literary award: "The endless philosophical debate seemed too remote, too abstract, for a poet of Pound's stature." Debating whether Pound should be honored led to "irresoluble debate [over] can a man's artistic achievement be separated from his morality and ideology? And if a moral yardstick is applied, whose morality is to be used?" The problem of which yardstick to apply becomes even more stark when one finds what Field Marshal Kesselring told Colonel Herbert Kappler after the Ardeatine Caves massacre. "I told him that I was to a certain extent grateful that ... matter had been settled in a way which was legally and morally above reproach." Heymann probably would object to Kesselring's yardstick, but if he could be flexible when thinking about an artist, why not do the same for a Field Marshal? The pragmatic Allies answered the question about Kesselring when he was sentenced at Nuremberg. However, in the multicultural world that Robert Orsi described, a common understanding of what is right or wrong remains elusive.

An eminent British philosopher and authority on ethical theory provided a way to think about the morality of bombing, and other matters, that differed from the absolutism of Anscombe and Rawls. According to R. M. Hare, "there will also be cases which are so much outside the ordinary run of cases that we may feel impelled to ask whether the general principles, sound though they may be for general use, ought not to be scrutinized before they are applied to these unusual circumstances. Into this category come a great many political situations (such as some of those on which Professor Anscombe has commented, as for example Truman's dilemma about dropping the bomb) It is not to be supposed that the simple general principles which are the soundest guide in private life can always be safely employed in political situations; and this is so, not because political decisions lie outside morality and are to be made only for 'reasons of State,' but because political situations differ in morally relevant respects from private situations, especially in their complexity and in the size of the calamities that it is possible to cause." Hare said, "I would include more people in the class of those whose sufferings are relevant to our moral decisions (for example, in the Hiroshima case, those that will die if the war is not ended quickly, as well as those actually killed by the bombing)."

Professor Hare considered the lesser of two evils — the thousands who would die at Hiroshima compared the hundreds of thousands more who would die if the war did not end. For those who see no shades of gray in history, Professor Hare's argument may seem too callous or too subtle. It was neither at the time for those confronting a difficult decision. That is why when evaluating Truman's decision to use the A-Bomb, or Pius XII's decisions, it is important to remember the context in which they were made, and that the greater the temporal distance from those decisions, the easier it becomes to judge them in the emotion driven terms found in the media or the abstract terms found in seminars and academic journals.[19]

* * *

How might one judge Pius XII to best fit the actual historic person? Some might depict him with a halo; others like Phayer have him trampling on a Jew, and Cornwell sees him as anti–Semitic. But the question

5—Afterword

goes beyond their cartoon descriptions to the more serious one of *judgment*. Like other historic figures from World War II who are tried in the court of history, a verdict is sought on Pius XII's performance during the war. Despite the passage of more than half a century, the case continues to be too complicated for scholars to finalize. Inevitably some pass judgment regardless of the pro and con evidence, but it may be best for history to have the case continued. Eventually the Vatican Archives should be open to researchers looking for evidence about Pius's reputation. By then the archives behind the old Iron Curtain as well as those in the West may have yielded relevant material and less passionate critics may adopt a more responsible voice toward the evidence. That does not mean that critics will necessarily reverse what seems to be the contemporary "consensus" judgment of the tenure of Pius XII. The elusive smoking guns they allude to might yet appear, but their lack will not discourage future disciples of Cornwell and Carroll from continuing to spin conspiracy theories. If David Brown's *Da Vinci Code* can entertain millions of readers with ruminations about the vast conspiracy known as Christianity, and James Carroll's *Constantine's Sword* can do the same for academics, the opportunities to flay Pius are endless, and profitable. More recently, in the spirit of Professor Goldhagen, Paul Elie asked readers to, "Consider Pope Pius XII, the now vilified wartime pope. It was Pius' pretension to be a statesman, not a fisher of men that led him to calculate about the fate of European Jews rather than telling his Church to stand up and do the right thing." The saturation of the media and revisionist history with such disinformation, if not mendacity, suggests that while the latest cycle of uninformed criticism of Pius XII may subside for a time, eventually a new version of Cornwell or Goldhagen will see that it resumes.

What Richard Posner said about public intellectuals in general can be said of many of the revisionists mentioned in these essays. No better description could be applied to Gary Wills, Goldhagen and other critics than Posner's description of a public intellectual: "A proclivity for taking extreme positions, a taste for universals and abstraction, a desire for moral purity, a lack of worldliness, and intellectual arrogance work together to induce in many public intellectuals selective empathy, a selective sense of justice, an insensitivity to context, and impatience with prudence and sobriety, a lack of realism and excessive self confidence."

The Vatican's policies have been an easy target, so the postwar avalanche of criticism it experienced should not be surprising. Its critics include academics who do not understand the European and Italian context in which the Vatican had to maneuver during the war. Others are understandably affected emotionally by the Holocaust and other events of the time and cannot accept that the pope did not make "flaming protests," and facts cannot have meaning for them. There are those who select facts they believe will incriminate the Vatican and serve as surrogates for their arguments with the Church. Many ignore or are not aware of the marginal role the Vatican actually played during the war. The famous Albert Schweitzer, for example, argued, "The Catholic Church bears a greater guilt for it was an organized, supra-national power in a position to do something, whereas the Protestant Church was an unorganized, impotent, national power. But it, too, became guilty, by simply accepting the terrible, inhuman fact of the persecution of the Jews." That was said in his preface to Rolf Hochuth's *The Deputy*. Schweitzer's celebrity allowed him to vilify Pius as accepting the destruction of the Jews, and both men exaggerated the Vatican's influence on countries like Nazi Germany and Croatia, the latter a country ruthless in its persecution of Jews and Serbs during the war, despite its reputed Catholicism.

After the dissolution of Yugoslavia many years later, Croatia continued its genocidal pursuit of Serbians. Why that happened deserves intense study, and soul searching on the part of Croatian and all Catholics, but it revealed the marginal influence of religion in Croatia's national politics. It was not only Croatia that ignored papal admonitions, according to Richard Lamb who discussed the situation in Rome and the atrocities committed during the German occupation: "Pope Pius XII's role was minor, although it has attracted much controversy." The list of similar cases could go on, suggesting that what George Bull said about the pope's diplomacy in the 1940s bore no better fruit in the 1990s. "The diplomacy of the Holy See — the universal prophet — can be effective only if the world's sovereign states are willing to accept its authority in matters where their own interests are at stake. They show little willingness to do so today, any more than during the war." Of course, he could also have said that about the United Nations.

It took almost a century for what are perhaps the best histories of the American Civil War to reach the publishers. Those books would not have been possible without relying not only on archives but on all the

5—Afterword

credentialed and non-credentialed writers that went before. Although that precedent should not stop writers from trying their hand at an assessment of the Vatican in World War II, what was true of Civil War history should be a cautionary tale for anyone seeking definitive answers that satisfy all parties to the current controversy. Perhaps the best one can do is to nibble at the margins of the controversy, asking questions, finding new evidence when possible, finding flaws in what purport to be factual accounts of Vatican actions during the war, or of its defense, eschewing advocacy in favor of a balanced presentation and avoiding historical interpretations based on contemporary fashions in politics and in history.[20]

Appendix A: On Historiography

> The modern manipulators of facts stand in the way of the historian. For history itself is destroyed, and its comprehensibility — based upon the fact that it is enacted by men and therefore can be understood by men — is in danger, whenever the facts are no longer held to be part and parcel of the past and present world, and are misused to prove this or that opinion.
> — Hannah Arendt, *The Origins of Totalitarianism*, 1951, 9

> Methodology does not dictate the conclusions that any particular study may reach, but it does dictate the parameters of the study: the way the research is conducted, how the findings are presented, even what are suitable subjects for study. A revolution in methodology is, therefore, of more than "academic" interest, as the invidious phrase has it — more than a technicality or a formality.
> — Gertrude Himmelfarb, *The New History and the Old*, 2004, 15

The innuendo and the direct accusations of papal complicity in the Holocaust have become repetitious in the niche field of World War II history. For years critics of the Vatican have recycled stories based on inferences and interpretations that fail to pass rigorous scrutiny. Reasonable alternative interpretations of issues such as papal "silence" have been ignored, not explored and not rebutted. Now part of popular and even academic "consensus" history, the result is a one-sided, revisionist consensus that violates the age-old canons of historical research. That is why it is important to spend time on what some would call minor matters such as the meaning of the word *stirpe*, or whether the pope told his staff orally

Appendix A

that Roman Jews were to be sheltered by the Church. Such matters loom large in books by papal critics and are repeated by the media, but an old adage is as true for history as in engineering: "The devil is in the details." If significant details are incorrect, or falsified, why assume that a writer's conclusions are correct? Some details may be of little importance, for example, missing a date by a day, and may be overlooked. However, some are vitally important because they can make a difference in our understanding of what actually happened.

The following comments address a few of the methodological problems found in the work of several Vatican critics. The use of qualifying statements, conjecture, assumptions and undocumented sources is a common problem in the books of several authors but nowhere more so than in the books of Mark Aarons and John Loftus, which are considered authoritative by many Vaticanologists. Their books about Vatican cooperation with "rat lines" or escape routes, are filled with references to intelligence reports found in the U.S. National Archives and elsewhere, plus interviews with presumably knowledgeable individuals. However, their narratives are replete with unidentified "our sources," and qualifiers such as "alleged," "claimed," and "probably." There may be good reasons why their sources wanted anonymity, but history is not journalism where sources may be protected. The authors' claims may be true and the sources reliable, but they *cannot be confirmed*. At first glance the result of their research, buttressed by extensive footnotes, is impressive, but too much of the narrative is speculation. Many of the intelligence reports referred to were so-called raw intelligence obtained by agents who were able to make at best only a cursory evaluation of the reliability of the source and the information.

Although an informant or agent might be reliable, and the information provided in good faith, it also could be mistaken, disinformation or a rumor. An effort is made to relate the agent's reports to other reports and to evaluate their reliability. However, from experience in counterintelligence it was clear that at times there was no way to cross-check information for authenticity, although it might seem highly probable that it was true. Pragmatically that may be enough for an intelligence agency to act, but it is not good enough for history. William Slany admitted when discussing Ustasha gold, "U.S. intelligence reports — many of them uncorroborated and speculative — portray the Croat underground in Rome as making use of a considerable quantity of gold." The strong implication in his study, and that of others, was that Ustasha gold ended in the Vatican. This was reminiscent of what seemed to be the excellent, credible information about the Vatican provided for years by Virgilio Scattolini of VESSEL fame who fooled the OSS and the *New York Times* among other newspapers foreign and domestic. Confirmed or not, an intelligence report rested in an archive until decades later it was available to researchers who could use it to "allege" or "claim" that something "probably" happened.

The authors of *The Fourth Reich: Klaus Barbie and the Neo-Fascist Connection* also wrote about Vatican involvement in postwar rat lines. Readers find detailed reports of how the Vatican aided the escape of wanted Ustashe war criminals that seem persuasive. The center of the operation was the Confraternity of San Girolamo, a Croatian religious institution in Rome headed by Father Krunoslav Draganovic, a questionable character who aided fellow Croat escapees. Not only did the Vatican refuse to act against the Confraternity when it sheltered escapees, according to the authors, "Indeed the pope signaled his support for Draganovic when he received a two man delegation from the institute in 1946; both men were close friends of Draganovic." Although the pope did not receive Hitler during his visit to Rome, many less than savory characters like SS General Karl Wolff were seen by the pope, who obviously did not endorse their policies. Claiming that the visit by two friends of Draganovic meant support for the Ustashe reveals the authors' credulity. Like the books of Aarons and Loftus this book by three journalists tells a disturbing story of how scores if not hundreds of war criminals were moved to South America, sometimes with the help of clergy in Rome, with the clear implication that it was under Vatican auspices or at least with its tacit approval. Like Aarons and Loftus the authors refer to Allied intelligence reports and make a seemingly strong case for the involvement of persons in or close to the Vatican. Their book has few references and instead refers to a "bibliography" listing books and "archival sources," the latter by their location in cities, and only occasionally are documentary sources in those places specified. Without more information there is no way to trace too many statements in the book to sources, plausible though they may seem. This is a "journalistic" fascinating tour de force, an account of the seamy side of postwar intelligence operations that provides "grist for the mill" of Vatican critics, *except it cannot be verified*.[1]

Appendix A

Testimony in a criminal case has to pass the bar of beyond a reasonable doubt. There have been too many cases when a thoughtful jury in good faith accepted the testimony of witnesses as reasonable and convicted someone, only to have the conviction reversed because of a DNA test. History does not have juries, although the guild's emphasis on "consensus" and peer review implies as much, nor does it have the equivalent of DNA testing that can be applied to raw intelligence. That is why readers need to be alert to unidentified sources, and "allegedly," "perhaps" and other conditional statements in history books. They also need to be alert to interesting books that give only very general or vague references to sources because they also sound a warning. Although such books avoid the clutter of citations, keep a narrative moving and may sound plausible, are their accounts accurate?

In *The Real ODESSA*, Uki Goni told about Vatican involvement in sheltering war criminals that would be disconcerting for anyone who believes that Vatican residents would never consort with war criminals. After extensive research Goni said that he found that the leader of the Catholic Church, "Pius XII was fully aware of the sanctuary provided to war criminals at Roman ecclesiastical institutions but also how he personally liaised with the Nazi-smuggling operation at the Croatian Confraternity of San Girolamo, was to aid Croat fugitives wanted by Tito's Yugoslavia, a connection long denied by the Vatican." The San Gerolamo operation was under Father Draganovic, and according to Goni, "Pius XII was understood to know everything about Father Draganovic's activities, otherwise he would never have stayed in his position, as one former British intelligence officer claimed." Following the style of John Loftus and Mark Aarons' "ground breaking" *Unholy Trinity*, Goni said the pope "was understood" (by whom?) to know about Draganovic's activities, and further, that an unidentified British officer "claimed" that was why Draganovic remained at San Girolamo. However, "Draganovic's usefulness to the Vatican expired only a few days after the death of Pius XII, a clear pointer as to the source of his great and mysterious power since his arrival in Rome in mid-war." In mid–October 1958, the CIA learned that he had been evicted from San Girolamo, "a humiliating final blow and again suggests who had been Draganovic's real master all along." Instead of this stealth approach, Goni might have been more direct and said that the master was Pius XII, which was the false message intended for the reader.

On Historiography

According to Goni, the pope was found to have "secretly pleaded with Washington and London on behalf of the notorious criminals and Nazi collaborators.... In at least one case, an appeal was made in the Pope's own name." The British Foreign Office was "shocked" that the Vatican would intervene seeking clemency for what were considered the minions of Hitler and Mussolini. Later Goni managed to note that appeals for commuting sentences were not requests for pardons. The British minister to the Vatican, D'Arcy Osborne, warned Cardinal Tardini that Yugoslavia would request the extradition of five men the British believed guilty who presumably were sheltered by the Vatican. Osborne told London that the pope would not order their surrender. These were the only five persons cited by Goni as sheltered by the Vatican, which does not necessarily mean they were in the Vatican proper or the only ones sheltered. However, of the large number he intimated were helped, only these five were identified. He might have added what Osborne said about the papal policy: "I think it likely, that some Fascist refugees were also helped and hidden when their time came to hide and be helped, but these would be exceptions; nothing like the wholesale protection of the victims of Fascism. And the Pope is on record that the authors of war crimes should pay for their evil-doing."[2]

Some historians who use primary and secondary sources do not explain them, leaving them in a vacuum by ignoring their context. Failing to report why some clergy working in the Vatican undoubtedly helped an unknown number of fugitives from Germany and its satellites to escape to South America is a case in point. Unfortunately, providing context can be tedious. The motivations of most of the clergy helping escapees probably were mixed and the actual numbers aided probably were fewer than some sensational accounts imply, but when any truly guilty person escaped justice, that was too many. Goni quoted a member of the British Foreign Office who said that "Black" Ustashi were returned to Yugoslavia while "Greys" were not. Yugoslavia wanted some 1800 extradited while the British turned over 50. Goni was outraged that any escaped extradition but did not tell the reader what was happening in Yugoslavia after the war, where "justice" for alleged war criminals, as well as for political opponents, was rough and swift. The British and Americans knew what happened when Yugoslavia occupied Trieste and engaged in political cleansing that killed thousands of their political opponents. For a time too many cases were based on mere allegations, but they were considered sufficient by the British and Americans to send individuals to foreordained verdicts, with or without one of Tito's show trials.

Considering what is known about the horrors of World War II, the British and Americans conducted a minuscule number of trials of war criminals. The Soviets gave little attention to legalisms and quickly doled out socialist justice. Raul Hilberg's section on "The Trials" makes it clear that several million Germans might have been charged with various degrees of war time offenses. That overwhelming number and the Allies' eagerness to return to peacetime pursuits after years of war were coupled with very limited resources to locate, investigate and try alleged criminals. With the Germans and Japanese they focused on so-called major war criminals. As a result a very large number of lesser figures were never charged although a relative few like Herbert Kappler were tried by countries like Belgium, France, Germany and Italy. Some notorious Nazis were sent to Poland and tried and executed. Gitta Sereny was critical of American occupation policy toward the pursuit of war criminals saying it "was often neither consistent nor, to go even further, morally defensible. It is equally true, however, that the occupation authorities were faced with problems of such magnitude as to be almost insuperable (not unlike those confronting the International Red Cross and, to some extent, the Vatican)." To her credit, Sereny was one of the few providing some context for what happened.

The daunting dimensions of the problems of dealing with war criminals is illustrated by two examples that confronted American tribunals in Germany. One involved 200 "flier" cases with about 600 defendants accused of killing nearly 1200 American airmen. Another involved more than 250 cases with more than 1,000 defendants who had staffed concentration camps. Among the latter cases was the Dachau case tried in late 1945. Of the forty individuals tried, 36 were sentenced to death and four received ten-year prison terms. A similar case in 1947 resulted in only one death sentence, 14 prison terms and four acquittals. The disparity in sentences was largely a product of the timing of the cases; the earliest ones received the most severe sentences, just as was the case in Italy. If, as Gitta Sereny said, it was equally true that the problems of dealing with war crimes were almost insuperable, while not always consistent, can history fairly accuse the program of being morally indefensible?[3]

The reasons for the declining number of war trials were complex. It was not, according to Donald Bloxham, "a simple lack of interest in putting together the evidence of the Holocaust, or the weariness with war and atrocities. Almost everywhere were very real political and sociocultural imperatives to direct attention away from the suffering of the Jews." Perhaps most important there was increasing evidence of what became known as the Cold War. Reduced interest in cooperation with the vengeful Soviets in the matter of "war criminals" stemmed from the American and British reaction to forcible repatriation. This rarely mentioned episode in postwar Europe was described by Hugh Thomas. Before the war ended, the Americans and British agreed to repatriate all POWs and found no problem doing so with their Japanese, Italian and most German POWs, who wished to return home. They knew that unless they returned all Soviet POWs, Stalin was capable of keeping Allied POWs as hostages. So willing or not, all Russians, even White Russians who left Russia in the early 1920s, were forced to return to the USSR. The status of those who joined the Vlasov army, which fought for the Germans, seemed clear, but the British and Americans were well aware that no mercy was given to Russians conscripted into German service as laborers who became Allied POWs. Some Russian POWs in American custody in the United States committed suicide rather than be forcibly returned to the Soviets. When the rest got home they were shot or sent to the gulag because to become a POW was considered treason. Episodes like the brutal treatment of an anti–Communist Cossack unit that fought with the Germans and moved into Northern Italy with its families before the war ended, were an eye-opener for Allied officers who protested what happened. At the time London and Washington had other priorities, and the practice of forcible repatriation continued for at least two or three years. As Soviet and Yugoslav policies became clearer, Allied enthusiasm to cooperate with them ebbed. With regard to the Yugoslavian returnees Milovan Djilas said, "There was no way in which the cases of twenty to thirty thousand people could have been reliably investigated. So the easy way out was to have them all shot." In April 1947, the British and American governments told Yugoslavia that they would surrender quislings found under their control, after deleting the phrase "And proved members of Ustasha" from their note. By May, however, the State Department "believed that the Yugoslav Government was meting out unduly harsh treatment to its political opponents and using charges of collaboration as a weapon in an increasingly severe campaign of repression against opposition elements." The return

Appendix A

policy finally stopped in Europe with American policy changing dramatically when hostilities ended in Korea. North Korea demanded the return of all of its POWs, but North Korean POWs who refused repatriation were not sent back because the United States knew what happened after World War II.

When the "rat lines" did not separate the goats from the sheep, sometimes deliberately and at other times through ignorance, it should be remembered that this was occurring in the climate of a devastated Europe. London and Washington were far from what was happening, with other priorities and little awareness of how the pursuit of war criminals often was a charade enabling victors to settle scores as well as hopefully achieve rough justice. In his introduction to articles on war crimes committed by the Italian military during the war, Claudio Pavone said, "The thirst for justice was genuine and profound, and the victorious powers as well as the liberation councils ... tried somehow to give this thirst a mantle of legality. At the popular level ... the action became more authentic but lurched toward vengeance." The authors that followed him detailed atrocities that happened in Greece and Yugoslavia, regretting that more war criminals, both German and Italian, who committed crimes in those places were not brought to justice. Similarly, Michale Battini regretted the lack of an Italian Nuremberg after the war. The atrocities committed under the command of major military figures now seem largely forgotten by later generations. Battini said that 9,364 fascists were killed without trial and 30,000 were tried by extraordinary Courts of Assizes. The immediate postwar situation in Italy was chaotic, which meant that nobody had plausibly exact numbers of how many Fascist "war criminals" or just potential political opponents, were killed, especially by Communist Partisans whose people's courts administered revolutionary justice. The figure could be several tens of thousands, and everyone knew what was happening. That was the climate in which the well meaning provided help, often unwittingly, to fugitive war criminals. At the same time others were knowingly helping Eichmann and his fellow criminals escape.

After Italians voted for a republic in 1946, there was a pattern of amnesties that commuted death sentences and reduced many long-term prison sentences. This was supported by all parties, and over the years successive amnesties further reduced sentences. For whatever reasons, there was broad popular support for this policy, and in a democratic society that must be recognized as important. Italy was trying to survive, which meant that there were more important priorities, such as coping with a host of orphans, and finding food and housing for its own refugees. Italy had few if any resources to pursue war crimes abroad, and to expect that there could have been an agreement with Yugoslavia about war crimes committed there by Italians, or against Italians in Trieste's hinterland that Italy lost to Yugoslavia, is sheer fantasy. The reality, for better or worse, is exemplified by what happened in Trieste in the late 1990s. A group wanted to memorialize those killed and buried in "foibe" or deep sinkholes outside the city while it was occupied by Yugoslavia. There was no question about the political and ethnic cleansing conducted by Tito's forces, but both governments wanted to close the books on a terrible atrocity. An Italian official of Italy's Foreign Ministry summed it up, saying that the matter was best left to the history books. If such episodes are to be left to history books they should tell the whole story. That criminals were not brought to justice is a significant part of history, but that fact alone should not be in the books with an implication of someone's moral failure. Historians who do not explain the why behind the fact at the least distort history and by omission at times they falsify history.[4]

* * *

The "Brown bishop," Alois Hudal, provides still another example of how writers have stretched the truth to implicate the Vatican in sleazy deals after the war. According to Uki Goni, "Bishop Hudal's probable contribution to Eichmann's escape was first disclosed in an article written in 1961 by Simon Wiesenthal. Hudal practically confirmed his participation in a subsequent interview." Hudal was quoted as saying, "I can't affirm or deny whether Eichmann was among those refugees, because none of them revealed to me their past during the Third Reich and because there were no photographs of them." He did admit helping more than 40 Germans. The bishop was not a nice man but Goni has him making a "probable" contribution to Eichmann's escape and then "practically" confirming helping Eichmann. Michael Phayer was more positive than Goni about Hudal's helping Eichmann, and in turn linked him to Pius. "Although Bishop Hudal knew that any number of the refugees he assisted had been, like Franz Stangl and Adolf Eichmann, central figures in the Holocaust, we cannot say that the pope himself or his Undersecretaries Montini and

Appendix A

Tardini knew this, but they had every reason to suspect it with Hudal as their agent." Despite the impressive end notes and diligence of both authors, what they present as definitive are really unsubstantiated opinions. Hudal is called the pope's "agent" to insure that readers understand their close relationship. Although Phayer hedged about the specifics of papal knowledge of aid to men like Eichmann, in the best tradition of Hochuth and Cornwell, without any evidence he indicted Pius for "suspecting" that Hudal aided Eichmann's escape. Whatever reason Professor Phayer might have to harbor such a suspicion about Pius, presenting his guess in a presumably serious scholarly work was historical fiction.[5]

* * *

Hitler's Willing Executioners and its successor, *A Moral Reckoning*, begin with modest introductions by Professor Daniel Goldhagen of Harvard University who pointed to the deficiencies of prior studies of the Holocaust, which, he told the reader, he intended to remedy. Despite more than half a century of scholarly exploration of the meaning of anti–Semitism, he found, "Studies of the Holocaust have been marred by a poor understanding and an under-theorizing of antisemitism." However, he provided no examples of such "poor understanding" that would help the reader understand the problem he intended to correct. Then in *A Moral Reckoning*, Goldhagen discovered that "academics elided almost all of the human beings from the investigation of the Holocaust's perpetrators, both empirically and conceptually." As the result of this failure by Hannah Arendt, for example, who did no "research worth speaking of about perpetrators," there were, "politically expedient and morally numbing—and therefore, for many people comforting claims" of why Germans cooperated in killing. He said Christopher Browning "latched on to Arendt and Milgram in order to try to lend universal significance to his faulty conclusions about the men in the one German police battalion. See his analytically confused concluding chapter in *Ordinary Men*." Again, there was no specification, but only an assertion that Browning was confused. What he did not say about Hannah Arendt, whose classic work will long outlast his criticism, is that in 1951 she understood the point that Goldhagen would make decades later. "We do not know the extent of character transformation under a totalitarian regime. We know even less how many of the normal people around us would be willing to accept the totalitarian way of life." That she may not have met the exacting criteria of Professor Goldhagen was by no means a "failure." Far from providing comforting claims about the origins of anti–Semitism, Arendt explored theories of its origin, including the "assumption of eternal antisemitism," a variant of which undergirds Goldhagen's explanation of German behavior.[6]

One need not agree with all of Arendt's conclusions about anti–Semitism to recognize that long before any significant development of the historiography of the tragedy of the Holocaust, she constructed a masterwork that endures. Although disparaged by Professor Goldhagen, Christopher Browning reminded readers that "the behavior of any human being is, of course, a very complex phenomenon, and the historian who attempts to 'explain' it is indulging in a certain arrogance." "In the long run," according to Peter Novick, "almost all scholars have come to accept Arendt's thesis that the typical Holocaust perpetrator was 'terrifyingly normal' and by no means a driven anti–Semitic.... Scholars of the Holocaust have rejected the argument of Daniel Jonah Goldhagen that generations of systematic socialization into murderous hatred of Jews was a necessary condition for the Holocaust."[7]

When he received an award in Germany in 1997, Professor Goldhagen explained that his book focused exclusively on the past, to explain why and how the Holocaust occurred. "My task was, therefore, not to render moral judgment but to explain why things happened." The pretense to explain was subordinated to his moral judgments in his next book. Because of the past myths explaining the Holocaust, he found it necessary to shift his inquiry to "the event's actors and to treat them as moral agents." Asserting, "It is time for the Catholic Church to be similarly reexamined," he made the surprising claim that during the war, "the Church was the most powerful institution remaining intact and independent in German-occupied and dominated Europe." How any historian could so characterize a situation that cost the lives of thousands of clergy defies reason. He also overlooked Gordon Zahn's work in this regard, although he mentioned him in another context. While Zahn was critical of the German Church, he did not stint when describing the situation it faced during war, which left it far from independent. If there is another edition of *A Moral Reckoning*, or other writing on the subject by Professor Goldhagen, he should read Kevin Slicer's *Resisting the Third Reich*, a study that describes the pressures placed on the clergy by the Nazis before and during the war.

Professor Slicer is not an apologist for the Church. He discusses the relatively few "brown priests" who supported the Nazis and criticized what he saw as the lack of guidance for dealing with the Nazis provided the clergy by the bishops and the Vatican. Nonetheless, he made clear the real situation the bishops and clergy faced in dealing with a ruthless government.[8]

That Professor Goldhagen showed no familiarity with the extensively documented wartime historic situation of the Church in countries like Poland and Germany is unusual for someone who extensively references his knowledge of that time. Evidently Professor Goldhagen never heard of Warthegau, an area in which the independence of the Church was nonexistent. That was only one of almost endless instances during the war in which the Church was impotent. After such a demonstrably untrue generalization, and similar generalizations abound in the book, he proceeded to conduct an inquiry into "the Church's and its clergy's moral character," with a foreordained conclusion. If one parsed the 292 pages of text in *A Moral Reckoning*, countless similar examples of rampant generalization would pop up, to say nothing of the blithe dismissal of contrary conceptualizations of the problems he pretended to approach in a scholarly manner.

Professor Goldhagen explained that he used evidence provided by other authors, although he did not necessarily agree with them. "Similarly," he said, "because this book is not a historiographic exercise, I do not carry on a running discussion with views that these authors or others may have that differ from my own. Their books and those of other interpreters are readily available for readers who wish to deepen their knowledge of the issues." It would be hard to find a franker acknowledgment of advocacy by a tendentious author who said he wanted social science research methods used by his colleagues. But he allowed himself an exception from the balance and fairness required in social science research. Two examples must suffice to show the cavalier treatment he accorded scholars with whom he disagrees. Referring to the *Actes et documents du Saint-Siège*, he called the multivolume work "a collection carefully selected by the Church's custodians of the Pope's reputation." Goldhagen is not the only one to question the *Actes* but he and the others to date have provided no evidence of the claimed selectivity.

There also was disagreement with Professor Ronald Rychlak, but it was not enough to merely disagree. The "unreliable" Rychlak was accused of "fawning praise" of the Pope and presenting "such praise falsely as determinative of evidence of historical facts. Rychlak's denial, omission, and misconstrual of basic facts is systematic and blatant." Most scholars adopt a more civil way of suggesting that another scholar is wrong or has cooked the evidence, but Goldhagen, without reference to chapter and verse, went for the jugular. In responsible scholarship the right to eviscerate someone guilty of Rychlak's alleged misbehavior depends on evidence, not mere assertions. It is regrettable that Professor Goldhagen seems to view historians with different views as adversaries to be demolished, going beyond spelling out their disagreement by denigrating their work.[9]

The caution that Richard Evans suggested when reading David Irving's books surely applies to Professor Goldhagen: "To the unwary reader — and there have been many such — Irving's books gave the appearance of scholarly solidity. The footnotes and sometimes the text cited innumerable archival sources, documents, interviews, and other material that seemed at first glance to conform to the normal canons of historical scholarship. All this conspicuous display of research was bolstered by Irving's extravagant self-promotion as a discoverer of new historical material and his arrogant denigration of other researchers in the field."[10]

Hitler's Willing Executioners was based upon Professor Goldhagen's doctoral dissertation, *The Nazi Executioners: A Study of Their Behavior and the Causation of Genocide*, which was completed at Harvard University in 1992. According to Professor Goldhagen, the dissertation was under the direction of Professors Stanley Hoffman, Peter Hall and Sidney Vera. Goldhagen's dissertation was awarded the 1994 American Political Science Associations's Gabriel A. Almond Award for the best dissertation in the field of comparative politics. A stern critique of Goldhagen's methodology by Harry Cargas pointed to some of the serious problems in the book caused by the kind of qualifiers that were mentioned above. If the dissertation contained what Cargas found in the book, which Goldhagen said was the basis for *Hitler's Willing Executioners*, the dissertation advisors and judges for that award did not notice Goldhagen's questionable generalizations and undocumented conclusions. They would have done so had this been an undergraduate's senior thesis. In most doctoral programs, the teacher's role is to be skeptical and force students to prove their case. If the book reflected the dissertation on which it is supposed to be based, the advisors may not have read the dissertation as carefully as Cargas read the book.

Appendix A

Whether this was the case could be determined by comparing the book with the dissertation. Unfortunately, that was not possible.

Ordinarily, obtaining a copy of a doctoral dissertation is easy. Virtually all doctoral dissertations in the United States have a copy at University Microfilm International (UMI) that can be obtained on request, a service that is an enormous contribution to scholarship. Lacking a UMI copy, a researcher wanting to consult a dissertation would have to travel to a distant university, something many students and faculty could not afford. The copy of Goldhagen's dissertation at Harvard University is not available through an interlibrary loan, which is not unreasonable. However, what is unusual is that neither is a copy of Daniel Goldhagen's 1992 dissertation available through UMI without Goldhagen's written authorization, which was not forthcoming although several requests were made over a period of several months. Because a copy is not available in the usual manner from UMI, there is not the comity expected between scholars. More important, it prevents the comparison of a prize-winning dissertation with a media-celebrated but controversial book.

* * *

Dealing with the memories of individuals requires a reasonable amount of skepticism. That became clear in what should be a cautionary tale for relying on survivor memories. The conviction of John Demjanjuk in Israel relied heavily on witnesses who identified him as "Ivan the Terrible," a sadistic guard in the Treblinka death camp. He lost his American citizenship, thanks to efforts by the Justice Department, and was extradited to Israel. His trial there led to a death sentence. On appeal and because of reasonable doubts about his identification as "Ivan the Terrible," the Israel Supreme Court reversed his conviction. He returned to the United States and regained his citizenship, but again the government sought his deportation. Few of the memories that historians deal with are as dramatic as those who testified in good faith against him in Israel, but an Israeli court found their identification unconvincing. That did not extend to the memories of what they suffered nor does it justify the case being more than a cautionary tale, but an important one for historians.

There is ample evidence that memoir writers can recast events in the most favorable light for their policies or reputations. This is what Alan Wald called the "politics of memory." However, it may be possible to validate memories by examining their context to evaluate whether one is dealing with sanitized or otherwise distorted memories. When an individual's memory contradicts another person's opinion, documentary evidence is best to confirm the memory. But it also may be possible to have other persons independently confirm that memory. That would not necessarily end the dispute, but ordinarily, multiple similar memories of an event ought not be dismissed out of hand and without reason.[11]

Professor Susan Zuccotti, who delved into claims that Pius XII directed aid to Jews during the war, is often cited by writers about the "silence" of Pius XII. As a putative authority on the subject, she was taken very seriously, for example, by the National Archives and by Professors Grover and Daniel Goldhagen. Acclaimed as such, it is worth examining how Zuccotti unmasked the lack of credible evidence that the pope gave a directive to help Roman Jews. An example is found in her questioning of an alleged papal directive to aid "persecuted Jews" reported in *L'Osservatore della Domenica* by a Jesuit, Paolo Dezza, the rector of the Gregorian University in Rome during the war. Because of his stature, she said, and his direct presence on the scene, "this claim deserves careful attention." She then proceeded to debunk his story. She considered it suspicious that he mentioned the pope's directive in only one article, and not in articles he wrote for *La Civiltà Cattolica*, the Jesuit semi-official Vatican journal. This led her to refer to him as an "alleged witness" to a papal directive to help Jews. Without directly accusing him of a faulty memory or lying, a reader would understand what Professor Zuccotti clearly implied. She also called "somewhat exaggerated" William Doino's translation of Paolo Dezza's account of the "alleged" directive by the pope. Doino translated "*Ma per gli altri ben volentieri: civili, ebrei perseguiti*" as "for the others, help them willingly, *especially help the poor* persecuted Jews" [Zuccotti's emphasis]. She fairly and correctly noted that the phrase "especially help the poor" is not in the Italian. While that phrase should not be in Doino's translation, is not the essential point an admonition to help "persecuted Jews"?[12]

Paolo Dezza had only one article in *Civiltà Cattolica* between 1945 and 1960, a ten-page article in 1957 on Catholic universities that did not refer to the "alleged" directive. Most of the journal's articles in those years were by the regular staff, and outsiders like Dezza appeared only occasionally. In the war's aftermath, and during the 1950s, the journal had surprisingly few articles dealing with what was happening to the Church behind the Iron Curtain and only one article about an event in World War II. Articles ranged from those about religious matters and philosophy to subjects such as art, education, and politics. Before the 1960s *Civiltà Cattolica* had no articles "defending" Pius XII or the Vatican, presumably because papal "silence" was not yet a hot issue. Calling Dezza an "alleged witness" without a shred of real evidence is not the way to do history.[13]

Professor Zuccotti made much of the fact that the Vatican told those sheltering Jews and others that their guests should not wear clerical garb. Apparently some places were not zealous in following those instructions if what I was told in January 1997 was correct. During a conversation with my elderly Jewish landlord in Rome, he said he dressed as a monk while in a monastery for six months during the occupation. We were in his kitchen with his wife as they reminisced about that terrible time. This happened during a casual conversation and not in a planned and recorded interview. How might Professor Zuccotti handle his account and my report? Without any documentation by the landlord should his story be dismissed as suspicious because it came from another "alleged witness," not to a papal directive, but to being sheltered in a religious house during the German occupation of Rome? Another reason for suspecting his veracity was his claim that he dressed as a monk, something that was not to happen according to the Vatican. Did he embroider his story, if indeed he had received shelter? Without a paper trail, even if reported by a person of "stature," which he was not, would what he said fail whatever was Professor Zuccotti's test of credibility? Would my report also be dismissed as lacking credibility because it did not measure up to Professor Zuccotti's criteria, whatever they were?

The case Professor Zuccotti created against the pope, Golda Meir, and others is based on speculation about the witnesses' supposedly tainted, even if well-intentioned, motivation in testifying. Following Zuccotti's unstated and untested protocols for credibility, Golda Meir must have fabricated or exaggerated for a political purpose. Therefore, she as well as scores of others lacked credibility, some because of alleged misunderstanding or self-serving and more because of the lack of a written document attesting to papal intervention. The manner in which the Italian witnesses were treated is in marked contrast to her treatment of French witnesses. Writing about some thirty Holocaust survisvors and rescuers she interviewed, she said their stories were "excruciatingly painful and intimate." "I asked them implicitly, to trust me to respect and record their memories accurately for the future." Other information about the experience of the Jews came from archives, letters, and so forth and it all makes for a painful story, but how was the information validated? Like the French witnesses we are asked to trust her to have reported accurately, just as Golda Meir might have expected that what she said would be trusted.[14]

A similar problem of validation emerged in Professor Andrea Grover's study of the contents of *L'Osservatore Romano* from January 1, 1933, to June 30, 1945. That research focused on how the Vatican's semi-official daily related to the "systematic slaughter of European Jewry." Seeking a multidimensional survey of the newspaper involved identifying its view of Palestine, Vatican diplomatic interests, fear of Communism, the pope's personal attitudes and the Vatican's subservience to Italy during the war. Grover began by noting that when Germany began its anti–Semitic campaign in March 1933, the paper had a story on March 22, 1933, about a concentration camp with the headline: "Communists and the like" (comunisti e simili). Professor Grover said the paper assumed that its readers would identify the word *simili* as "Jews." Furthermore, this "perpetuated the stereotypical linkage of Jews with Communists," and that trend continued throughout the war.

When Professor Grover assumed that the word *simili* in this context really meant "Jews," that was the foundation for the charge of anti–Semitism. However, the word *simili* (or "similar"), is not evidence that it necessarily referred to Jews. *Simili* could refer to socialists and members of other parties the Nazis deemed enemies. That this could be the case is found in the diary of Rudolph Hoss, who became the Kommandant of Auschwitz. He described how in the early days of the Nazi regime, the Dachau concentration camp held almost all political prisoners, "Bavarian Communists, Social Democrats, or members of the Bavarian Peoples Party." He did not mention Jews. But reference to his diary would not be necessary by scholars familiar with the political situation in Germany as the Nazis consolidated power, with Kristallnacht coming several years later. With such an alternative interpretation readily available, it is surprising that it was either ignored or overlooked. Another assumption was that when the Vatican newspaper quoted Hitler, who said that almost all Communist agitators were Jewish, that ipso facto reflected the paper's negative

Appendix A

attitude toward Jews. On March 22, 1933, the *New York Times* headlined a story on the anti–Jewish boycotts accompanied by violence that were spreading in Germany: "Boycott Spreads in Reich but Hitler Bans Violent Acts." The story went on to say that Hitler supported the boycott and said that protests abroad would hurt the Jews. When the *New York Times* quoted Hitler's reference to Jews, why might that story be interpreted differently than a story in the Vatican paper? If there is a reason for doing so, readers are entitled to know why an author reached a conclusion that branded a paper anti–Semitic.

Beyond assumptions presented as facts, there was a lack of context for the research. The author's lack of understanding of the situation of the Vatican in wartime Rome was shown by a surprising comment about *L'Osservatore*: "It failed to follow the lead of such papers as the *Manchester Guardian*, which reported in October 1942 that between one and two million Jews were believed to have already been destroyed." To compare a wartime British paper with one in Rome on this issue is fatuous as well as grossly unfair. Grover could have easily discovered that at the time, British and American authorities, as well as Jewish agencies in those countries, were reluctant to credit the authenticity of such then unimaginable figures. However, newspapers in Allied countries had no hesitation printing unconfirmed reports that were confirmed much later, but there were good reasons for hesitation on the part of the Vatican. Professor Grover may have wanted it otherwise, but that was no reason to insulate readers from the factual situation facing such newspapers. In simple fairness the context of events in the past should not be omitted from the record. Otherwise one is doing something other than history.[15]

Using the cloak of history (extensive footnotes and so forth), Holocaust deniers and revisionists continue to publish a surprising number of books and articles, as well as web sites, especially in Europe. One domestic Holocaust revisionist who denied there was a German policy of exterminating the Jews is Professor Arthur Butz, who was an unlikely and unwelcome apologist for the Vatican. "It is no more necessary, here," he said, "to explain why Pius XII did not speak up about the extermination of the Jews, than it is necessary to explain why he did not protest the extermination of Eskimos." Butz made unwarranted assumptions about statements by persons he quoted and drew conclusions on sketchy "evidence." An example was his quibbling over the meaning of the word *sopprimere* (suppress). In a conversation with Franz Von Papen, the German ambassador to Turkey, the then Vatican Nuncio to Turkey, Msgr. Angelo Roncalli, who later became pope, used the word "suppress" when referring to Jews sent to Poland. Although Butz agreed that the word *sopprimere* means killing, he said, "To apply sopprimere to a large group of people carries an implication only of large numbers of killings, and may or may not mean 'extermination' depending on the context. Thus one must allow the possibility that Roncalli was thinking of something other than the sort of extermination claims that the Allies had made, and which Roncalli had certainly heard by then." In a textbook example of sophistry, Butz went on to imply that Roncalli was taken in by Allied propaganda about the supposed extermination policy of the Germans.[16]

True believers, such as Butz, David Irving, Robert Faurison and others, continue to question the reality of the Holocaust. By conducting a so-called analysis of the construction of execution chambers, they seek to show they really were for disinfecting clothing, or they find differing accounts of witnesses about techniques used in executions. One might concede that they may have a point about some witnesses or about a technical matter, such as whether fumes from gasoline or diesel engine were used to kill people. However, they deliberately ignore the overwhelming evidence that there was a Final Solution, evidence that overshadows debates about technology or the conflicting reports of witnesses. That evidence comes from the demographics of Europe after the war. When more than a thousand Roman Jews were deported in October 1943, fifteen returned to Rome. Primo Levi was with 650 men when he was sent to Germany; he was one of only six who returned to Italy. What happened to all the others? What happened to the Dutch deportees and the Jews taken from Hungary? The few survivors of the deportations to death camps, where most died because of gassing, starvation or disease, testify to a reality that only minds warped by prejudice can deny.

* * *

Why there is a seeming consensus about the Vatican's performance in World War II finds at least a partial explanation through social network analysis (SNA), a method used in the social sciences and other academic disciplines revealing how network members communicate and affect others. Most networks are informal, and members do not have to know each other or communicate personally in order to be influenced and influence others inside and outside the network. Some networks tend toward dominance and the monopoly of information. They can become insulated from outside influences and fail to heed critical information from outsiders. An example of missing such critical information is found in Professor Michael Phayer's hard hitting criticism of Pius XII that appeared in 2000. It does not refer to Pierre Blet's *Pius XII and the Second World War* that appeared in 1997 and is found in the library of Marquette University where he teaches, and in twenty other Wisconsin libraries. He also dismissed Robert Graham as a "Vatican operative," ignoring his many writings about a period Phayer researched so intensively. He was not alone, of course, because John Cornwell also made no reference to Blet's book, nor did he refer to Robert Graham. Professor Goldhagen made a brief reference to the "carefully selected" documents in *Actes et documents du Saint-Siège* but overlooked Pierre Blet's book in Harvard's library and the work of Robert Graham. There is nothing surprising about such selectivity in social networks once one begins to think about them.

Although sometimes more structured, academic networks are little different from others, including UFO enthusiasts and music fans. Articles and books, as well as the Internet in recent years, maintain the exchange of information. If SNA is applied to the coterie of writers who have been the most critical of Pius XII, one will find a mutually reinforcing group that shares approaches and ideas, resists outside information, and constitutes the core of the academic and media "consensus" about the pope's wartime behavior. For a long time they have been the favored informants whom journalists consider authorities when writing about matters such as papal "silence." That vastly extends the range of the academic network's intellectual influence. Going against the tide of that "consensus" in academia is difficult. No counter to Professor Goldhagen's or John Cornwell's profitable blockbuster attacks on Pius XII would receive their kind of attention, let alone reviews in major journals. Knowing this, professors, who are as risk aversive as anyone else, are reluctant to confront a "consensus" in contemporary history. Only a major figure in the field could do that, and to date that has not happened. While the so-called defenders of Pius have done excellent scholarship, they are not members of the historical establishment and their message has not received a fair hearing.

Readers will decide the merit of evaluating the seemingly "minor" distorted details in much of the writing of critics of the wartime pope. They also will need to decide why Professor Goldhagen ignored reliable contrary evidence when writing his books and how Professor Zuccotti justified questioning the integrity of John Carroll-Abbing, Paolo Dezza and Golda Meir. Why, based on no evidence, did the National Archives Web site imply a connection between Swiss gold and Pius XII? Why did the University of Washington warn its library patrons that "Catholic" Web sites about Pius XII might be biased and why did the National Security Agency question whether Pius XII offered to help Rome's Jewish community raise the gold extorted by the Nazis? These and other questions do not imply an academic and media conspiracy that created the contemporary virtual consensus about the wartime Vatican's behavior. They do suggest that instead of vigorous debate about what happened, a social network gained the high ground in contemporary history based on questionable scholarship. Hochuth's myth was aided by a virtual cottage industry of Vatican critics. There has been and can be fair scholarly criticism, some of it harsh, of Vatican policies during World War II. With some exceptions that scholarly historical tradition has been replaced by the "Pius Wars" in which sensationalism evokes media interest and newer myths like *Hitler's Pope* flourish. That is not the way to do honest history for the public.

Appendix B:
The Vatican Archives

> The modern manipulators of facts stand in the way of the historian. For history itself is destroyed, and its comprehensibility — based upon the fact that it is enacted by men and therefore can be understood by men — is in danger, whenever the facts are no longer held to be part and parcel of the past and present world, and are misused to prove this or that opinion.
>
> — Hannah Arendt, 1951

The completeness and authenticity of the *Actes et documents du Saint-Siège relatifs à la seconde guerre mondiale* have been questioned, sometimes directly but mostly by indirection, with the evident intent of persuading readers to doubt their credibility. Pierre Blet, S.J., the last surviving member of the team that spent years preparing the *Actes*, had the following to say about how the work was done, in "The Myth in the Light of the Archives: The Recurring Accusations against Pope Pius XII." This account, with its original notes, is reproduced with the permission of *La Civiltà Cattolica* in which it first was published.*

* * *

When he died on 9 October 1958, Pius XII was the object of unanimous tributes of admiration and gratitude: "The world," declared President

---

*Pierre Blet, S.J. "La leggenda alla prova degli archivi," *La Civiltà Cattolica* 144, vol. 1, no. 3546 (March 21, 1998): 531–541. Reprinted by permission. The English version is in J.D. Bindenagel, ed., *Washington Conference on Holocaust-Era Assets, November 30–December 3, 1998, Proceedings*, "Appendix O" (Washington, D.C.: U.S. Department of State, Department of State Publication 10603, 1999), 1067–1078.

Eisenhower, "is now poorer since the death of Pius XII." Golda Meir, then Foreign Minister of the State of Israel: "The life of our times was enriched by a voice speaking out about great moral truths above the tumult of daily conflict. We mourn a great servant of peace."[1] A few years later however, beginning in 1963, he had become the subject of a black legend: during the War, it was claimed, due to political calculation or faintheartedness, he remained impassive and silent in the face of crimes against humanity, which would have been prevented had he intervened.

When accusations are based on documents, it is possible to discuss the interpretation of texts, verify whether they have been misunderstood, received in a non-critical way, misrepresented or chosen selectively. But when a legend is created from unrelated elements and with the aid of imagination, discussion is meaningless. The only thing possible is to counter the myth with the historical reality proved by incontestable documentation. For this reason, Pope Paul VI, who as Substitute of the Secretariat of State had been one of the closest collaborators of Pius XII, as early as 1964 authorized the publication of the documents of the Holy See relating to the Second World War.

The Layout of Actes et Documents

The Archives of the Secretariat of State preserve the files in which it is often possible to follow day by day, sometimes hour by hour, the activity of the Pope and his offices. Here are found the messages and addresses of Pius XII; the letters exchanged between the Pope and civil and ecclesiastical authorities, notes of the Secretariat of State, service notes from junior officials to their superiors to communicate information and suggestions and, in addition, private notes (in particular, those of Monsignor Domenico Tardini, who had the habit, most fortunate for historians, of thinking with pen in hand), the correspondence of the Secretariat of State with the Holy See's representatives abroad (Apostolic Nuncios, Internuncios and Delegates) and the Diplomatic Notes exchanged between the Secretariat of State and Ambassadors or Ministers accredited to the Holy See. These documents are for the most part sent with the name and signature of the Secretary of State or the Secretary of the First Section of the Secretariat of State: this does not detract from their expressing the intentions of the Pope.

On the basis of these documents it would have been possible to write a work describing the attitude and policy of the Pope during the Second World War. Or an official report could have been produced to demonstrate the groundlessness of the accusations against Pius XII. Since the main charge was that of silence, it would have been particularly easy to use the documents to illustrate the Holy See's activity on behalf of war victims and particularly on behalf of the victims of racist persecutions. It was considered more suitable to undertake a complete publication of the documents relating to the War. Various collections of diplomatic documents already existed, many volumes of which dealt with the Second World War: Documenti diplomatici italiani; Documents on British Foreign Policy: 1919–1939; Foreign Relations of the United States, Diplomatic Papers; Akten zur deutschen auswärtgen Politik 1918–1945. Given the existence of these collections and on the lines of such models, it seemed useful to allow historians to study from the documents the role and activity of the Holy See during the War. With this perspective the publication of the collection entitled *Actes et documents du Saint-Siège relatifs à la seconde guerre mondiale* was begun.[2]

The difficulty lay in the fact that for this period the archives both of the Vatican and of other States were closed to the public and also to historians. The particular interest in the events of the Second World War, the desire to write its history on the basis of the documents, and not only from more or less direct accounts or testimonies, had led the States involved in the conflict to publish the documents still inaccessible to the public. Trustworthy persons charged with such a task are subject to certain rules: not to publish documents which would call into question people still living or which, if revealed, would hamper current negotiations. On the basis of these criteria the volumes of the Foreign Relations of the United States relating to the Forties were published, and the same criteria were followed in the publications of the documents of the Holy See.

The task of publishing the documents of the Holy See relating to the War was entrusted to three Jesuit priests: Angelo Martini, editor of *La Civiltà Cattolica*, who had already access to the secret archives of the Vatican, Burkhart Schneider and the author of the present article, both professors in the Church History Faculty of the Pontifical Gregorian University. The work began in the first days of January 1965, in an office near the storeroom containing the archives of the then Congregation for Extraordinary Ecclesiastical Affairs and First Section of the Secretariat of State; documents relating to the War were normally kept there.

In such conditions, the work was both easy and difficult. The difficulty was that since the archives were not open to the public there were no systematic inventories geared to research, documents were not classified, either in chronological or strictly geographical order. Those of a political nature, and hence relating to the War, were sometimes stored with documents of a religious, canonical or even personal nature, placed in fairly manageable boxes but sometimes with widely differing contents. Information relating to Great Britain could be found in files on France, if the information had been sent through the Nuncio in France, and naturally interventions on behalf of Belgian hostages were in the boxes of the Nuncio in Berlin. It was therefore necessary to examine every box and go through the entire contents in order to identify the documents relating to the War. The research was simplified, however, thanks to an old rule of the Secretariat of State in force since the time of Urban VIII: Nuncios were to deal with only one subject in each letter.

Despite such difficulties, certain circumstances made our task easier. Since we were working in an office of the Secretariat of State and as members of the Commission, we were not bound by the conditions placed on researchers given access to the public storerooms in the consultation areas; one of us would take the boxes of documentation directly from the storeroom shelves. Our task was also made considerably easier by the fact that the documentation was for the most part typewritten and had been stored as separate letters (except for manuscripts to be typed for the printing office). Thus when a particular document was recognized as pertaining to the War it could simply be removed and photocopied, and the photocopy together with explanatory notes — as scholarly work requires — given to the printing office.

Although in the winter of 1965 the work was proceeding quickly enough, we decided to ask the help of Father Robert Leiber, who had retired to the German College after serving for more than thirty years as private secretary of Pacelli, first when the latter was Nuncio, then Secretary of State and finally Pope Pius XII. Leiber had followed the situation in Germany very closely, and it was he who had told us of the existence of drafts of Pius XII's letters to the German Bishops. These became the material of the second volume of the series and are the documents that best reveal the thoughts of the Pope.

The Individual Volumes

The first volume, which covers the first seventeen months of the Pontificate (March 1939–July 1940) and which reveals Pius XII's efforts to stave off war, was published in December 1965 and was given a generally positive reception. In 1966, while Father Schneider was busy preparing the volume of the letters to the German Bishops, Father Robert A. Graham, an American Jesuit of the magazine *America* who had already published a work on the diplomacy of the Holy See (Vatican Diplomacy), asked for information covering the period on which we were working. In reply to his request, he was invited to join our group, especially as we had learned of the ever more frequent contacts of Pius XII with Roosevelt and since we were coming across documents in English fairly frequently. He worked directly on the preparation of the third volume, which was devoted to Poland and modeled on the second volume, concerning the relationships of the Holy See with the Bishops. But the direct exchange of letters with other Bishops proved much less intense, with the result that volumes two and three (in two parts) remained the only ones of their kind. Thus we decided to divide the documents into two sections: one was to be a continuation of the first volume, for questions primarily diplomatic in nature, as indicated by their title *Le Saint-Siège et la guerre en Europe, Le Saint-Siège et la guerre mondiale*. These were volumes 4, 5, 7 and 11. Volumes 6, 8, 9 and 10, entitled *Le Saint-Siège et les victimes de la guerre*, present in chronological order documents pertaining to the efforts of the Holy See to help all suffering in body or spirit because of the War, prisoners separated from their families and exiled far from their loved ones, peoples subjected to the devastation of the War, and victims of racial persecution.

The work lasted more than fifteen years; the group divided the workload according to the planned volumes and the time that each member could give. Father Leiber, whose help had been so valuable to us, was taken from us by death on 18 February 1967. Father Schneider, after the publication of the letters to the German Bishops and while continuing to teach

Appendix B

Modern History at the Gregorian University, had devoted himself to the section on the victims of the War. With the help of Father Graham he prepared volumes 6, 8 and 9, which were completed at Christmas 1975. But in the summer of that same year he had been stricken by the illness from which he would die the following May. Father Martini, who had devoted himself full-time to this work and had in some way worked on every volume, did not have the satisfaction of seeing the work completed in its entirety: he was only able to see the proofs of the last volume, at the beginning of the summer of 1981, before he himself passed away. Volume 11 (the last of the series) came out towards the end of 1981, under the auspices of Father Graham and myself. Thus Father Graham, although the oldest among us, was able to work until the project was brought to completion. During those fifteen years he was also able to work on related research and publications, which mainly came out as articles in *La Civiltà Cattolica*, and which themselves also constitute a source of information which historians of the Second World War can profitably consult. He left Rome on 24 July 1996 to return to his native California, where he ended his days on 11 February 1997.

Since the beginning of 1982, I had resumed my own research on seventeenth century France and papal diplomacy. But seeing that after fifteen years our volumes remained unknown even to many historians, I devoted the years of 1996–1997 to putting the essence and conclusions of that work into a single column of modest size, but as complete as possible.[3] A dispassionate reading of this documentation clearly brings to light in its concrete reality the attitude and conduct of Pius XII during the World War and, consequently, the unfoundedness of the accusations made against him. The documentation clearly shows that he did everything he possibly could in the area of diplomacy to avoid the War, to dissuade Germany from attacking Poland, to convince Mussolini's Italy to dissociate itself from Hitler. There is no trace of the alleged pro–German partiality that he is purported to have developed while he was at the Nunciature in Germany. His efforts, joined with those of Roosevelt, to keep Italy out of the conflict, the solidarity telegrams of 10 May 1940 to the Sovereigns of Belgium, the Netherlands and Luxembourg after the invasion of the Wehrmacht, his courageous admonition to Mussolini and to King Victor Emanuel calling for a separate peace certainly do not point in that direction. It would be unrealistic to think that with the halberds of the Swiss Guard, or even with the threat of excommunication, he would have been able to stop the tanks of the Wehrmacht.

But the accusation which is often repeated is that he remained silent about the racial persecution aimed at the Jews; even when this was carried to its ultimate consequences, and that he thus left the way open for the Nazi atrocities. The documentation, however, shows the Pope's unfailing and constant efforts to oppose the deportations, the outcome of which was the subject of ever increasing suspicion. The apparent silence hid a clandestine activity on the part of the Nunciatures and Bishops to circumvent, or at least limit, the deportations, the violence, and the persecutions. The rationale behind this caution is clearly explained by the Pope himself in different speeches, in the letters to the German Bishops, and in consultations within the Secretariat of State. Public denunciations would have been of no use: they would have only served to make the fate of the victims worse and to increase their actual number.

Recurring Accusations

In an effort to obscure this evidence, the detractors of Pius XII have cast doubts upon the seriousness of our publication. Quite remarkable in this regard is an article published in a Paris evening newspaper on 3 December 1997: "Those four Jesuits have produced [!] in the *Actes et documents* texts which have absolved Plus XII of the omissions with which he is charged. But those *Actes et documents* are far from being complete." It is insinuated that we had omitted documents that might prejudice the memory of Pius XII and the Holy See.

First, it is not clear how the omission of certain documents would help to clear Pius XII of the failures of which he has been accused. On the other hand, to state peremptorily that our publication is not complete is to state something impossible to prove: to do so, one would have to compare our publication with the archival material and indicate documents present in the archives but missing in our publication. Even though the pertinent archival material is still closed to the public, some people have gone so far as to furnish alleged proofs of such gaps in the *Actes et documents*. In doing so they have shown their scanty knowledge of research into archival collections, the opening of some of which they are demanding.

Appendix B

Repeating an identical statement in a Roman daily newspaper on 11 September 1997, the 3 December article states that the correspondence between Pius XII and Hitler is missing from our publication. Let us first note that the letter in which the Pope informed the Head of State of the Reich of his election is the last document published in the second volume of the *Actes et documents*. As for the rest, if we did not publish any correspondence between Pius XII and Hitler it is because such correspondence exists solely in the imagination of the journalist. The latter mentions contacts between Pacelli, then Nuncio in Germany, and Hitler, but he should have checked his dates: Hitler came to power in 1933 and thus would only have been able to meet the Apostolic Nuncio after that date. But Archbishop Pacelli had returned to Rome in December 1929; Pius XI had created him a Cardinal on 16 December 1929 and Secretary of State on 16 January 1930. Most importantly, had such correspondence ever existed, the Pope's letters would have been preserved in the German archives and it would be natural for some trace of them to be found in the archives of the Foreign Ministry of the Reich. Hitler's letters would have ended up in the Vatican, but some mention of them would be found in the instructions given to the German Ambassadors, Bergen and then Weitzacker, who were charged with delivering them, and in the reports filed by these diplomats confirming that they had in fact transmitted them to the Pope or the Secretary of State. There is no trace of any of this. In the absence of such references, it must be said that the seriousness of our publication has been impugned without a shred of evidence. These observations about the alleged correspondence between the Pope and the Führer are also applicable to other documents, ones which actually existed. Very frequently documents from the Vatican, e.g., notes exchanged with ambassadors, are attested to by other archives. One can presume that many telegrams from the Vatican were intercepted and deciphered by the information services of the warring powers, and that copies can be found in their archives. Consequently, had we in fact attempted to hide certain documents it would be possible to establish their existence and thus have a basis for casting doubt on the seriousness of our work. The same article in the Paris newspaper, after imagining relations between Hitler and the Nuncio Pacelli, refers to an article in the Sunday Telegraph in July 1997, which accuses the Holy See of having used Nazi gold to help war criminals flee to Latin America, and in particular the Croat Anton Pavelic: "Some studies support this thesis" (!). One is amazed at the casualness with which journalists can content themselves with documenting statements. Historians, who often labor for hours in order to verify their references, will envy them. One can understand that a journalist will trust a colleague, especially when the English name of the paper gives him an air of respectability. But there are two other statements which deserve to be studied separately, namely the arrival in the Vatican coffers of Nazi gold, or more exactly the gold belonging to Jews and stolen by the Nazis, and its use to facilitate the flight of Nazi war criminals to Latin America.

Some American dailies had in fact produced a document from the U.S. Treasury Department in which the Department was informed that the Vatican had received, through Croatia, Nazi gold of Jewish origin. The fact that the document was "from the Treasury Department" might appear impressive, but one has to read what is printed beneath the headline and one discovers that it is a note based on the "report of a trustworthy Roman informant." Those who take such statements for gospel truth should read Father Graham's article on the exploits of the informant V. Scattolini, who made a living out of "information" concocted in his own imagination which he then passed on to all the Embassies, including the American Embassy, which dutifully forwarded it to the State Department.[4] In our search of the archives of the Secretariat of State, we found no mention of the alleged entrance into Vatican coffers of gold stolen from Jews. Obviously those who make such statements have a responsibility to furnish documented proof, for example a receipt, not kept in the Vatican archives, as in the case of the alleged letters of Pius XII to Hitler. In the archives themselves, one finds only the prompt response of Pius XII when the Jewish communities of Rome were subjected to extortion by the SS, which demanded that they hand over fifty kilograms of gold. At that time the Chief Rabbi turned to the Pope to ask him for the fifteen kilograms needed to make up the amount, and Pius XII immediately ordered his offices to make the necessary arrangements.[5] Recent checks of the archives have discovered nothing further.

Nor is the report about Nazi criminals fleeing to Latin America with the alleged help of the Vatican something new. Obviously we cannot exclude the naiveté of some Roman cleric who may have used his position to facilitate the escape of a Nazi. The sympathies of Bishop Hudal, Rector of the German national church in Rome, for the Great Reich are well-known; but on these grounds to imagine that the Vatican organized a large-scale escape of Nazis to Latin America would be to attribute heroic charity to the Roman clergy, as the Nazi plans for the Church and the Holy See were well-known in Rome. Pius XII referred to them in his Consistorial Address of 2 June 1945, recalling that the persecution by the regime of the Church had been intensified by the War, "when its adherents still entertained the illusion that, following a military victory, they would eliminate the Church once and for all."[6] The authors referred to by our journalist have a rather lofty idea of the forgiveness of wrongs practiced in papal circles, if they imagine that a number of Nazis were sheltered in the Vatican and thence taken to Argentina, under the protection of the Peron dictatorship, and then on to Brazil, Chile and Paraguay, as a way of salvaging whatever could be salvaged of the Third Reich: thus a "Fourth Reich" would have been created in the pampas.

In these reports it is hard to differentiate fact and fiction. For those who like to read fiction we can recommend Ladislas Farago's *Aftermath: Martin Bormann and the Fourth Reich*. The phrase "the Fourth Reich" says it all. The author takes us from Rome and the Vatican to Argentina, Paraguay and Chile on the trail of the Reichsleiter and other fleeing Nazi leaders. With the attention to detail of an Agatha Christie, he describes the exact position of each character at the moment of the crime, indicates the numbers of the hotel rooms occupied by the fleeing Nazis and the Nazi hunters hot on their trail and paints a picture of the green Volkswagen which transported them. One is struck by the modesty of the author, who presents his book as "a typically French investigative report, a study that is serious yet without pretensions to pure scholarship" (!).

Conclusion

The reader will understand that the Vatican archives may contain nothing of all that, even if it actually happened. If Bishop Hudal did help some prominent Nazis to escape, he certainly would not have gone seeking the Pope's permission. And if he had later confided to him what had happened, we would know nothing of it now. Among the things which the archives will never reveal we must mention the conversations between the Pope and his visitors, with the exception of the ambassadors who reported on them to their governments, or de Gaulle who speaks of them in his memoirs. This does not mean that when serious historians wish personally to check the archives from which published documents have been drawn their desire is not legitimate and praiseworthy. Even after a publication carried out as accurately as possible, consultation of the archives and direct contact with the documents makes for historical understanding. It is one thing to cast doubt on the seriousness of our research, and another altogether to wonder if something perhaps escaped us. We have not deliberately ignored any significant document on the grounds that it seemed to us to damage the image of the Pope and the reputation of the Holy See. But in an undertaking such as this the person doing the work is the first to wonder whether he has forgotten something. Without Father Leiber, the existence of the drafts of Pius XII's letter to the German Bishops would have gone unnoticed, and the collection would have been deprived of the text which are perhaps the most valuable of all for an understanding of the Pope's thinking.[7] Yet those letters do not contradict in any way what we had learnt from the notes and diplomatic correspondence. In them, we see more of Pius XII's concern to depend upon the teaching of the Bishops in order to put German Catholics on their guard against the perverse seductions of National Socialism, more dangerous than ever in time of war. This correspondence, published in the second volume of the *Actes et documents*, therefore confirms the tenacious opposition of the Church to National Socialism, though we knew already of the first warnings of German Bishops like Faulhaber and von Galen, of many religious and priests, and finally the encyclical letter *Mit Brennender Sorge*, read in all the churches of Germany on Palm Sunday 1937, despite the Gestapo.

We can therefore only consider as a pure and simple lie the claim that the Church supported Nazism, as a Milan newspaper wrote on 6 January 1998. Moreover, the texts published in the fifth volume of the *Actes et documents* deny outright the idea that the Holy See supported the Third Reich because it was afraid of Soviet Russia. When Roosevelt sought the Vatican's help to overcome the opposition of American Catholics to his plan to extend to Russia at war against the Reich the support already granted to Great Britain, he was listened to. The Secretariat of State charged the Apostolic Delegate in Washington to entrust to American Bishops the task of explaining that the encyclical *Divini Redemptoris*

Appendix B

which enjoined Catholics to refuse the hand held out by the Communist parties did not apply to the current situation and did not forbid the USA to help Soviet Russia's war effort against the Third Reich. These are unassailable conclusions.

Therefore, without wishing to discourage future researchers, I very much doubt whether the opening of the Vatican archives of the War years will change our understanding of the period. In the archives, as we have explained earlier, the diplomatic and administrative documents are mixed with documents of a strictly personal character; and this demands a longer closure than in the archives of the Foreign Ministries of the various States. Those who do not want to wait but wish to study in depth the history of that convulsed period can work fruitfully in the archives of the Foreign Office, the Quai d'Orsay, the State Department, and in the archives of the other States which had representatives accredited to the Holy See. Better than the notes of the Vatican's Secretariat of State, the dispatches of the British Minister Osborne evoke the situation of the Holy See, surrounded by Fascist Rome which then fell under the control of the German army and police.[8] It is by devoting themselves to such research without asking for a premature opening of the Vatican archives, that they will show that are really seeking the truth."

Chapter Notes

Chapter 1

1. L. Zaccagnini, *Il ghetto di Roma* [The Roman Ghetto] (Albano di Roma: Fratelli Strini, 1929), 8; Giuliana Albini Mantovani, "La Communita Ebraica in Cremona Nel Sec. XV e le Origini del Monte di Pieta" [The Jewish Community in Cremona in the XV Century and the Origin of the Monte di Pieta], *Nuova Rivista Storica* 59 (Maggio-Agosto 1975): 378–405; Robert Bonfil, *Rabbis and Jewish Communities in Renaissance Italy* (London: The Litman Library of Jewish Civilization, 1993); Sergio Della Pergola, *Anatomia dell'ebraismo italiano* [The Anatomy of Italian Judaism] (Assisi/Rome: Beniamino Carucci Editore, 1976), 56; *Compendio Statistico Italiano 1939-XVIII. Vol. III* [Summary of Italian Statistics 1939-XVIII, Vol. III] (Rome: Istituto Poligrafico Dello Stato), A. XVII, 29. Tav. VI; and Joachim Prinz, *Popes from the Ghetto: A View of Medieval Christendom* (New York: Horizon Press, 1966), 48.

2. Andrew M. Canepa, "Emancipation and Jewish Responses in Mid-Nineteenth-Century Italy," *European History Quarterly* 16, no. 4 (October 1986): 429. The Haskalah was a movement promoting the "modernization" of Judaism that began in the last half of the 1700s.

3. Paolo Bernardini, "The Jews in Nineteenth Century Italy: Toward a Reappraisal." *Journal of Modern Italian Studies* 1, no. 2. (Spring 1996): 292–310; Lois C. Dubin, "Trieste and Berlin: The Italian Role in the Cultural Politics of the Haskalah," in *Toward Modernity: The European Jewish Model*, ed. Jacob Katz, 189–224 (New Brunswick, NJ: Transaction Books, 1987). Although dated, chapter 11, 509–553. In Cecil Roth, *History of the Jews of Italy* (Philadelphia: Jewish Publication Society of America, 5706-1946) 509–553; Barbara Armani and Guri Schwarz, "Ebrei Borghesi" [Middle Class Jews], *Quaderni Storici* 38, no. 3 (2003): 621–652; "Ebrei Sotto Processo." [Jews on Trial], *Quaderni Storici* 33 (December 3, 1998); Philip V. Cannistraro and Brian R. Sullivan, *Il Duce's Other Woman* (New York: William Morrow and Company, 1993), 20–28; Vivian, B. Mann, ed. *Gardens and Ghettos: The Art of Jewish Life in Italy* (Berkeley: University of California Press, 1989); H. Stuart Hughes, *Prisoners of Hope: The Silver Age of the Italian Jews, 1924–1974* (Cambridge, MA: Harvard University Press, 1983), 1–28; and Meir Michaelis, "The Holocaust in Italy: Areas of Inquiry," in *The Holocaust and History: The Known, the Unknown, the Disputed, and the Reexamined,* ed. Michael Berenbaum and Abraham J. Peck, 439 (Bloomington: Indiana University Press, 1998).

4. *Enciclopedia italiana di scienze, lettere, ed arte*, Vol. 13 [The Italian Encyclopedy of Science, Letters and Art, Vol. 13] (Milano: Rizzoli, 1932), 329. "La definizione del razzismo come 'roba da biondi' no l'ho letto in nessun documento. L'ho attinta direttamente dalla bocca di Mussolini. "Il Mussolini del '32." ["The definition of racism as 'the stuff of blonds' I did not read in any document, I heard it directly from Mussolini, the Mussolini of 1932."] Indro Montanelli in *Corriere della Sera*, April 13, 1997, 35. Orestano quoted in: Denis Mack Smith, *Mussolini's Roman Empire* (New York: The Viking Press, 1976), vi.

5. Civil Affairs Training Program, "The Jews of Italy" (Madison: University of Wisconsin) 1; *VII Censimento generale della*

popolazione. 21 Aprile 1931, IX, Vol. IV. Relazione generale. [VII General Census of Population, April 21, 1931, IX. Vol. IV. General Summary] (Rome: Istituto Generale Di Statistica del Regno D'Italia, 1935), 90; *VIII Censimento della popolazione, 1936 XIV, Vol. V. Libia, isole italiane dell'Egeo, Tientsin* [VIII Census of Population, 1936, XIV. Vol. V. Libya. Italian Islands in the Agean, Tientsin] (Rome: Istituto di Statistica, 1936), Tavola 30, 104.

6. Tracy Koon, *Believe, Obey, Fight: Political Socialization of Youth in Fascist Italy 1922-1943* (Chapel Hill: University of North Carolina Press, 1985), 287. Aldo Capasso, *Idee chiare sul razzismo* [Ideas about Racism] (Rome: Edizioni Augustea, 1942), 12, 33. Ugo Giorgio Andaldo, *Razza, nazione, guerra* [Race, Nation, War] (Bologna: Edizione SIA, 1940), 67.

7. Michele Sarfatti, *Mussolini contro gli Ebrei: Cronaca dell'elaborazione delle leggi del 1938* [Mussolini Against the Jews: Summary of the Development of the Laws of 1938] (Torino: Silvio Zamorani Editore, 1994), 164. Sarfatti also provides the progression of official actions that led to the final legislation, as well as copies of the relevant documents. Note that the regular national census of 1936 *did not* enumerate Jews in Italy itself.

8. Royal Decree (RD) 5 September 1938, N. 1390, regarding schools; RD 7 September 1938, N. 1381, foreign Jews; RD 17 November 1938, N. 1728, marriages and definition of Jews; RD 15 November 1938, N. 1779, education (Fascist Grand Council, October 6, 1938). Also, Ugo Caffaz, *Discriminazione e persecuzione degli Ebrei nell'Italia fascista* [Discrimination and Persecution of Jews in Fascist Italy] (Consiglio Regionale della Toscana, 1988); and Giorgio Sacchetti, "Arezzo: Presenze ebraiche fra XIX e XX Secolo" [The Jewish Presence in Arezzo between the XIX and XX Century], in *Presenze ebraiche nell'Aretino dal XIV al XX Secolo* [The Jewish Presence in the Aretino from XIV to the XX Century], ed. Roberto G. Salvadori (Firenze: Leo S. Olschki Editore, 1990).

9. David I. Kertzer, *The Popes Against the Jews: The Vatican's Role in the Rise of Modern Anti-Semitism* (New York: Alfred A. Knopf, 2001), 282-283; and Giovanni Miccoli, *I dilemmi e i silenzi di Pio XII* [The Dilemmas and Silences of Pius XII] (Milano: Rizzoli, 2000), 303

10. Liliana Picciotto Fargion, "La ricerca del Centro di documentazione ebraica contemporanea sugli Ebrei deportati dall'Italia." [The Research of the Center for Contemporary Jewish Documentation on the Jews Deported from Italy], in *Italia Judica: Gli ebrei nell'Italia unita 1870-1945*, 474-486 [Jewish Italy: The Jews in United Italy 1870-1945] (Rome: Ministero per i Beni Culturale e Ambientali, 1993); and Robert Katz, *Black Sabbath: A Journey through a Crime Against Humanity* (Toronto: The Macmillan Company, 1969). Also Giacomo DeBenedetti, *16 Ottobre 1943* (Palermo: Sellerio editore, 1993).

11. Maria de Blasio Wilhelm, *The Other Italy: Italian Resistance in World War II* (New York: WW. Norton & Company, 1988), chapter 7, "Fighting Back: The Jews of Italy," 148-172. There were 8,000 deportees to concentration camps, of whom just less than 1,000 survived, 171. Meir Michaelis, "Fascism, Totalitarianism and the Holocaust: Reflections on Current Interpretations of National Socialist Anti-Semitism," *European History Quarterly* 19 (1989): 85-103; and Arthur R. Butz, *The Hoax of the Twentieth Century: The Case against the Presumed Extermination of European Jewry* (Costa Mesa, CA: Institute for Historical Review, 1977). He does not deny that there were deaths caused by sickness and brutality, but denies that there was any German policy to exterminate Jews. Details of the racial laws about education can be found in "Cronica contemporanea," *La Civiltà Cattolica* 89, no. 3 (September 17, 1938): 558-563. Giancarlo Sacerdote, *Ricordi di un Ebreo bolognese: illusioni e delusioni 1929-1945* [Memories of a Jew of Bologna: Illusions and Delusions 1929-1945] (Rome: Bonacci Editore, 1983); Alexander Stille, *Benevolence and Betrayal: Five Italian Jewish Families under Fascism* (New York: Summit Books, 1991); Paolo Ravenna, "La persecuzione e i giovani, la scuola ebraica di via Vignatagliata" [The Persecution and Youth: The Jewish School of Via Vegnatagliata] in *Le legge razziali del 1938*, Atti del Convegno di Ferrari, 20 Novembre 1988 [The Racial Laws of 1938,

Conference of Ferrara, November 20, 1988], 41 (Ferrara: Spazio Librio Editore, 1988), 75.

12. Fabio Bertini, "Il fascismo e gli Ebrei: dalla marcia su Roma alle leggi razziali del 1938 e alla deportazione" [Fascism and the Jews: From the March on Rome to the Racial Laws of 1938 and Deportations] in *Figure della memoria* [Figures in Memory], 27–42 (Pisa: Regione Toscana Giunta Regionale, Pisa University Press, 2004); Vera Jarach and Eleonora W. Smolensky, *Colectividad judia italiana a la Argentina (1937–1943)* [The Italian Jewish Community in Argentina (1937–1943)] (Buenos Aires: Centro Editor de America Latina S.A., 1993), 9. The number of Jewish immigrants is found in Haim Auni, *Argentina and the Jews: A History of Jewish Immigration* (Tuscaloosa, AL: University of Alabama Press, 1991), 170; Fabio Della Seta, *The Tiber Afire* (Marlboro, VT: The Marlboro Press, 1991).

13. Angelo Ara, "Gli Ebrei di Trieste, 1850–1918" [The Jews of Trieste, 1850–1918], *Rivista Storica Italiana* 102, no. 1 (1990): 53–86, urban contribution, 83; racial laws, 82.

14. Luigi Villari, *Italian Foreign Policy under Mussolini* (New York: Devin-Adair Company, 1956), 202. The Via Rasella incident in Rome in 1944 involved the bombing of a German police unit. The reprisal led to the Ardeatine Caves massacre of 335 Italians, many of whom were Jewish. For Villari's account see his *The Liberation of Italy 1943–1947* (Appleton, WI: C. G. Nelson Publishing Company, 1959), 111–114. There are few English-language postwar defenses of Mussolini and Fascism. Villari's well-written and highly selective books, by someone who knew the United States, could seem convincing to casual readers. Gene Bernardini, "The Origins and Development of Racial Anti-Semitism in Fascist Italy," *Journal of Modern History* 49, no. 3, 432; Michael A. Ledeen, "The Evolution of Italian Fascist Antisemitism," in *The Final Solution outside Germany*, Vol. 1, ed. Michael Marrus, 240–254 (Westport, CT: Meckler, 1989). For "Blood-Honor," see www.portal-ns.com//thecensure. *Annuario statistico italiano* [Italian Statistical Abstract] (Rome, 1951). Quoted by Guido Bedarida, *Ebrei d'Italia* (Livorno: Società Editrice Terrena, 1950), 294. There was a discrepancy between the 58,412 persons of "razza ebraica" reported by the 1938 census and the 51,893 quoted by Bedarida from other official Italian statistics. John M. Lord, *Civilian Casualties in Western Europe and Italy in World War II: France, Germany, Belgium, the Netherlands, and Italy* (Washington, DC: Special Operations Office, The American University, 1966), 5; Nicholas Kristof, review of *Mao: The Unknown Story*, *The New York Times*, October 23, 2005, p. 1; Susan Zuccotti, *The Italians and the Holocaust: Persecution, Rescue, Survival* (New York. Basic Books, 1987), 201–228; L. Poliakov, "Mussolini and the Extermination of the Jews," *Jewish Social Studies* 12 (1948): 250.

Chapter 2

1. Leon Trotsky, *The Revolution Betrayed* (New York: Pathfinder Press, 1972), 222; Ivo Herzer, ed., *The Italian Refuge: Rescue of Jews during the Holocaust* (Washington, DC: The Catholic University of America Press, 1989), 3; and MacGregor Knox, *Hitler's Italian Allies, Royal Armed Forces, Fascist Regime, and the War of 1940–1943* (Cambridge: Cambridge University Press, 2000), 174–175. Knox is exceptionally knowledgeable about the Italian military of World War II. Richard Lamb, *War in Italy 1943–1945: A Brutal Story* (New York: St. Martin's Press, 1994); Padre Romualdo Formato, *L'Eccidio di Cephalonia* [The Massacre at Cephalonia] (Milano: Mursia e C. 1968); Ministero della Difesa, *Le operazioni della unita italiane nel Settembre-Ottobre 1943* [The Operations of Italian Units in September–October 1943] (Rome: Ufficio Storico, Stato Maggiore dell'Esercito, 1975).

2. Menachem Shelah, *Un debito di gratitudine: Storia dei rapporti tra l'esercito italiano e gli Ebrei in Dalmazia (1941–1943)* [A Debt of Gratitude: History of the Relations of the Italian Army and the Jews in Dalmatia 1941–1943] (Rome: Ufficio Storico, Stato Maggiore dell'Esercito, 1991); Jonathan Steinberg, *All or Nothing: The Axis and the*

Holocaust, 1941–1943 (New York: Routledge, 2002); Reitlinger, Liliana Picciotto Fargion, *Il libro della memoria, gli Ebrei deportati dall'Italia (1943–1945)* [The Book of Memory: The Jews Deported from Italy (1943–1945)] (Milano: Mursia, 1991); and Susan Zuccotti, *The Italians and the Holocaust: Persecution, Rescue, and Survival* (New York: Basic Books, 1987). She was harshly criticized for poor methodology and historical judgment by Deborah Dwork in *Journal of Modern History* 62, no. 2 (June 1990): 409–411. Meir Michaelis, "The 'Duce' and the Jews: An Assessment of the Literature on Italian Jewry under Fascism (1922–1945)," in *The "Final Solution" Outside Germany: The Nazi Holocaust,* Vol. 4, ed. Michael Marrus, 191–216 (Westport, CT: Meckler Corporation, 1989); Meir Michaelis, "The Holocaust in Italy: Areas of Inquiry," in *The Holocaust and History: The Known, the Unknown, the Disputed, and the Reexamined,* ed. Michael Berenbaum and Abraham J. Peck, 439–462 (Bloomington: Indiana University Press, 1998); Meir Michaelis, "Italy," in *The World Reacts to the Holocaust,* eds. David S. Wyman and Charles H. Resenzweig, 514–553 (Baltimore, MD: The Johns Hopkins University Press, 1996); Gerald Reitlinger, *The Final Solution: The Attempt to Exterminate the Jews of Europe 1939–1945* (New York: A. S. Barnes & Company, 1961), 357.

3. Archivio, Ufficio Storico, Stato Maggiore dell'Esercito (AUSSME) Rep. H-2, Rac. 2. Pro memoria per S.E. Sabastini. Rome, 5 Luglio 1938. XVI. "Allievi Israeliti nelle scuole e academic militare" [Jewish Students in Military Schools and Academies] Promemoria per S.E. Il Capo del Governo" [Memo for His Excellency The Head of Government] Rome, 28 Giugno 1938 XVI. Also Rep. H-1, Rac. 1. Separation of Jewish Soldiers, Rep. H-1, Rac. 2, Cart. 1, Ministry of War, Memo 21413, December 10, 1938. Documents in the Italian military archive in Rome are referenced as follows: AUSSME (Archivio, Uflicio Storico, Stato Maggiore dell'Esercito); Repertorio (alphanumeric code), Fondo (subject), Raccolta (folders-boxes), Carteggio (file). For example, AUSSME, Rep. H-2, Fondo, Rac. 2, Cart. 6. The subject repertorio H-2 is Partisans, 1943–1945, and it includes eight raccolta in each of which are several files containing documents.

4. E. Rubin, *140 Jewish Marshals, Admirals and Generals* (London: De Vero Books, 1952), 157, list, 12–13; Giancarlo Sacerdote, *Ricordi di un Ebreo bolognese, illusioni e delusioni 1929–1945* [Memories of a Jew of Bologna: Illusions and Delusions 1929–1945] (Rome: Bonacci Editore, 1983), 75; Sergio Della Pergola, quoted in *Conseguenze culturali delle legge razziali in Italia* [Cultural Consequences of the Racial Laws in Italy] (Rome: Academia Nazionale dei Lincei, 1989), 63; Luciano Tas, *Storia degli Ebrei italiani* [History of the Italian Jews] (Rome: Newton Compton Editori, 1987); AUSSME, Rep. H-1, Rac., Letter of Giancarlo Lombroso Finzi to Ministero di Guerra, 23 Agosto 1943. The reply regretted that it was not possible because, "le legge razziale tuttore in vigore" ["the racial laws were still in force"]. Nicolo Caracciolo, *Gli Ebrei e l'Italia durante la guerra 1940–1945* [The Jews and Italy during the War, 1940–1945] (Rome: Bonacci, 1986), 188.

5. Mario Toscano also said that the Badoglio government's delay in rescinding the laws was due to the German presence during the forty-five days between Mussolini's fall and the Armistice. Mario Toscano, ed., *L'Abrogazione delle leggi razziali in Italia (1943–1987): Reintegrazione dei diritti dei cittadini e ritorno ai valori del Risorgimento* [The Abrogation of the Racial Laws in Italy (1943–1987): Reintegration of the Rights of Citizens and Return to the Values of the Risorgimento] (Rome: Collana del Servizio Studi delSenato Della Repubblica, 1988), 33.

6. Guido Fubini, "Dalla legislazione antiebreica al'legislazione riparatoria: Orientamenti giuisprudenziali nell'Italia post fascista" [From the Anti-Jewish Legislation to the Reparation Legislation: Jurisprudence in Post Fascist Italy], *La rassegna mensile di Israel: Le leggi contro gli Ebrei* [The Monthly Israel Review. The Laws against the Jews] 54, no. 1–2 (January 1988): 477–93; Fabio Levi, "L'Applicazione delle leggi contro Ebrei (1938–1946)" [The Application of the Laws against Jews (1938–1946)], *Studi Storici* 36, no. 3 (Luglio-Settembre 1995): 845–62. A good summary of the process and its

results as well as a comparison to similar German laws. Meir Michaelis, *Mussolini and the Jews: German-Italian Relations and the Jewish Question in Italy 1922-1945* (Oxford: The Clarendon Press, 1978), 305.

7. Guido Bedarida, *Ebrei d'Italia* [The Jews of Italy] (Livorno: Società Editrice Terranea, 1950), 35; Susan Zuccotti, *The Italians and the Holocaust: Persecution, Rescue, and Survival* (New York: Basic Books, 1987). Dan Vittorio Segre, *Memoirs of a Fortunate Jew: An Italian Story* (Northvale, NJ: Jason Aronson, 1995), 77-78; Menachem Shelah, *Un debito di gratitudine* [A Debt of Gratitude], 9; Carlo Falconi, *The Silence of Pius XII* (Boston: Little, Brown and Company, 1965): 219-220; Roatta, 319, re: Filipovic, see Stella Alexander, "Croatia: The Catholic Church and Clergy, 1919-1945," in *Catholics, the State, and the European Radical Right*, eds. Richard J. Wolf and Jorg K. Hoesch, 31-66, 54 (Highland Lakes, NJ: Atlantic Research and Publications, 1987).

8. Nicola Caracciolo, *Gli Ebrei e l'Italia durante la guerra 1940-1945* [The Jews and Italy During the War 1940-1945] (Rome: Bonacci Editore, 1986), 113-123. The episode involving the Weisers is mentioned by Renzo De Felice although he did not have their names. I happened to come across their story and names in the archives of the Italian Army's Ufficio Storico. See Nicola Caracciolo, *Gli Ebrei e l'Italia durante la guerra 1940-45*, 11.

9. Branko Bokun, *Spy in the Vatican 1941-45* (New York: Praeger Publishers, 1973), 137.

10. Donatello De Luigi, *Il processso Roatta, i documenti* [Documents of the Trial of Roatta] (Rome: Universale De Luigi, 1945), 68.

11. Attilio Ascarelli, *Le Fosse ardeatine* [The Ardeatine Caves] (Rome: Fratelli Palombi Editore, 1945), Table 17. "Dio mio grande Padre, noi ti preghiamo affinche tu possa proteggere gli ebrei dalle barbare persecuzioni. Un paternoster, dieci avemarie, un gloria Patri." ["Great God we pray that You will protect the Jews from brutal persecution. An Our Father, ten Hail Marys and a Gloria."] Ascarelli noted that of the identified victims, 247 were Catholics, 2 were of an unknown religion and 73 were Jews, 52. Later information placed the number of Jews at 77.

12. Raul Hilberg, *The Destruction of the European Jews: Revised and Definitive Edition*, vol. 2 (New York: Olmes and Meier, 1985), 715; Heinz Hohne, *The Order of the Death's Head* (New York: Coward McCann, 1969), 345-397. Hohne was quoted by Renzo De Felice re: Todt, the German labor organization, 460. Gerald Reitlinger, *The Final Solution: The Attempt to Exterminate the Jews of Europe 1939-1945*, discussed the situation of the Jews in Italian occupied France, 321-326; in Italy, 352-357; in Yugoslavia, 358-370; and in Greece, 375-376. He noted that the refusal to deport the Jews in the Italian zone in Yugoslavia came from General Roatta, 367. Menachem Shelah, *Un debito di gratitudine*, 160. For more on rescue efforts in Italy, see Martin Gilbert, *The Righteous: The Unsung Heroes of the Holocaust* (New York: Henry Holt And Company, 2003), 356-380. A 1950 study revealed something about the attitudes of Italian university students toward "razzismo." The research replicated *The Authoritarian Personality*, a study of anti-Semitism in the United States. These Italian students had their elementary and secondary education under Fascism where they were exposed to anti-Jewish propaganda. Although on certain stereotypical statements about Jews these Italians scored higher than those in the original study, they rejected overt discriminatory measures against the Jews, as well as the stereotypes of the Jews as communistic and unpatriotic. Charles T. O'Reilly, *Race Prejudice among Catholic College Students in the United States and Italy* (Notre Dame, IN: University of Notre Dame, PhD diss., 1954); Theodor W. Adorno, Else Frenkel-Brunswik, Daniel J. Levinson and R. Nevitt Sanford, *The Authoritarian Personality* (New York: Harper and Brothers, 1950); Susan Zuccotti, *The Holocaust, the French, the Jews* (New York: Basic Books, 1993), 180-189.

13. John Bierman, "How Italy Protected the Jews in the Occupied South of France, 1942-1943." in *The Italian Refuge: Rescue of Jews during the Holocaust*, ed. Ivo Herzer, 226 (Washington, DC: Catholic University of America Press, 1989); Leon Poliakov and Jacques Sabille, *Jews under Italian*

Occupation (New York: Howard Fertig, 1983); Meir Michaelis, *Mussolini and the Jews*, 309. Luciano Tas, *Storia degli Ebrei italiani* [The History of Italian Jews] (Rome, Newton Compton Editore, 1984), 150.

14. Giuseppe Mayda, *Ebrei sotto Salo: La persecuzione antisemita 1943–1945* [Jews under Salo: The Anti-Semitic Persecution 1943–1945] (Milano: Feltrinelli Editore, 1978), 55; Nora Levin, *The Holocaust: The Destruction of European Jewry 1933–1945* (New York: Thomas Y. Crowell Company, 1968), 449–454; Alberto Cavaglion, *Nella notte straniera: Gli Ebrei di S. Martin Vesubie e il Campo di Borgo S. Dalmazzo 8 Settembre — 21 Novembre 1943* [In the Alien Night: The Jews of San Martin Vesuble and Borgo San Dalmazzo September 8–November 21, 1943] (Cuneo: Edizione L'Arciere, 1981).

15. Pearl L. Preschel, *The Jews of Corfu* (New York: New York University, PhD diss., 1984), 129; Hermann Langbein, *Against All Hope: Resistance in the Nazi Concentration Camps, 1938–1945* (New York: Paragon House, 1994), 190; and Eugene Davidson, *The Trial of the Germans* (New York: Collier Books, 1966), 572.

16. Giuseppe Mayda, *Ebrei sotto Salo* [Jews under Salo], 55; Harriet Pass Freidenreich, *The Jews of Yugoslavia: A Quest for Community* (Philadelphia: The Jewish Publication Society of America, 1979), 192.

17. Dominique Eudes, *The Kapetanios: Partisans and Civil War in Greece, 1943–1949* (New York: Monthly Review Press, 1972), 49; *Actes et documents du Saint-Siège relatifs à la seconde guerre mondiale. La Saint-Siège et la guerre mondiale Novembre 1942-Decembre 1943* [Records and Documents of the Holy See Regarding the Second World War. The Holy See and the World War November 1942–December 1943] (Città del Vaticano: Libreria Editrice Vaticana, 1973), 339–343; Deborah Dwork and Robert Jan van Pelt, *Holocaust: A History* (New York: W.W. Norton & Company, 2002), 120, 123; and Charles F. Delzell, "The Italians and the Holocaust," *Italian Quarterly* 132, no. 123–124 (Winter-Spring 1995): 91.

18. Renzo De Felice, in Caracciolo, *Gli Ebrei e l'Italia durante la guerra 1940–1945* [The Jews and Italy during the War 1940–1945], 11; Cavaglion, *Nella notte straniera* [The Alien Night], 134.

19. Lamb, *War in Italy, 1943–1945*, 4; Cannistraro and Sullivan, *Il Duce's Other Woman*, 30; Eugen Dollman, *Roma Nazista* [Nazi Rome] (Milano: Longnesi, e C. 1949), 342; Ermano Amicucci, *I 600 giorni di Mussolini* [The 600 Days of Mussolini], 4th ed. (Rome: Editrice "Faro," 1948), 192.

20. Salvatore Loi, "Quante Lacune da Colmare!" [How Many Gaps to Fill!], in *L'immagine delle forze armate nella scuola italiana* [The Image of the Armed Forces in the Italian Schools], Ministero della Difesa, 196 (Rome: Archivio, Ufficio Storico, Stato Maggiore dell'Esercito, 1986); Poliakov, op. cit., 258. With regard to textbooks, see Mino Milani, "L'Immagine delle forze armate nell manualistica scolastica: le antologie letterarie," in *L'immagine delle forze armate* [The Image of the Armed Forces], Ministero della Difesa, 77–86. Enrico Deaglio, *The Banalty of Goodness: The Story of Giorgio Perlasca* (Notre Dame, IN: University of Notre Dame Press, 1998), 10.

21. Daniel Jonah Goldhagen, "Ordinary Men or Ordinary Germans?" in *Holocaust and History: The Known, the Unknown, the Disputed, and the Reexamined*, eds. Michael Berenbaum and Abraham J. Peck, 305 (Bloomington: Indiana University Press, 1998). Quoted by Guido Bedarida, *Ebrei d'Italia* [The Jews of Italy] (Livorno: Societa Editrice Terrena, 1950), 294. Regarding harsh treatment, see Frank P. Verna, "Notes on Italian Rule in Dalmatia under Bastiniani, 1941–1943," *International History Review* 12, no. 3 (1990) 528–547.

Chapter 3

1. Cornwell, *Hitler's Pope*; Phayer, *The Catholic Church and the Holocaust;* Georges Passelecq and Bernard Suchecky, *The Hidden Encyclical of Pius XI* (New York: Harcourt Brace & Company, 1997); Michael O'Carroll, *Pius XII: Greatness Dishonored* (Chicago, IL: Franciscan Herald Press, 1980); William Doino, Jr., "An Annotated

Notes — Chapter 3

Bibliography of Works on Pius XII, the Second World War, and the Holocaust," in *The Pius Wars: Responses to the Critics of Pius XII*, eds. Joseph Bottum and David G. Dalin, 97–280 (Lanham, MD: Lexington Books, 2004); Rolf Hochhuth, *The Deputy* (Baltimore: The Johns Hopkins Press. 1997), 287; Eric Foner, ed., *The New American History* (Philadelphia, PA: Temple University Press. 1990), vii; Stanley Fish quoted by Michiko Kakutani in *The New York Times*, Jan 17, 2006, B-8; Barton J. Bernstein, ed., *Toward a New Past: Dissenting Essays in American History* (New York: Pantheon Books, 1968); John W. Dower, "Triumphal and Tragic Narratives of the War in Asia," *Journal of American History* 82, no. 3 (1997): 1124; Jack E. Davis, "New Left, Revisionist, In-Your Face History," in *Oliver Stone's USA, Film History, and Controversy*, ed. Robert Brent Tomlin, 36 (Lawrence: University Press of Kansas, 2000); Sidney Lens, *The Maginot Line Syndrome: America's Hopeless Foreign Policy* (Cambridge, MA: Ballinger Publishing Company, 1982), 135; re: Farrell, see Alan M. Wald, *The New York Intellectuals: The Rise and Decline of the Anti-Stalinist Left from the 1930s to the 1980s* (Chapel Hill: The University of North Carolina Press, 1987), 256; John J. McCloy, "From Military Government to Self-Government," in *Americans as Proconsuls, United States Military Government in Germany and Japan, 1944–1952*, ed. Robert Wolfe, 122 (Carbondale: Southern Illinois University Press, 1984). See Philip Green and Sanford Levinson, eds., *Power and Community: Dissenting Essays in Political Science* (New York: Pantheon Books, 1969). viii, ix. The "Pius Wars" is a niche subject in academic history although it receives major attention from the media. *The American Historical Review (AHR)* is a leading historical journal. The interest of historians in the Pius Wars can be gauged for the number of articles about the topic in the AHR. In 2003 it carried an average of five major articles in each of its four issues, none of which touched on aspects of the Pius Wars. Each of the journal's quarterly issues reviewed an average of 162 books and of the 649 books reviewed that year, only one was directly related in some way to the wartime papacy, whereas two or three others made peripheral references to the wartime Vatican.

2. John L. Allen, *All the Pope's Men: The Inside Story of How the Vatican Really Thinks* (New York: Doubleday, 2004), 7; Martin Gleeson, *The Story of the Force-Landing of "Traveling Trollop" at Lahinch, Co. Clare, 10 July 1943* (Cork: Warplane Research Group of Ireland, 1993), 8; Anthony Cave Brown, *The Last Hero: Wild Bill Donovan* (New York: Times Books, 1982), 684–685; Martin S. Quigley, *Peace without Hiroshima: Secret Action at the Vatican in the Spring of 1945* (Lanham, MD: Madison Books, 1991). The dates of Harada's messages to Tokyo are in a letter Quigley sent to Robert Graham, June 20, 1985. Graham's papers are in the library of *Civiltà Cattolica* in Rome. Quigley's papers are at Georgetown University. P. Blet, A. Martini, R.A. Graham, and B. Schneider, eds., *Actes et documents du Saint-Siège relatifs à la seconde guerre mondiale* [Records and Documents Regarding the Second World War], 11 vols. in 12 parts (two parts for vol. 3) (Città del Vaticano: Libreria Editrice Vaticana, 1963–81). Giorgio Gariboldi has a lengthy account of the Vassalli episode. See Giorgio Angelozzi Gariboldi, *Pio XII, Hitler e Mussolini: Il Vaticano fra le dittature* [Pius XII, Hitler and Mussolini: The Vatican between the Dictators] (Milano: Mursia, 1995), 248–250. Re: Darlan: A. E. Campbell, "Franklin Roosevelt and Unconditional Surrender," in *Diplomacy and Intelligence during the Second World War: Essays in Honour of F. H. Hinsley*, ed. Richard Langhorne, 226 (Cambridge, Cambridge University Press, 1985). Robert Graham reported the peace efforts late in the war, referring to VESSEL and regretting that the Allies failed to use the Vatican as a conduit to Japan. He surmised that to do so would be politically impossible for Washington. See Robert Graham, S.J., "Contatti di pace fra Americani e Giaponesi in Vaticano nel 1945" [Peace Contacts Between the Americans and Japanese in the Vatican in 1945], *Civiltà Cattolica* (April 1971), II. 31–42. For Operation SUNRISE, Kolko, Smith, Bradley and Elena Aga-Rossi quoted in O'Reilly, *Forgotten Battles*, 288–290. Re: Darlan, see Michael Beschloss, *The Conquerors: Roosevelt, Tru-*

man and the Destruction of Hitler's Germany, 1941–1945 (New York: Simon & Schuster, 2002), 101; Lisle A. Rose, *The Long Shadow: Reflections on the Second World War Era* (Westport, CT: Greenwood Press, 1978), 90; Dante A. Puzzo, *The Partisans and the War in Italy* (New York: Peter Lang, 1992), 63.

3. Lukacs, John. *June 1941: Hitler and Stalin* (New Haven: Yale University Press, 2006), 112; Cornwell, *Hitler's Pope*, 7; Michael Phayer, *The Catholic Church and the Holocaust, 1930–1965* (Bloomington: Indiana University Press, 2000); David I. Kertzer, *Prisoner of the Vatican: The Pope's Secret Plot to Capture Rome from the New Italian State* (Boston: Houghton Mifflin Company, 2004), 292; Giovanni Miccoli, *I dilemmi e i silenci di Pio XII (The Dilemmas and the Silences of Pius XII)* (Milan, Rizzoli, 2000); Anthony Read, *The Devil's Disciples: Hitler's Inner Circle* (New York: W.W. Norton & Company, 2003), 323; Anthony Rhodes, *The Vatican and the Dictators (1922–1945)* (New York: Holt, Rinehart and Winston, 1973), 183.

4. Georges Passelecq and Bernard Suchecky, *The Hidden Encyclical of Pius XI* (New York: Harcourt Brace & Company, 1997); Robert Leiber, S.J., "Pio XII e gli Ebrei di Roma 1943–1944" [Pius XII and the Roman Jews 1943–1944], *Civiltà Cattolica* 1 (25 febraio 1961): 458; Andrea Tornielli, *Pio XII: Il Papa degli Ebrei* [Pius XII: The Pope of the Jews] (Casale Monferrato: Edizione Piemme, 2001), 146–152; re: Manifesto, *L'Osservatore Romano*, Rome, July 17, 1938, p. 1; re: *Non abbiamo bisogno*, Anne Freemantle, ed., *The Papal Encyclicals in Their Historical Context* (New York: G.P. Putnam's Sons, 1956), 249; David I. Kertzer, *The Popes against the Jews: The Vatican's Role in the Rise of Modern Anti-Semitism* (New York: Alfred A. Knopf, 2001), 282; Saul Friedlander, *Nazi Germany and the Jews*, vol. 1, *The Years of Persecution, 1933–1939* (New York: Harper Collins, 1997), 251; Gitta Sereny, *Into That Darkness: From Mercy Killing to Mass Murder* (New York: McGraw-Hill Book Company, 1974), 294; Daniel Jonah Goldhagen, *A Moral Reckoning: The Role of the Catholic Church in the Holocaust and Its Unfulfilled Duty of Repair* (New York: Alfred A. Knopf, 2002), 40–43.

5. I.S.O. Playfair and C.I.C. Molony, *The Mediterranean and Middle East*, vol. IV, *The Destruction of the Axis Forces in Africa* (London: His Majesty's Stationery Office, 1966), xvi. The encyclicals of Pius XI that are most relevant to this time period are *Non abbiamo bisogno* (June 29, 1931), which dealt with Fascism and Catholic Action; *Mit Brennender Sorge* (March 14, 1937), which dealt with Nazism; and *Divini Redemptoris* (March 19, 1937), which dealt with atheistic communism. Those of Pius XII are *Summi Pontificatus* (October 20, 1939) dealing with the role of the state in the modern world, thus with Nazism, Fascism and Communism, and *Mystici Corporis* (June 29, 1943) on the "Mystical Body," which emphasized the unity of humanity.

6. Peter Godman, *Hitler and the Vatican: Inside the Secret Archives that Reveal the New Story of the Nazis and the Church* (New York: Free Press, 2004). "Notorious silence," 162. A bit of evidence that supports Leiber's account is the draft of the title page for the encyclical that shows editing by the then Cardinal Pacelli. See Andrea Tornielli, *Pio XII: Il Papa degli Ebrei* [Pius XII: The Pope of the Jews] (Edizione Piemme, 2000), 379; Anthony Rhodes, *The Vatican in the Age of the Dictators (1922–1945)* (New York: Holt, Rinehart and Winston, 1973); Giorgio Cosmacini, *Gemelli: Il Machiavelli di Dio* [Gemelli: God's Machiavellian] (Milano: Rizzoli, 1985), 245; Caracciolo, *Gli Ebrei e l'Italia durante la guerra 1940–45* [The Jews and Italy during the War 1940–1945], 203–205.

7. Alexander Ramati, *The Assisi Underground: The Priest Who Rescued Jews* (New York: Stein and Day, 1978). For the hazardous and dramatic story of what happened in Genoa, see Stille, *Benevolence and Betrayal*, 223–278. Odaliso Galli in a personal communication to the author. Robert A. Graham, S. J., "Pfeiffer's List," *Soggiorno* (June 1994): 70–73. Robert A. Graham, "La Santa Sede e la difesa degli Ebrei durante la seconda guerra mondiale" [The Vatican and the Defense of the Jews during the Second World War], *La Civiltà Cattolica* 141, no. 3 (1990): 208–206; Robert A. Graham, S.J.

"Il 'Protocolo di Auschwitz' e il Vaticano nel 1944" [The Auschwitz Protocol and the Vatican in 1944], *La Civiltà Cattolica* 147, no. 4 (1996): 330–337; Re: "Vatican operative:" Phayer, *The Catholic Church and the Holocaust, 1930–1965*, 166. A word should be said about casting unsupported suspicion of the work of another scholar. Several authors have questioned the credibility of members of the scholarly team that produced the *Actes* as well as those who have "defended" the Vatican and Pius XII. That the latter group came to different conclusions about contested events was enough to have their credibility questioned, which means questioning their scholarly integrity. One of those questioned both as a member of the *Actes* team and as an individual writing for the "defense" of Pius was the late Robert Graham. There is no evidence that Robert Graham, to whom I often refer, ever fudged, doctored data or otherwise engaged in scholarly malfeasance. While working on another project after his death, I had the opportunity to view some of his work papers in Italy and compare them with other secondary and primary sources. I found no discrepancies that would alert any scholar to his trifling with evidence. Admittedly, I did not do this systematically or because of any suspicion of malfeasance, and this is only anecdotal evidence of his scholarly integrity. The comparisons I made happened before I was aware of the claims of his critics who offer only opinions based on no evidence, anecdotal or otherwise. It is unfortunate and of questionable professionalism when the reputation of any scholar is unfairly tainted by unsupported accusations of violating the canons of historical scholarship. John Cornwell, *Hitler's Pope: The Secret History of Pius XII* (New York: Viking, 1999), has all the paraphernalia of scholarship although it hardly is a "secret history" because most of its revelations have been known for years. United States Holocaust Museum, *Fifty Years Ago: Revolt amid the Darkness* (Washington, DC: United States Government Printing Office, 1993), 90–91. Robert A. Graham, S.J., "Il Vaticano e gli Ebrei profughi in Italia durante la guerra" [The Vatican and Jewish Refugees during the War], *La Civiltà Cattolica* 138, no. 1 (1987): 417–428.

8. Silvio Bertoldi, *I Tedeschi in Italia* [The Germans in Italy] (Milano: Rizzoli, 1964); George O. Kent, "Pope Pius XII and Germany: Some Aspects of German-Vatican Relations, 1933–1943," *American Historical Review* 70, no. 1 (1964): 59–78; Eugenio Dollman, *Roma Nazista* [Nazi Rome] (Milano: Loganesi, E. C. 1949). See also Eugen Dollman, *The Interpreter: Memoirs of Doktor Eugen Dollman* (London: Hutchinson and Company, 1967); Lamb, *War in Italy*, 46–48. Re: Verolini, see Richard Sale, S.J., "La Santa Sede e lo stermino degli Ebrei ungheresi" [The Holy See and the Extermination of the Hungarian Jews], *Civiltà Cattolica* 15 (January 2005): I, 114–127. Per Anger, *With Raoul Wallenberg in Budapest: Memories of the War Years in Hungary* (New York: Holocaust Library, 1981), 145, 152.

9. Eugen Dollman, quoted in O'Reilly, *Forgotten Battles*, 196. Giorgio Angelozzi, *Pio XII, Hitler e Mussolini: Il Vaticano fra le Dittature* [Pius XII, Hitler and Mussolini: The Vatican between the Dictators] (Milano: Mursia, 1995), chapter 8, "Minacce a Pio XII: Le Deportazione" [Threats to Pius XII: The Deportation]; Lamb, *War in Italy 1943–1945: A Brutal Story*, 48.

10. Robert A. Graham, "Bernardo Attolico e la 'Guerra antibolscevica'" [Bernardo Attolico and the "Anti-Bolshevik War"], *La Civiltà Cattolica* 143, III (1992): 262–271. Michael Phayer, "The Priority of Diplomacy: Pius XII and the Holocaust during the Second World War," in *Christian Responses to the Holocaust, Moral and Ethical Issues*, ed. Donald J. Deitrich, 93 (Syracuse, NY: Syracuse University Press, 2003).

11. Angelo Martini, "Due nuovi volumi dei documenti della Santa Sede relative alla seconda guerra mondiale" [Two New Volumes of the Documents of the Holy See Regarding the Second World War], *La Civiltà Cattolica* 124, II (7 Aprile 1973): 44–45. Re: Vatican note, Giovanni Sale, S.J., "Roma 1943: Occupazione nazista e deportazione degli Ebrei romani" [Rome 1943: Nazi Occupation and the Deportation of Roman Jews], *La Civiltà Cattolica* IV (decembre 2003): 424; Robert Dallek, *Franklin D. Roosevelt and American Foreign*

Notes — Chapter 3

Policy, 1932–1945 (New York: Oxford University Press, 1995), 123; Giovanni Miccoli, "Sante Sede e il Terzo Reich: A proposito di uno libro recente" [The Holy See and the Third Reich: With Regard to a Recent Book], *Studi Storici* 45, no. 2 (Aprile-Giugno 2004): 498.

12. John H. Waller, *The Unseen War in Europe: Espionage and Conspiracy in the Second World War* (New York: Random House, 1996), 374–377.

13. Giovanni Sale, "Roma 1943: Occupazione nazista e deportazione degli Ebrei romani" [Rome 1943: Nazi Occupation and Deportation of Roman Jews], 420. Elena Agarossi's *A Nation Collapses: The Italian Surrender of September 1943* (Cambridge: Cambridge University Press, 2000), has a succinct and excellent account of the critical situation in Italy in 1943. The Vatican was keenly aware of the delicacy of its situation in Rome. "The Italian government could switch off its electric light, its water supply or even its food. If the Vatican broke its side of the treaty by interfering in Italian politics, Italy had an easy and instant answer." Chadwick, *Britain and the Vatican during the Second World War*, 131–132; Robert Katz, *The Fall of the House of Savoy* (New York: The Macmillan Company, 1971), 371; Dante A. Puzzo, *The Partisans and the War in Italy* (New York: Peter Lang, 1992), 41, 89. See also Massimo Legnani, "L'Italia partigiana" [Partisan Italy], *Studi Storici* 8, no. 3 (1967): 612–620; Roberto Battaglia, *La seconda guerra mondiale: Problemi e nodi cruciale* [The Second World War: Critical Knotty Problems] (Rome: Edizioni Riuniti, 1960), 258; Luigi Longo, *Chi ha tradito la resistenza* [Who Betrayed the Resistance] (Rome: Editore Riuniti, 1975), 16; Guido Quazza, "The Politics of the Italian Resistance," in *The Rebirth of Italy, 1943–1950*, ed. S.J. Woolf, 18 (London: Longman, 1972); Spencer M. Discala, "Resistance Mythology," *Journal of Modern Italian Studies*, 4, no 1 (Spring 1999): 67–72.

14. Jose M. Sanchez, "The Popes and Nazi Germany: The View From Madrid," *Journal of Church and State* 38, no. 2 (March 1996): 365–376; John F. Morley, *Vatican Diplomacy and the Jews during the Holocaust, 1939–1943* (New York: Ktav Publishing House, 1980): 208–209; John T. Pawlikowski, "The Catholic Response to the Holocaust," in *The Holocaust and History: The Known, the Unknown, the Disputed, and the Reexamined*, ed. Michael Berenbaum and Abraham J. Pick, 561 (Bloomington: Indiana University Press, 1998): Giovanni Macalli, "Santa Sede e chiesa italiana di fronte alle leggi antiebraiche del 1938" [The Holy See and Church Confront the Anti-Semitic Laws of 1938], *Studi Storici* 29, no. 4 (1988): 821–902; F. Cavalli, S.J., "La relazione diplomatiche fra la S. Sede e Giappone (1922–1942)" [Diplomatic Relations between the Holy See and Japan 1922–1942], *Civiltà Cattolica* 100, no. 2 (1949): 393–408; *Foreign Relations of the United States, Diplomatic Papers* (Washington DC: U.S. Government Printing Office, 1966), 961–962. For the evolution of the strategy of the PCI, from supporting the position that we are allies from 1944 to the policy of anti-imperialism as the Cold War developed, see Dilvio Pons, "Unione Sovietica nella politicas estera di Togliatti (1944–1949)" [The Soviet Union in the Foreign Policy of Togliatti 1944–1949], *Studi Storici* 33, no. 2/3 (Aprile-Settembre 1992): 435–456.

15. Pawlikowski, "The Catholic Response to the Holocaust," 363; Nora Levin, *The Holocaust: The Destruction of European Jewry, 1933–1945* (New York: Thomas Y. Crowell Company, 1968), 691; Monty Noam Penkower, *The Jews Were Expendable: Free World Diplomacy and the Holocaust* (Urbana: University of Illinois Press, 1983), 215. Later, Penkower said, "The holder of the Keys of St. Peter, who had moved so cautiously to save the Jews, tried to distinguish between a minority of war criminals and a docile, deluded majority of the German nation (at least 50 percent Catholic) reported Great Britain's delegate to the Holy See," 300. Roberto Sani, "Un laboratorio politico e culturale: *La Civiltà Cattolica*" [*La Civiltà Cattolica*: A Political and Cultural Laboratory], in Riccardi, *Pio XII*, 409–436; Eric Sterling, "Indifferent Accomplices," in *Problems Unique to the Holocaust*, Henry James Cargas, 118 (Lexington: The University Press of Kentucky, 1999).

16. Pawlikowski, op. cit., 559; Jozef Tischner, *Marxism and Christianity: The Quarrel and the Dialogue in Poland* (Washington,

DC: Georgetown University Press, 1981), xvii, 164.

17. Ray Moseley, *Mussolini: The Last 600 Days of Il Duce* (Lanham, MD: First Taylor Trade Publishing, 2004), 104. The opinions of Katz and Moseley are contradicted by many who have studied the sequence of events that led to an overnight move of victims to the Caves. The newspaper article Moseley cited had no bearing on the Vatican's knowledge of what was to happen that day, and as a veteran reporter, Moseley knew better than to suggest that it was connected to the Pope's supposed prior knowledge of the massacre. Morley, *Vatican Diplomacy and the Jews during the Holocaust, 1939–1943*, 208–209. Graham also noted Morley's mistaken statement that the Vatican only interceded for baptized Jews. Robert A. Graham, *La Civiltà Cattolica* 132, no. 1-3 (Gennaio 1981): 98–99; Sir Llewellyn Woodward, *British Foreign Policy in the Second World War*, vol II (London: Her Majesty's Stationery Office, 1971), 189; Giovanni Macalli, "Santa Sede e chiesa italiana di fronte alle leggi antiebraiche del 1938" [The Holy See and the Vatican Confront the Anti-Semitic Laws of 1938], *Studi Storici* 29, no. 4 (1988): 821–902; John T. Pawlikowski, O.S.M., "The Catholic Response to the Holocaust," in *The Holocaust and History: The Known, the Unknown, the Disputed, and the Reexamined*, eds. Michael Berenbaum and Abraham J. Pick, 563, 559 (Bloomington: Indiana University Press, 1998); Raul Hilberg, *Perpetrators Victims Bystanders: The Jewish Catastrophe 1933–1945* (New York: Harper Collins Publishers, 1992), 265. Another useful and more balanced discussion of Vatican policy is found in Peter C. Kent, "A Tale of Two Popes: Pius XI, Pius XII, and the Rome–Berlin Axis," *Journal of Contemporary History* 23, no. 4 (1988): 589–608. For an interesting review of many of the recent books in this niche area, see Joe Bottum, "The End of the Pius Wars," *First Things*, April 2004, 18–25.

18. Cornwell, *Hitler's Pope*, re: Graham and "claim." James Carroll, *Constantine's Sword, The Church and the Jews: A History* (Boston: Houghton Mifflin Company, 2001), 45.

19. Sanchez, op. cit., 208–209. Domenico Tardini, *Memories of Pius XII* (Westminster, MD: The Newman Press, 1961), executives, 83; Erik H. Erikson, *Dimensions of a New Identity*, The 1973 Jefferson Lectures in The Humanities (New York: W. W. Norton & Company, 1974), 12; Kevin Madigan, review of *Hitler's Pope: The Secret History of Pius XII*, by John Cornwell. H-Holocaust, H-Net Reviews, April 2000.

20. Anthony Read, *The Devil's Disciples: Hitler's Inner Circle* (New York, W. W. Norton & Company, 2003), 814–815; Martin Gilbert, *The Holocaust: A History of the Jews of Europe during the Second World War* (New York: Holt, Rinehart & Winston, 1985), 622–623; Deborah Dwork and Robert Jan van Pelt, *Holocaust: A History* (New York: W.W. Norton & Company, 2002), 333, 423; Sam Waagenaar, *The Pope's Jews* (La Salle, IL: Open Court Press, 1974), 367, 414, 416, 423, 426; Susan Zuccotti, "Pope Pius XII and the Holocaust in Italy," in *The Italian Refuge: Rescue of Jews During the Holocaust*, ed. Ivo Herzer, 256 (Washington, DC: Catholic University of America Press, 1989); R. Leiber, S.J., "Pio XII e Gli Ebrei di Roma, 1943–1944," *La Civiltà Cattolica* 1 (1961): 449–458; regarding Tagliacozzo: Lamb, *War in Italy 1943–1945*, 41; Charles F. Delzell, "Pius XII, Italy, and the Outbreak of War," *Journal of Contemporary History* 2, no 4 (October 1967): 160. Taking into consideration when he wrote, his references to this opinion were to Robert Katz, Saul Friedlander and Rolf Hochhuth. Fabio Della Seta, "The Jew Rediscovered," in *The Italian Jewish Experience*, ed. Thomas P. DeNapoli, 30 (Stony Brook, NY: Forum Italicum Publishing, 2000); Stanislao G. Pugliese, " Reflections on the Priebke Affair on Massacres, Trials, History and Memory," in DeNapoli, *The Italian Jewish Experience*, 117; Uki Goni, *The Real ODESSA* (London: Granata Books, 2002), 255.

21. Re: Vatican note, Giovanni Sale, S.J., "Roma 1943: Occupazione Nazista e deportazione degli Ebrei Romani" [Rome 1943: Nazi Occupation and Deportation of Roman Jews], *La Civiltà Cattolica* IV (decembre 2003): 424; Susan Zuccotti, "*L'Osservatore Romano* and the Holocaust," *Holocaust and Genocide Studies* 17, no. 2 (2003): 264; Spinosa, *Mussolini razzista riluttante* [Mussolini Reluctant Racist],

7–10; Gariboldi, *Pio XII, Hitler e Mussolini: Il Vaticano fra le Dittature* [Pius XII, Hitler and Mussolini: The Vatican between the Dictators], chapter 9, "Le Fosse ardeatine" [The Ardeatine Caves], 225–255; Re: "Ridiculous Dogmas," see Peter Godman, *Hitler and the Vatican: Inside the Secret Archives that Reveal the New Story of the Nazis and the Church* (New York: Free Press, 2004): 222–223. For definitions of "stirpe," see Fernando Palazzi, *Novissimo dizionario della lingua italiana* [New Dictionary of the Italian Language] (Milano: Casa Editrice Ceschina, 1949), 1172.

22. Robert J. Hanyok, *Eavesdropping on Hell: Historical Guide to Western Communications Intelligence and the Holocaust, 1939–1945*, 2nd ed. (Fort George C. Meade, MD: National Security Agency, Center for Cryptologic History, 2005), 111; Leonidas Hill, "The Vatican Embassy of Ernst Von Weizsacker, 1943–1945," *Journal of Modern History* 39, no. 2 (1967), 150; Jane Scrivener, *Inside Rome with the Germans* (New York: The MacMillan Company, 1945), 31; re: gold, see Della Seta, "The Jew Rediscovered," 30; Zuccotti, *The Italians and the Holocaust*, re: "seems," 126, "almost certainly," 128; Andrea Grover "*L'Osservatore Romano* and the Holocaust, 1933–45," in *Why Didn't the Press Shout? American and International Journalism during the Holocaust*, ed. Robert Moses Shapiro, 360, 361, 363 (Jersey City, NJ: Yeshiva University Press, 2003); Re: foreknowledge, Susan Zuccotti, "Pope Pius XII and the Holocaust: The Case in Italy," in Herzer, *The Italian Refuge*, 258; Berel Lang, "'Not Enough' vs 'Plenty': Which Did Pius XII Do," *Judaism*, September 1, 2001, vol. 50, no. 4; Kevin Madigan, "What The Vatican Knew about the Holocaust, and When," *Commentary* 112, no. 3 (October 1, 2001): 43–52; Leonidas Hill, "The Vatican Embassy of Ernst Von Weizsacker, 1943–1945," *Journal of Modern History* 39, no. 2 (1967): 150; Robert Katz, "The Mollhausen Telegram, the Kappler Decodes, and the Deportation of the Jews of Rome: The New CIA-OSS Documents, 2000–2002," in *Jews in Italy under Fascist and Nazi Rule, 1922–1945*, ed. Joshua D. Zimmerman, 238–239 (Cambridge: Cambridge University Press, 2005).

Chapter 4

1. Richard J. Evans, *Lying About Hitler: History, Holocaust, and the David Irving Trial* (New York: Basic Books, 2001), 102, 238–247; Francesco Prefetti, "Prefazione," in Spinosa, *Mussolini razzista riluttante* [Mussolini, Reluctant Racist], 7–10; Gariboldi, *Pio XII, Hitler e Mussolini: Il Vaticano fra le Dittature* [Pius XII, Hitler and Mussolini: The Vatican Between the Dictators], chapter 9, "Le Fosse ardeatine" [The Ardeatine Caves], 225–255; Meir Michaelis, *Mussolini and the Jews: German-Italian Relations and the Jewish Question in Italy, 1922–1945* (Oxford: The Clarendon Press, 1978), Vatican's actions, 364–378, 424–426; Rolf Hochhuth, *The Deputy* (New York: Grove Press, 1964); Gary Wills, *Papal Sin: Structures of Deceit* (New York: Doubleday, 2000), 66; Eugen Dollman, *Roma nazista* [Nazi Rome] (Milano: Longanesi, e C. 1951). "La responsibilità principale per l'ordine eseguito da Kappler alle Fosse ardeatine ricade indiscuttilmente su Hitler, da lui partirono gli l'ordine di esecuzion" ["The principal responsibility for the order followed by Kappler at the Ardeatine Caves falls unquestionably on Hitler, who gave the execution order"]. 236.

2. Deborah E. Lipstadt, "Moral Bystanders," *Society* March–April, 1983, 26; Robert Katz, *The Battle for Rome: The Germans, the Allies, the Partisan and the Pope, September 1943–June 1944* (New York: Simon & Schuster, 2003), 546; Owen Chadwick, *Britain and the Vatican during the Second World War* (Cambridge: Cambridge University Press, 1986), 211; Lamb, *War in Italy*, 72; Gariboldi, op. cit., 225–255.

3. Zuccotti, *The Italians and the Holocaust*, 133; Michael Phayer, *The Catholic Church and the Holocaust, 1930–1965* (Bloomington: Indiana University Press, 2000), 219; Michael Phayer, "The Priority of Diplomacy: Pius XII and the Holocaust during the Second World War," in *Christian Responses to the Holocaust, Moral and Ethical Issues*, ed. Donald J. Deitrich, 97 (Syracuse, NY: Syracuse University Press, 2003); Jose M. Sanchez, "The Popes and Nazi Germany: The View from Madrid,"

Journal of Church and State 38, no. 2 (March 1996): 365–376; Richard Pipes, *Russia under the Bolshevik Regime* (New York: Alfred A. Knopf, 1993), 337; Felix Corley, *Religion in the Soviet Union: An Archival Reader* (New York: New York University Press, 1996); Christopher Andrew and Vasili Mitrokhin, *The Sword and the Shield: The Mitrokhin Archive and the Secret History of the KGB* (New York: Basic Books, 1999), 499; R.J.B. Bosworth, *Mussolini's Italy: Life under the Dictatorship 1915–1945* (New York: Penguin Press, 2006), 373. Another interesting opinion of Bosworth was reported by Gerhard Weinberg, who reviewed Bosworth's *Explaining Auschwitz*: "The only new point made about Hiroshima is Bosworth's regret that the Japanese did not have atomic bombs to drop on San Francisco, San Diego and Los Angeles." Gerhard L. Weinberg, Review of Bosworth's *Explaining Auschwitz and Hiroshima: History Writing and the Second World War*, by R.J.B. Bosworth, *Journal of Military History* 59. no. 3 (July 1995): 553–554. Jonathan Luxmoore and Jolanta Babiuch, *The Vatican and the Red Flag: The Struggle for the Soul of Eastern Europe* (London: Geoffrey Chapman, 1999), see chapter 1; Christopher L. Zugger, *The Forgotten: Catholics of the Soviet Empire from Lenin through Stalin* (Syracuse: Syracuse University Press, 2001).

4. John Loftus and Mark Aarons, *The Secret War Against The Jews: How Western Espionage Betrayed the Jewish People* (New York: St. Martin's Press, 1994), 13; Paul I. Murphy with R. Rene Arlington, *La Popessa* (New York: Warner Books, 1983), 52, 310.

5. Carlo D'Este, review of *The Battle for Rome*, by Robert Katz, *The New York Times*, January 11, 2004; Robert Katz, "The Mollhausen Telegram, the Kappler Decodes, and the Deportation of the Jews of Rome: The New CIA-OSS Documents, 2000–2002." in *Jews in Italy under Fascist and Nazi Rule, 1922–1945*, ed. Joshua D. Zimmerman, 231 (Cambridge: Cambridge University Press, 2005); Robert Graham, S.J., "Il 'Concordatismo' del Card. Pacelli Secondo Giovanni Spadolini" [The "Concordatism" of Cardinal Pacelli According to Giovanni Spadolini], *La Civiltà Cattolica* 125, no. III, (21 Settembre 1974), 495–499. Papal reliance on the Concordat is key to understanding much of the Vatican's policy toward Germany in the 1930s. Especially for a diplomat like Pacelli, the "rule of law" was paramount, and it guided much of his dealings with Berlin. He would have been comfortable at the League of Nations and later at the United Nations. Unfortunately, Hitler's only rule was winning by any means, whereas the Vatican's attitude, for far too long, was based upon the illusion that they were dealing with someone who valued international law. Mauro Cappelletti, John H. Merryman and Joseph M. Perillo, *The Italian Legal System: An Introduction* (Stanford, CA: Stanford University Press, 1967), 174.

6. Richard L. Rubenstein, "Pius XII and the Shoah," in *Pope Pius XII and the Holocaust*, eds. Carol Rittner and John K. Roth, demographic elimination, 177, it is my conviction, 198.

7. John T. Pawlikowski, "The Catholic Response to the Holocaust," in *The Holocaust and History: The Known, the Unknown, the Disputed, and the Reexamined*, eds. Michael Berenbaum and Abraham J. Pick, 556 (Bloomington: Indiana University Press, 1998); Anthony Rhodes, *The Vatican and the Dictators (1922–1945)* (New York: Holt, Rinehart and Winston, 1973), 357; Hugh Trevor-Roper, ed., *Final Entries 1945: The Diaries of Joseph Goebbels* (New York: G. P. Putnam's Sons, 1978), 173; James McMillan quoted by Kevin Passmore, "Catholicism and Nationalism: The Federation republicaine, 1927–39," in *Catholicism, Politics and Society in Twentieth-Century France*, ed. Kay Chadwick, 49 (Liverpool: Liverpool University Press, 2000); Richard J. Wolff, "A Reexamination of the Relationship between Catholicism and Fascism," *Italian Quarterly* 23, no. 89 (Summer 1982): 67–71.

8. Jean Claude Favez, *Mission Impossible: The Red Cross and the Holocaust* (Cambridge: Cambridge University Press, 1999); Levin, *The Holocaust*, 693–698; Walter Laquer, *The Terrible Secret: The Suppression of the Truth about the Holocaust* (Boston: Little Brown and Company, 1980). 60; Levin, *The Holocaust*, 693–698, principal of victory, 698; Vasilis Vourkoutiotis, *Prisoners of*

War and the German High Command: The British and American Experience (New York: Palgrave Macmillan, 2003), see especially his chapter 6, "Final Assessments"; Raul Hilberg, *The Destruction of the European Jews. Revised and Definitive Edition,* vol. 1 (New York: Holmes & Meier, 1985), 334; Robert A. Graham, S.J., "La Sante Sede e la difesa degli Ebrei durante la seconda guerra mondiale" [The Holy See and the Defense of the Jews during the Second World War], *La Civiltà Cattolica* 141, no. III (4–18 agosto 1990): 225. According to Steven Paskuly, who edited Rodolph Hoss's diary, in September 1944, a Red Cross delegate visited Auschwitz but was not allowed to enter the camp, talk to prisoners or verify rumors about gassing. See Paskuly, *Death Dealer: The Memoirs of the SS Commandant at Auschwitz,* 364.

9. Phayer, *The Catholic Church and the Holocaust,* 218. Camille M. Cianfarra, *The Vatican and the War* (New York: E. P. Dutton & Company, 1944), 22. Before World War II Cianfarra was a New York Times reporter in Rome. John K. Roth, "An American Protestant's Reflection," in *Pope Pius XII and the Holocaust,* eds. Carol Rittner and John K. Roth, 269.

10. Rittner and Roth, eds., *Pope Pius XII and the Holocaust,* 251.; John P. Carroll-Abbing, *But for the Grace of God* (New York: Delacorte Press, 1965), 267; Aryeh L. Kubovy, "The Silence of Pope Pius XII and the Beginnings of the 'Jewish Document,'" in *Yad Vashem Studies on the European Jewish Catastrophe and Resistance, VI,* eds. Nathan Eck and Aryeh Leon Kubovy, 81 (Jerusalem: Jerusalem Post Press, 1967); Martin Stannard, *Evelyn Waugh: The Later Years 1930–1966* (New York: W.W. Norton & Company, 1992), 140. Soviet archival material released in 1992 contained a letter from Lavrenti Beria to Stalin that recommended the liquidation of 25,700 officers and other Polish POWs including the men whose bodies were found at Katyn. That only confirmed what was known 50 years earlier. See Patel Sudodplatov and Anatoli Sudodplatov, *Special Tasks: The Memoirs of an Unwanted Witness—A Soviet Spymaster* (Boston: Little Brown and Company, 1994), 277, 476–478. Given the information about Katyn that was available long before the mid 1960s when he wrote, it is interesting to read Gabriel Kolko's apologia for Katyn that was published in 1968. He presents what happened as something the Polish government in exile brought on itself. See his *The Politics of War: The World and United States Foreign Policy 1943–1945.* (New York: Random House, 1968), 104–106.

11. Frans Josef van Beek, S.J., "Denying Communion to Politicians: A Theologian Explains Why It Is Wrong," *Commonweal,* June 6, 2004, 19; Goldhagen, *A Moral Reckoning.* 296; Frank J. Coppa, "Review, Pope Pius XII: Architect for Peace," *Journal of Church & State* 42, no. 4 (Autumn 2000): 864–865; Coppa, "failure," ibid., 188; Frank J. Coppa, "The Papal Responses to Nazi and Fascist Anti-Semitism: From Pius XI to Pius XII," in Joshua D. Zimmerman, op. cit., 279; Jose M. Sanchez, *Pius XII and the Holocaust: Understanding the Controversy* (Washington, DC: The Catholic University, 2002), 120. For the story of Marzabotto, see Lamb, *War in Italy,* 68–69.

12. Dean Acheson, *Present at the Creation: My Years at the State Department* (New York: W.W. Norton & Company, 1969), 38; George F. Kennan, *American Diplomacy, 1900–1950* (New York: Mentor Books, 1952), 83.

13. David Alvarez and Robert A. Graham, S.J., *Nothing Sacred: Nazi Espionage against the Vatican, 1939–1943* (London: Frank Cass, 1997), 112. Gitta Sereny reported Hudal's helping some Jews during the war. See her *Into That Darkness,* 314. Hudal's help to forty persons is in Goni, *The Real ODESSA,* 299. Owen Chadwick, *Britain and the Vatican during The Second World War* (Cambridge: Cambridge University Press, 1986), O'Flaherty, 293–294. According to Chadwick, by June 1944 the number helped was 3,925 Allied ex-prisoners (p. 299); Papal charity, 315; Inga Clendinnen, *Reading the Holocaust* (Cambridge: Cambridge University Press, 1999), 108. Clendinnen has a thoughtful, if in her own words not scholarly discussion of the Holocaust. However, it certainly is the work of a competent scholar, although one must question her assertion that Pius XII protected Hudal when he aided SS men to escape. Re:

Notes — Chapter 4

Priebke, see Lorenzo Rosso, *Il "caso" Priebke: Un ofessa alla memoria* [The Priebke Case: An Offense to Memory] (Rome: Edizione EdiDiGi, 1996); Robert A Graham, "Pfeiffer's List," *Soggiorno*, June 1994, 70–73.

14. Peter Godman, *Hitler and The Vatican: Inside the Secret Archives that Reveal the New Story of the Nazis and the Church* (New York: Free Press, 2004), 170. Mark Aarons and John Loftus, *Unholy Alliance: The Vatican, the Nazis and the Swiss Banks* (New York: St. Martins Griffin, 1998), 108. Mark Aarons and John Loftus, *Ratlines* (London: Mandarin House, 1991), 108; John Loftus and Mark Aarons, *The Secret War Against the Jews: How Western Espionage Betrayed the Jewish People* (New York: St. Martins Press, 1994); re: Huttenback, *Holocaust Education: Approaches That Work* (Greensburg, PA: National Center for Holocaust Education, Seton Hill College, 1997), 16. Sturzo's letter is in Aryeh L. Kubovy, "The Silence of Pope Pius XII and the Beginnings of the 'Jewish Document,'" in *Yad Vashem Studies on the European Jewish Catastrophe and Resistance*, VI, eds. Nathan Eck and Aryeh Leon Kubovy, 12 (Jerusalem: Jerusalem Post Press, 1967), 12. Chadwick, *Britain and the Vatican*, 315.

15. Godman, *Hitler and the Vatican*, 170; Margherita Marchione, *Consensus & Controversy: Defending Pope Pius XII* (New York: Paulist Press, 2002), 63; Robert A. Graham, S.J., "Goebbels e il Vaticano nel 1943, un enigma resolto" [Goebbels and the Vatican in 1943: A Puzzle Resolved], *La Civiltà Cattolica* 125, no 4 (19 ottobre 1974), 130–140; and Hilberg, *Perpetrators Victims Bystanders*, 268.

16. re: Tardini, Michael O'Carroll, *Pius XII, Greatness Dishonoured: A Documented Study* (Chicago: Franciscan Herald Press, 1980), 135–136. Re: Warthegau, see Robert A. Graham, S.J., "Il piano straordinario di Hitler per distruggere la chiesa" [Hitler's Extraordinary Plan to Destroy the Church], *La Civiltà Cattolica* 146, no I (18 marzo 1995): 544–552. Bouscaren, *A World to Reconstruct*. On OSS report in Aarons and Loftus, see Robert, A. Graham, S.J., "Una trappola per gli storici. Il falso sul Vaticano: 1939–1945" [A Trap for Historians: Falsehoods About the Vatican, 1939–1945], *La Civiltà Cattolica* 143, no. 1 (1992): 232–237.

17. re: von Weizsacker, Robert Leiber, S.J., "Pio XII e gli Ebrei di Roma 1943–1944" [Pius XII and the Jews of Rome 1943–1945], *La Civiltà Cattolica* 1 (1961): 449. Anthony Rhodes, *The Vatican in the Age of the Dictators, 1922–1945* (New York: Holt Rinehart and Company, 1974), 272–273.

18. Phayer, *The Catholic Church and the Holocaust*.

19. Myron Taylor, see: "Le delegue apostolique a Washington Cicognani au cardinal Maglione" [The Apostolic Delegate Cicognani in Washington to Cardinal Maglione], 17 juin 1941, 555–558. En Europe, Juin 1940–Juin 1941." *Actes et documents du Saint-Siège relatifs à la seconde guerre mondiale, 4, le Saint-Siège et la guerre en Europe, Juin 1940–Juin 1941* (Città del Vaticano: Libreria Editrice Vaticana, 1967); Falconi, *The Silence of Pius XII*, 138; Steven M. Avella, "The Rise and Fall of Bernard Sheil," in *Catholicism, Chicago Style*, ed. Ellen Skerett (Chicago: Loyola University Press, 1993), 104; *Records and Documents of the Holy See Relating to the Second World War. The Holy See and the War in Europe, March 1939–August 1940* (Washington: Corpus Books, 1968), 353.

20. Fiorello Cavalli, S.J., "La Santa Sede contro le esportazione degli Ebrei dalla Slovacchia durante la seconda guerra mondiale" [The Holy See Opposition to the Expulsion of the Slovak Jews during the Second World War], *La Civiltà Cattolica* (1961): III, 4.

21. Phayer, *The Catholic Church and the Holocaust*, 162; Owen Chadwick, *Britain and the Vatican during the Second World War* (Cambridge: Cambridge University Press, 1986); Mark Aarons and John Loftus, *Rat Lines: How the Vatican's Nazi Networks Betrayed Western Intelligence to the Soviets* (London: Mandarin Paperbacks, 1991). The book was published in the United States as *Unholy Trinity*. A revised edition came out in 1998, *Unholy Trinity: The Vatican, the Nazis and the Swiss Banks* (New York: St. Martin's Press, 1998). Aaron Freiwald with Martin Mendelsohn, *Josef Schwammberger and the Nazi Past* (New York: W.W. Norton & Company, 1994), 120.

22. Daniel Jonah Goldhagen, *Hitler's Willing Executioners: Ordinary Germans and the Holocaust* (New York: Alfred A. Knopf, 1996), 390. His book created controversy in Europe and the United States. While calling it a valuable contribution to Holocaust studies, Joseph Joffe criticized Goldhagen's circular reasoning that indicted the German people. See "Hitler's Willing Executioners: An Exchange," *New York Review of Books*, February 6, 1997, 40. James Carroll, *Constantine's Sword: The Church and the Jews* (Boston: Houghton-Mifflin, 2001). Re: primordial sin, James Carroll, *Toward a New Catholic Church* (New York: Houghton Mifflin, 2002), 10. Norman Finkelstein and Ruth Bettina Birn, *A Nation on Trial: The Goldhagen Thesis and Historical Truth* (New York: Henry Holt and Company, 1998). Finkelstein and Birn give no leeway to Goldhagen, with scathing criticism of his scholarship and conclusions. Claudio Pavone, *Una guerra civile: Saggio storico sulla moralità nella resistanza* [A Civil War: An Historical Essay on the Morality of the Resistance] (Torino: Bollati Boringhieri, 1991); Geoff Eley, ed., *The "Goldhagen Effect": History, Memory, Nazism–Facing the German Past* (Ann Arbor: The University of Michigan Press, 2000).

23. Christopher R. Browning and Jurgen Matthaus, *The Origins of the Final Solution: The Evolution of Nazi Jewish Policy, September 1939-March 1942* (Lincoln: University of Nebraska Press, 2004); see also Christopher R. Browning's *Ordinary Men: Reserve Police Battalion 101 and the Final Solution in Poland* (New York: Harper Collins, 1992).

24. Jonathan Luxmoore and Jolanta Babiuch, *The Vatican and the Red Flag: The Struggle for the Soul of Eastern Europe* (London: Geoffrey Chapman, 1999), 173. Also chapter 1 in Peter Novick, *The Holocaust in American Life* (Boston: Houghton Mifflin, 2000), 142. Zuccotti, *The Italians and the Holocaust*, 128.

25. Chadwick, *Britain and the Vatican*, 315–316.

26. Harold H. Tittmann, Jr., *Inside the Vatican of Pius XII: The Memoir of an American Diplomat during World War II* (New York: Doubleday, 2004), personally, 122, arguments 118–123, Mueller, 212; Hilberg, *Perpetrators Victims Bystanders*, 264; Robert A. Graham, "Alle origini degli 'Actes et documents du Saint-Siège'" [The Origin of the Records and Documents of the Holy See], in *Pio XII*, ed. Andrea Riccardi, 273 (Bari: Editore Laterza, 1984).

27. Re: Roberto Farinacci, in Paolo Moglia, *Il regime fascista: La Stampa quotidiana nella Repubblica Social Italiana* [The Fascist Regime: The Daily Press in the Italian Social Republic] Tesi di Laurea, Roma, Università degli Studi di Roma "La Sapienza," 307.

Chapter 5

1. James Edward Miller, Book Review, *International History Review* 24, no. 2 (June 2002): 474, 1986; Gerhard L. Weinberg, *A World at Arms: A Global History of World War II* (Cambridge: Cambridge University Press, 1994), 925; Norman Tutorow, ed., *War Crimes, War Criminals and War Crimes Trials* (New York: Greenwood Press, 1986).

2. Giovanni Miccoli, *I dilemmi e i silenci di Pio XII* [The Dilemmas and the Silences of Pius XII] (Milan: Rizzoli, 2000). Several Italian critics are found in an issue of *Studi Storici* devoted to "Ebrei italiani, memoria e antisemitismo" [Italian Jews, Memory and Anti-Semitism]. It was introduced by Giovanni Miccoli's "Antisemitismo e ricerca storica" [Anti-Semitism and Historical Research], 605–618. See *Studi Storici* 41, no 3 (Luglio-Settembre 2000). Andrea Riccardi, *Pio XII* [Pius XII] (Rome: Editori Laterza, 1984). Re: USSR, see Riccardi, "Governo e profezia nei Pontificato di Pio XII" [Governing and Prophesy in the Pontificate of Pius XII], 65.

3. Richard Breitman and Timothy Naftali, *Report to the IWG on Previously Classified OSS Records* (Washington, DC: National Archives and Records Administration, July 7, 2000); Susan Zuccotti, "Rescue of Jews during the Holocaust," in *Pope Pius XII and the Holocaust*, eds. Rittner and Roth, 213. Re: Wolff, "Brani della testimonianza del generale Otto Wolff al processo di beatificazione de Pio XII" [Extracts from the

Notes — Chapter 5

Testimony of General Otto Wolff at the Hearing on the Beatification of Pius XII], *30 Giorni* (September 2001). Re: Freeman, Alfred D. Chandler, ed., *The Papers of Dwight David Eisenhower: The War Years, III* (Baltimore, MD: The Johns Hopkins Press, 1970), 1563, Re: message to Mussolini, Robert Dallek, *Franklin D. Roosevelt and American Foreign Policy, 1932–1945* (New York: Oxford University Press, 1979), 220. Discussing the preparation of the *Actes et documents du Saint-Siège relatifs à la seconde guerre mondiale*, one of the editors, Pierre Blet, noted that "Trustworthy persons charged with such a task are subject to certain rules: not to publish documents which would call into question people still living or which, if revealed, would hamper current negotiations. On the basis of these criteria the volumes of the *Foreign Relations of the Unites States* relating to the Forties were published, and the same criteria were followed in the publications of the documents of the Holy See." Pierre Blet, S.J., "Appendix O: The Myth in the Light of the Archives," *Washington Conference on Holocaust-Era Assets*, 1069. Harold Mattingly, *Roman Imperial Civilization* (Garden City, New York: Doubleday, 1959), xvi.

4. Cornwell, *Hitler's Pope*; Ronald J. Rychlak, *Hitler, the War and the Pope* (Columbus, MS: Genesis Press, 2000); Margherita Marchione, *Consensus and Controversy: Defending Pope Pius XII* (Mahwah, NJ: The Paulist Press, 2002); Phayer, *The Catholic Church and the Holocaust*; University of Washington, http://www.lib.washington.edu/subject/History/bi/hist498-felak. The University library has books by Marchione, Phayer and Cornwell but not by Rychalak. Ralph McInerny, *The Defamation of Pius XII* (South Bend, IN: St. Augustine's Press, 2001); Jose M. Sanchez, *Pius XII and the Holocaust: Understanding the Controversy* (Washington, DC: The Catholic University of America Press, 2002).

5. www.archives.gov.//research holocaust//finding-aid/civilian/part-1-notes.html. Admiring the professionalism of the archivists at NARA, I doubt there was any effort to lead researchers in any direction. However, this effort to be helpful has an obvious imbalance that does not belong in a government or private resource. Jean Ziegler, *The Swiss, the Gold, and the Dead* (New York: Harcourt Brace & Company, 1997), 48–49; William Z. Slany, *U.S. and Allied Efforts to Recover and Restore Gold and Other Assets Stolen or Hidden by Germany during World War II. Preliminary Study* (Washington, DC: U.S. Government Printing Office, May 1997), v. See also William Slany, *U.S. and Allied Wartime and Postwar Relations and Negotiations with Argentina, Portugal, Spain, Sweden, and Turkey on Looted Gold and German External Assets and U.S. Concerns about the Fate of the Wartime Ustasha Treasury* (Washington, DC: Department of State Publication 10557, 1998); Itmar Levin, *The Last Deposit: Swiss Banks and Holocaust Victims' Accounts* (Westport, CT: Praeger, 1999), 153; Helen B. Junz, "Confronting Holocaust History: The Bergier Commission's Research on Switzerland's Past," Jerusalem, Center for Public Affairs, *Post-Holocaust and Anti-Semitism* 8 (May 1, 2003), http//www.jcpa.org//phas/phas/-8.htm; J.D. Bindenagel, ed., *Washington Conference on Holocaust-Era Assets, November 30–December 3, 1998, Proceedings*, "Appendix O" (Washington, DC: U.S. Department of State. Department of State Publication 10603, 1999); "Transcript Eizenstat Briefing on New Report on 'Nazi Gold,'" 06/02/98, USIS Washington File; Greg Bradsher, "Investigative Reporters, the National Archives, and the Search for 'Nazi Gold' and other Treasures," Speech at annual meeting of Investigative Reporters and Editors, Kansas City, MO, June 5, 1999; Greg Bradsher, "Turning History into Justice: The Search for Records Relating to Holocaust-Era Assets at the National Archives," Speech at annual meeting of the Society of American Archivists, Pittsburgh, PA, August 27, 1999.

6. Carol Rittner and John K. Roth, eds., *Pope Pius XII and the Holocaust* (London: Leicester University Press, 2002), 4–9; David Dalin, *The Myth of Hitler's Pope: How Pope Pius XII Rescued Jews from the Nazis* (Washington, DC: Regnery Publishing, 2005). Rittner and Roth criticized Dalin's earlier articles that provide the base for his book. James Carroll, *Toward a New Catholic Church* (New York: Houghton Mifflin

Company, 2002); Gary Wills, *Bare-Ruined Choirs, Doubt, Prophesy and Radical Religion* (Garden City, NY: Doubleday & Company, 1972); Gary Wills, *Papal Sin: Structures of Deceit* (New York: Doubleday, 2000). John Cornwell, *Breaking Faith: The Pope, the People and the Fate of Catholicism* (New York: Viking Company, 2001), 18. Obviously Rittner and Roth did not read Gary Wills' *Papal Sin: Structures of Deceit* as did Msgr. George G. Higgins ("My Take on Gary Wills' New Book"): "Wills' literary conceit here is that virtually everything the church did before and has done since Vatican Council II has been duplicitous." See: http://www.catholiclabor.org/higgins/higgins-72.htm. For status conscious, see "Part II: Popes, Politics, and Reform Resentment and the Holocaust," *U.S. Catholic Historian* 20, no. 2 (Spring 2002): 53–117.

7. Primo Levi, *If This Is a Man* (London: Little Brown and Company, 1987), 15–16; Daniel Jonah Goldhagen, *A Moral Reckoning: The Role of the Catholic Church in the Holocaust and Its Unfilled Duty of Repair* (New York: Alfred A. Knopf, 2002), 12; Novick, *The Holocaust in American Life*, 275; D.D. Guttenplan, *The Holocaust on Trial* (New York: W. W. Norton & Company, 2001), 307–308; Kubovy, "The Silence of Pope Pius XII and the Beginnings of the 'Jewish Document,'" 19. The medieval philosopher William of Occam advanced the idea of parsimony or economy in explaining phenomena. His razor removes the extraneous and unnecessary when studying theories or models, which is what faces scholars of the wartime Vatican.

8. Susan Zuccotti, "Pope Pius XII and the Rescue of Jews in Italy: Evidence of a Papal Directive?" *Holocaust and Genocide Studies* 18, no. 2 (2004): 255–273; J. Patrick Carroll-Abbing, *But for the Grace of God* (New York: Delacorte Press, 1965), 7, 24, 33, 34, 45, 78. A partial explanation for the lack of more detail in Carroll-Abbing's account of his experiences may be what he said on page 30: "When the occupation was over, many of us wondered why it was that we had never kept a diary." Re: Carroll-Abbing, Doino is quoted, December 23, 2004, in http:/www.zenit.org/english/visualizza.plum?sid=64050. We will never know whether this expatriate Irishman used a touch of blarney when talking to William Doino, assuming of course, because there is only the Web site record but not a written or printed archival record to confirm Doino's account, that the exchange actually did occur. Therefore, how acceptable would this evidence be? I found Carroll-Abbing credible based on a meeting with him in 1950 in Rome while studying postwar services for children in Italy. We did not discuss his wartime activities except in relation to abandoned children. He was friendly, plain spoken and appeared credible in a professional relationship, which suggests he was not the kind of person to concoct that story about the Pope. The lack of a paper trail was a favorite gambit of historian David Irving who claimed that Hitler did not learn about the mass extermination of the Jews until it was well underway. Irving made much of the fact that there was no archival evidence that Hitler ordered the "Final Solution." However, for years scholars have dismissed such reliance on an absent paper trail. According to historian John Evans, who made a detailed analysis of Irving's writings: "Irving's argument that Hitler did not know or approve of actions against the Jews thus clearly rested on a substantial number of historical falsifications." Hitler was directly involved in such matters as the Führer Order commanding the execution of Allied commandos and the execution of captured Italian soldiers who resisted the Germans after the Armistice of September 1943, and he personally ordered fifty hostages executed for every dead German in the Via Racially bombing. German headquarters in Italy was able to reduce the number executed to ten hostages for each dead German.

9. Daniel Jonah Goldhagen, *A Moral Reckoning: The Role of the Catholic Church in the Holocaust and Its Unfulfilled Duty of Repair* (New York: Alfred A. Knopf, 2002), 40.

10. Saul Friedlander, *Nazi Germany and the Jews: The Years of Persecution, 1933–1939*, vol. 1 (New York: Harper Collins, 1997), 2; Gerda Lerner, "Making History Her Story Too," *The New York Times*, July 20, 2002, A-17.

11. Susan Zuccotti, "L'Osservatore

Romano and the Holocaust," *Holocaust and Genocide Studies* 17, no. 2 (2003): 249–269.

12. For objections to interlopers, see "Part II: Popes, Politics, and Reform: Resentment and the Holocaust," *U.S. Catholic Historian* 20, no. 2 (Spring 2002): 53–117. Objecting to intrusion by non-historian outsiders was common in the 1995 controversy that roiled the media for months and took on new life in late 2003 when the Enola Gay, the aircraft that bombed Hiroshima, was displayed near Dulles Airport. The controversy began over how the Smithsonian Institution planned to mark the fiftieth anniversary of the end of the Pacific war. When veterans objected to the proposed exhibit, a committee of prominent historians as well as the Organization of American Historians and the American Historical Association waded into the debate on the basis of the "consensus" of historians, as if majority opinion decided acceptable history. See Charles T. O'Reilly and William A. Rooney, *The Enola Gay and the Smithsonian Institution* (Jefferson, NC: McFarland & Company, 2005).

13. Robert G. Weisbord and Wallace P. Sillanpoa, *The Chief Rabbi, the Pope, and the Holocaust: An Era in Vatican-Jewish Relations* (New Brunswick, NJ: Transaction Publishers, 1992), 7; Walter Laquer, *The Terrible Secret: Suppression of the Truth about Hitler's "Final Solution"* (Boston: Little Brown and Company, 1980), 208; David S. Wyman, *The Abandonment of the Jews* (New York: Pantheon Books, 1984); David S. Wyman, "Why Auschwitz Wasn't Bombed," in *Anatomy of the Auschwitz Death Camp*, eds. Yisrael Gutman and Michael Berenbaum, 569–587 (Bloomington: Indiana University Press, 1994); Larry Ceplair, *The Shadow of War: Fascism, Anti-Fascism, and Marxists* (New York: Columbia University Press, 1987), 206.

14. Michael Beschloss, *The Conquerors, Roosevelt, Truman and the Destruction of Hitler's Germany* (New York: Simon & Schuster, 2002), "moral statement," 65, 284; Michael Beschloss speech at Commonwealth Club, San Francisco, December 5, 2002. Re: James McDonald and Severin Hochberg, see Neil A. Lewis, "Nazis and Jews: Insights from Old Diary," *The New York Times* (April 22, 2004), A3. Dallek, *Franklin D. Roosevelt*, 443–448, 543–545. See also Monty Noam Penkower, *The Jews Were Expendable: Free World Diplomacy and the Holocaust* (Urbana: University of Illinois Press, 1983), 216–217; Martin Gilbert, *Auschwitz and the Allies* (New York: Holt, Rinehart and Winston, 1981), 299–323; James H. Kitchens, "The Bombing of Auschwitz Re-Examined," *Journal of Military History* 58 (1994): 233–266; William D. Rubenstein, *The Myth of Rescue: Why the Democracies Could Not Have Saved More Jews from the Nazis* (London: Routledge, 1997). Like Finkelstein and Birn, Rubenstein has been criticized not as much for his analysis but for contesting the prevalent theory of Allied inaction. Richard Breitman, *Official Secrets: What the Nazis Planned, What the British and Americans Knew* (New York: Hill and Wang, 1998), 232. Michael J. Neufeld and Michael Berenbaum, *The Bombing of Auschwitz: Should The Allies Have Attempted It?* (New York: St. Martin's Press, 2000). German Version of the History of the Italian Campaign, Headquarters, U.S. Fifth Army, 1945, 216. German logistics at the Gothic Line (Apennines Operation) are covered, 159–174. Italian Partisans in the North told the OSS that between April 2, 1945, and April 8, 1945, 843 freight cars came into Italy via Tarviso carrying coal and munitions and 2050 freight cars, 1500 of them empty, went from Italy to Germany. In the same period 521 loaded freight cars came into Italy via the Brenner route and many more were sidetracked because of bombing. Although this was only a trickle of supplies for the retreating Germans it shows that they were able to use railroads to some extent almost to the last days of the war. NARA, RG 226/Entry 190/ Caserta/OSS. Deborah E. Lipstadt, "The Failure to Rescue and Contemporary American Jewish Historiography of the Holocaust: Judging from a Distance," in *The Bombing of Auschwitz: Should the Allies Have Attempted It?* eds. Michael J. Neufeld and Michael Berenbaum, 227–236 (New York: St. Martin's Press, 2000); John K. Roth, "Reflections on Post-Holocaust Ethics," in *Problems Unique to the Holocaust*, ed. Harry James Cargas, 175 (Lexington: University Press of Kentucky, 1999);

Notes — Chapter 5

quoting Gerald Fleming, "Engineers of Death," *The New York Times*, July 18, 1993; re: Institute for Historical Research, www.ihr.org/jhr/v16/v16n6p11; Martin Bunzl, "Counterfactual History," *The American Historical Review* 109, no. 3 (June 2004): 845–858.

15. Peter C. Kent, *The Lonely Cold War of Pope Pius XII: The Roman Catholic Church and the Division of Europe, 1939–1950* (Montreal: McGill-Queens University Press, 2002), 22; John Keegan, *The Battle for History: Re-Fighting World War II* (New York: Vintage Books, 1995), 25–26; Richard Wolff and Jorg K. Hoesch, eds., *Catholics, the State, and the European Radical Right* (Highland Lakes, NJ: Atlantic Research and Publications, 1987); Jonathan Luxmore and Jolanta Babiuch, *Red Flag: The Struggle for the Soul of Eastern Europe* (London: Geoffrey Chapman, 1999), especially chapter 2; Dermot Keogh, "Ireland and the Vatican, 1921–1949," in *Papal Diplomacy in the Modern Age*, eds. Peter C. Kent and John F. Pollard, 87–104 (Westport, CT: Praeger 1994); Rudolph Hoss, *Death Dealer: The Memoirs of the SS Kommandant at Auschwitz*, ed. Steven J. Paskuly (New York: DaCapo Press: 1996), 12; Pipes, op. cit., 337; Hilberg, *Perpetrators, Victims, Bystanders*, 263; Goldhagen, op. cit., 132–133; Gordon Zahn, *In Solitary Witness: The Life and Death of Franz Jagerstatter* (New York: Holt, Rinehart and Winston, 1964), 197, 203; Jacques Nobecourt, "Pius XII's Biased Trial?" *Etudes*, July–August, 1999; Wolff, "A Reexamination of the Relationship between Catholicism and Fascism," foe of Fascism, 70.

16. Michael R. Marrus, "Essential Themes," in *Pope Pius XII and the Holocaust*, ed. Rittner and Roth, 54; Arthur Koestler, *Scum of the Earth* (New York: Macmillan, 1941).

17. Kenneth Macksey, *Military Errors of World War Two* (London: Arms and Armor Press, 1993), 238; Robert A. Graham, "Introduction: Reflections on Vatican Diplomacy," in *Papal Diplomacy in the Modern Age*, eds. Peter C. Kent and John F. Pollard, 7 (Westport, CT: Praeger, 1994); Re: Orsenigo, see Pierre Blet, S.J., *Pius XII and the Second World War According to the Archives of the Vatican* (New York: Paulist Press, 1997), 149.

18. Frank J. Coppa, "The Papal Response to Nazi and Fascist Anti-Semitism: From Pius XI to Pius XII," in *Jews in Italy under Fascist and Nazi Rule, 1922–1945*, ed. Joshua D. Zimmerman, 279 (New York: Cambridge University Press, 2005). Phayer, op. cit., 219; Keegan, *The Battle for History*, "weak pope," 106; Mark Aarons and John Loftus, *Unholy Trinity: How The Vatican's Nazi Networks Betrayed Western Intelligence to the Soviets* (New York: St. Martin's Press, 1991), 287.

19. G.E.M. Anscombe, *Ethics, Religion and Politics: The Collected Philosophical Papers of G. E. M. Anscombe*, vol. III (Oxford: Basil Blackwood, 1981); John Rawls, "Fifty Years after Hiroshima," *Dissent* 42, no. 3 (1995): 323–327; Robert Orsi in Richard Wrightman Fox and Robert B. Westbrook, eds., *In the Face of the Facts: Moral Inquiry in American Scholarship*, (Cambridge: Cambridge University Press and Woodrow Wilson Center Press, 1998); Richard Posner quote in Gertrude Himmelfarb, "Judging Judge Posner," *Commentary* 113, no. 2, 43. a review of Posner's *Public Intellectuals: A Study in Decline*; C. David Heymann, *Ezra Pound, the Last Rower: A Political Profile* (New York: Viking Press, 1976), 310–311; O'Reilly, *Forgotten Battles*, 210; R.M. Hare, *Essays in Political Theory* (Oxford: Clarendon Press, 1989), 59; R.M. Hare, *Essays in Political Morality* (Oxford: Clarendon Press, 1989), 63.

20. Paul Elie, "The Year of Two Popes," *The Atlantic Monthly* 297, no. 1 (Jan–Feb 2006), 92; Albert Schweitzer, "Preface," June 30, 1963. In Rolf Hochhuth, *The Deputy* (Baltimore: The Johns Hopkins University Press, 1997). no page number; Richard A. Posner, *Public Intellectuals: A Study in Decline* (Cambridge, MA: Harvard University Press, 2001), 75; for Gary Wills' background, see Patrick Allitt, *Catholic Intellectuals and Conservative Politics in America, 1950–1985* (Ithaca, NY: Cornell University Press, 1993), 243–288; Lamb, *War in Italy*, 6; George Bull, "The Vatican, the Nazis and the Pursuit of Justice," *International Affairs*, 47, no. 2 (April 1971): 353–358.

Appendix A

1. Hanna Arendt, *The Origins of Totalitarianism* (New York: Harcourt, Brace, 1951), 9; Gertrude Himmelfarb, *The New History and the Old: Critical Essays and Reappraisals*, rev. ed. (Cambridge: Harvard University Press, 2004), 15; Magnus Linklater, Isabel Hilton and Neal Ascherson, *The Fourth Reich: Klaus Barbie and the Neo-Fascist Connection* (London: Cornet Books Hodder & Stoughton Ltd, 1985), 243; William Slany, *U.S. and Allied Wartime and Postwar Relations with Argentina, Portugal, Spain, Sweden and Turkey on Looted Gold and German External Assets and U.S. Concerns About the Fate of the Wartime Ustasha Treasury* (Washington, DC: Department of State Publication 10557, 1998), 150. Regarding Scatolini, see Robert A. Graham, S.J., "Una trappola per gli storici. I falsi nel Vaticano 1939–1945" [A Trap for Historians: Falsehoods about the Vatican], *La Civiltà Cattolica* 143, no. I (1 Febbraio 1992): 232–237.

2. Uki Goni, *The Real ODESSA: Smuggling the Nazis to Peron's Argentina* (London: Granata Books, 2002), 328.

3. Hilberg, "The Trials," *The Destruction of the European Jews*, vol. III, 1060–1109; Gitta Sereny, *Into That Darkness: From Mercy Killing to Mass Murder* (New York: McGraw-Hill Book Company, 1974), 268; re: Draganovic, according to Gitta Sereny, Draganovic was abducted by the Yugoslavs in 1967 and executed. However, according to Richard Wolff and Jorg K. Hoensch, Dr. Krunoslav Draganovic returned to Yugoslavia in the 1970s and died in 1983. See their *Catholics, the State and the European Radical Right, 1919–1945* (Boulder: Social Science Monographs, 1987), 234. John Mendelsohn, "War Crimes Trials and Clemency in Germany and Japan," in *Americans as Proconsuls: United States Military Government in Germany and Japan, 1944–1952*, ed. Robert Wolfe, 228–229 (Carbondale: Southern Illinois University Press, 1984).

4. Hugh Thomas, *Armed Truce: The Beginnings of the Cold War 1945–1946* (New York: Atheneum, 1987), 218–221; Slany, op. cit., 153; Donald Bloxham, "From Streicher to Sawoniuk: The Holocaust in the Courtroom," in *The Historiography of the Holocaust*, ed. Dan Stone, 403 (New York: Palgrave-Mcmillan, 2004); Milovan Djilas, quoted by Hugh Thomas, ibid., 221; Claudio Pavone, "Introduction, The Hidden Pages of Contemporary Italian History: War Crimes, War Guilt and Collective Memory," *Journal of Modern Italian Studies* (9. 3. 2004): 271–279; Michale Battini, "Sins of Memory: Reflections on the Lack of an Italian Nuremberg and the Administration of Internal Justice after 1945," *Journal of Modern Italian Studies* 9, no. 3 (2004): 349–362, for collaboration, 309.

5. Goni, *The Real ODESSA*, 299; Phayer, *The Catholic Church and the Holocaust*, 168.

6. Daniel Jonah Goldhagen, *A Moral Reckoning: The Role of the Catholic Church in the Holocaust and Its Unfulfilled Duty of Repair* (New York: Alfred A Knopf, 2000), elided, 9, re: Arendt, 10, en 10, 205; Hannah Arendt, *The Origins of Totalitarianism* (New York: Harcourt, Brace and Company, 1951), 7, 413.

7. Christopher R. Browning, *Ordinary Men: Reserve Police Battalion 101 and the Final Solution in Poland* (New York: Harper Collins, 1992), 188; Peter Novick, *The Holocaust in American Life* (Boston: Houghton Mifflin, 2000), 137.

8. Daniel Jonah Goldhagen, "National History, Democracy, and Internationalization in Germany," in *Aus der Geschichte Lernen: How to Learn from History*, eds. Karl D. Bredthauer and Arthur Heinrich, 76 (Bonn: Blatter 2, 1997); Goldhagen, *A Moral Reckoning*, 11, 12; Kevin P. Slicer, *Resisting the Third Reich: The Catholic Clergy in Hitler's Berlin* (DeKalb: Northern Illinois University Press, 2004).

9. Goldhagen, *A Moral Reckoning*, 12, 296.

10. Richard J. Evans, *Lying About Hitler: History, Holocaust, and the David Irving Trial* (New York: Basic Books, 2001), 103.

11. Harry James Cargas, "Afterword," in *Problems Unique to the Holocaust*, ed. Harry James Cargas, 182–189 (Lexington: University Press of Kentucky, 1999); Alan M. Wald, *The New York Intellectuals: The Rise and*

Decline of the Anti-Stalinist Left from the 1930s to the 1980s (Chapel Hill: University of North Carolina Press, 1987), 13–14. The convoluted and controversial Demjanjuk case is mentioned because it illustrates the importance of accurate identification in a politically sensitive case involving the death penalty. Opinions and facts about the case can be found on a host of web sites on theInternet. About forty books have been written about the case.

12. Susan Zuccotti, "Pius XII and the Rescue of Jews in Italy: Evidence of a Papal Directive," in Zimmerman, op. cit., 293–294.

13. See Paolo Dezza, S.J., "Le Universita Cattoliche Nel Mondo" [Catholic Universities in the World], *La Civiltà Cattolica* 108, no. 4 (1957): 589–598.

14. Zuccotti, re: Doino, op. cit., 304; re: French Jews, Susan Zuccotti, *The Holocaust, the French, the Jews* (New York: Basic Books, 1993), xiv.

15. Andrea Grover, "L'Osservatore Romano and the Holocaust, 1933–45," in *Why Didn't The Press Shout? American and International Journalism During the Holocaust*, ed. Robert Moses Shapiro, 360, 349, 350, 351, 362 (Jersey City, NJ: Yeshiva University Press, 2003); Hoss, *The Death Dealer: The Memoirs of the SS Kommandant at Auschwitz*, 243.

16. Arthur R. Butz, *The Hoax of the Twentieth Century: The Case against the Presumed Extermination of European Jewry* (Costa Mesa, CA: Institute for Historical Review, 1977), 288–289. According to Fernando Palazzi's *Novissimo dizionario della lingua italiana* (Milano: Casa Editrice Ceschina, 1949), "sopprimere" means "uccidere" [kill].

Appendix B

1. *L'Osservatore Romano*, 9 October 1958.

2. P. Blet, A. Martini, R.A. Graham, and B. Schneider, eds., *Actes et documents du Saint-Siège relatifs à la seconde guerre mondiale*, 11 vols. in 12 parts (two parts for vol. 3) (Città del Vaticano: Libreria Editrice Vaticana, 1963–81).

3. Cfr. P. Blet, *Pie XII et la seconde guerre mondiale d'après les archives du Vatican* [Pius XII and the Second World War in the Archives of the Vatican] (Paris: Perrin, 1997).

4. Cfr. R. A. Graham, "Il vaticanista falsario: L'incrediblile successo di Vittorio Scatolini" [The False Vaticanist: The Incredible Success of Vittorio Scatolini], *La Civiltà Cattolica* (1973 III): 467–478.

5. Cfr. *Actes et documents*, vol. 9, 491 and 494.

6. Pius XII, "Consistorial Address" (June 2, 1945), *Acta Apostolicae Sedis* (1945): 159–168.

7. Thus when we prepared the first volume, it was not known who edited Pius XII's appeal for peace on August 24, 1939, opportunely corrected and approved by the Pope. Only later research allowed us to discover that the editor had been Monsignor Montini (cfr. B.Schneider, "Der Friedensappell Papst Pius XII. Vom 24 August 1939" [The Appeal for Peace by Pius XII, August 24, 1939], *Archivum Historiae Pontificiae* 6 (1968): 415–424, although it is difficult to attribute particular sections to the two authors.

8. Cfr. O. Chadwick, *Britain and the Vatican during the Second World War* (Cambridge: Cambridge University Press, 1986).

Selected Bibliography

Aarons, Mark, and John Loftus. *Ratlines: How the Vatican's Networks Betrayed Western Intelligence to the Soviets.* London: Heinemann, 1991.
Actes et documents du Saint-Siège relatifs à la seconde guerre mondiale [Records and Documents of the Holy See Regarding the Second World War]. Città del Vaticano: Libreria Editrice Vaticana, 1967.
Allen, John L. *The Inside Story of How the Vatican Really Thinks.* New York: Doubleday, 2004.
Andaldo, Ugo Giorgio. *Razza, nazione, guerra* [Race, Nation, War]. Bologna: Edizione SIA, 1940.
Ara, Angelo. "Gli Ebrei di Trieste, 1850–1918" [Trieste's Jews, 1850–1918]. *Rivista Storica Italiana* 102, no. 1, 1990, 53–86.
Armani, Barbara, and Guri Schwarz. *Ebrei Borghesi* [Middle Class Jews]. *Quaderni Storici* 38, no. 3, 2003, 621–652.
_____, and _____. *Ebrei sotto processo* [Jews on Trial]. *Quaderni Storici* 33. Milano: Fondazione Giangiacomo Feltrinelli, December 3, 1998
Ascarelli, Attilio. *Le Fosse Ardeatine* [The Ardeatine Caves]. Rome: Fratelli Palombi Editore, 1945.
Bedarida, Guido. *Ebrei d'Italia* [Italy's Jews]. Livorno: Società Editrice Terranea, 1950.
Berenbaum, Michael, and Abraham J. Peck, eds. *The Holocaust and History: the Known, the Unknown, the Disputed, and the Reexamined.* Bloomington: Indiana University Press, 1998.
Blet, Pierre, S.J. *Pius XII and the Second World War According to the Archives of the Vatican.* New York: Paulist Press, 1997.
Bottom, Joseph, and David G. Dalin, eds. *The Pius Wars: Responses to the Critics of Pius XII.* Lanham, MD: Lexington Books, 2004.
Breitman, Richard. *Official Secrets: What the Nazis Planned, What the British and Americans Knew.* New York: Hill and Wang, 1998.
Browning, Christopher R., and Jurgen Matthaus. *The Origins of the Final Solution: The Evolution of Nazi Jewish Policy, September 1939–March 1942.* Lincoln: University of Nebraska Press, 2004.
Caffaz, Ugo. *Discriminazione e persecuzione degli Ebrei nell'Italia fascista* [Discrimination and Persecution of the Jews in Fascist Italy]. Consiglio Regionale della Toscana, 1988.
Canepa, Andrew M. "Emancipation and Jewish Responses in Mid-Nineteenth-Century Italy." *European History Quarterly* 16, no. 4, October 1986, 403–439.
Caracciolo, Nicolo. *Gli Ebrei e l'Italia durante la guerra 1940–1945* [The Jews and Italy during the War, 1940–1945]. Rome: Bonacci, 1986.

Bibliography

Cardoza, Anthony L. *Benito Mussolini: The First Fascist.* New York: Pearson-Longman, 2006.
Chadwick, Owen. *Britain and the Vatican During the Second World War.* Cambridge, England: Cambridge University Press, 1986.
Clendinnen, Inga. *Reading the Holocaust.* Cambridge, England: Cambridge University Press, 1999.
Compendio statistico italiano 1939 — XVIII. Vol. III [Summary of Italian Statistics 1939 — XVIII (Year 18 of the Fascist Era)]. Vol. III. Rome: Istituto Polografico dello Stato, 1939.
Coppa, Frank J. *The Modern Papacy since 1789.* New York: Addison Wesley Longman, 1998.
Cornwell, John. *Hitler's Pope: The Secret History of Pius XII.* New York: Viking, 1999.
DeBenedetti, Giacomo. *16 Ottobre 1943* [October 16, 1943]. Palermo: Sellerio editore, 1993.
Della Pergola, Sergio. *Anatomia dell'ebraismo italiano* [Anatomy of Italian Judaism]. Assisi/Rome: Beniamino Carucci Editore, 1976.
Dubin, Lois C. "Trieste and Berlin: The Italian Role in the Cultural Politics of the Haskalah." In *Toward Modernity: The European Jewish Model*, edited by Jacob Katz, 189–224. New Brunswick, NJ: Transaction Books, 1987.
Dwork, Deborah, and Robert Jan van Pelt. *Holocaust: A History.* New York: W.W. Norton & Company, 2002.
Evans, Richard J. *In Defense of History.* NY: W.W. Norton & Company, 1999.
Falconi, Carlo. *The Silence of Pius XII.* Boston: Little, Brown and Company, 1965.
Fargion, Liliana Picciotto. *Il libro della memoria: Gli Ebrei deportate dall'Italia (1943–1945)* [The Book of Memory: The Jews Deported from Italy (1943–1945)]. Milan: Mursia, 1991.
_____. "La ricerca del Centro di documentazione ebraica contemporanea sugli Ebrei deportati dall'Italia" [The Research of the Center of Documentation of Contemporary Judaism on the Jews Deported from Italy]. In *Italia Judica: Gli Ebrei nell' Italia unita 1870–1945* [Jewish Italy: The Jews in United Italy 1870–1945], 474–486. Rome: Ministero per i Beni Culturale e Ambientali, 1993.
Friedlander, Saul. *Nazi Germany and The Jews: The Years of Persecution, 1933–1939.* Vol. 1. New York: Harper Collins, 1997.
Fubini, Guido. "Dalla legislazione antiebreica al'legislazione riparatoria: Orientamenti giurisprudenziali nell'Italia post fascista" [From the Anti-Jewish Legislation to the Reparation Legislation: Jurisprudence in Post Fascist Italy]. *La Rassegna Mensile di Israel: Le Leggi contro gli Ebrei* [The Monthly Review of Israel: The Laws Against the Jews], Vol. 54. (Jan. 1988), 477–493.
Gallo, Patrick J., ed. *Pius XII, the Holocaust and the Revisionists: Essays.* Jefferson, NC: McFarland & Company, Inc., Publishers, 2005.
Gariboldi, Giorgio Angelozzi. *Pio XII, Hitler e Mussolini: Il Vaticano fra le dittature* [Pius XII, Hitler and Mussolini: The Vatican Between the Dictators]. Milan: Mursia, 1995.
Gilbert, Martin. *Auschwitz and the Allies.* New York: Holt, Rinehart & Winston, 1981.
_____. *The Holocaust: A History of the Jews of Europe during the Second World War.* New York: Holt, Rinehart & Winston, 1985.
Godman, Peter. *Hitler and The Vatican: Inside the Secret Archives That Reveal the New Story of the Nazis and the Church.* New York: Free Press, 2004.

Bibliography

Goldhagen, Daniel Jonah. *Hitler's Willing Executioners: Ordinary Germans and the Holocaust.* New York: Alfred A. Knopf, 1996.

_____. *A Moral Reckoning: The Role of the Catholic Church in the Holocaust and Its Unfulfilled Duty of Repair.* New York. Alfred A. Knopf, 2002.

Graham, Robert A., S.J. "Come e perche Hitler blocco il Vaticano in Russia" [How and Why Hitler Blocked the Vatican in Russia]. *La Civiltà Cattolica* 123, Vol. IV (November 4, 1972): 241–52.

_____. "I progetti di Hitler per la chiesa e l'atteggiamento di Pio XII" [Hitler's Plans for the Church and the Attitude of Pius XII]. *La Civiltà Cattolica* 138, Vol. III. (August 1–15, 1987): 209–221.

_____. "Ideologia nazi-communista nella seconda guerra mondiale" [Nazi-Communist Ideology in the Second World War]. *La Civiltà Cattolica* 145, Vol. II (May21, 1994): 35.

_____. "Il 'Protocollo di Auschwitz' e il Vaticano nel 1944" [The Protocol of Auschwitz and the Vatican in 1944]. *La Civiltà Cattolica* 147, Vol. IV (November 16, 1996): 330–37.

_____. "Il Vaticano e gli Ebrei profughi in Italia durante la guerra" [The Vatican and Jewish Refugees in Italy during the War]. *La Civiltà Cattolica* 138, Vol I (March 7, 1987): 429–43.

_____. "La rappresaglia nazista alle Fosse Ardeatine: P. Pfeiffer, messaggero della carità di Pio XII" [The Nazi Reprisal at the Ardeatine Caves: Padre Pfeiffer, Messenger of the Charity of Pius XII]. *La Civiltà Cattolica* 124, Vol. IV (December 1, 1973): 467–74.

_____. "La Santa Sede e la difesa degli Ebrei durante la seconda guerra mondiale" [The Holy See and the Defense of the Jews During the Second World War]. *La Civiltà Cattolica* 141, Vol. III (August 4–18, 1990): 209–28.

_____. "Una trappola per gli storici: i falsi sul Vaticano: 1939–1945" [A Trap for Historians: Falsehoods about the Vatican]. *La Civiltà Cattolica* 143, Vol I (February 1, 1992): 232–37.

Herzer, Ivo, ed. *The Italian Refuge: Rescue of Jews during the Holocaust.* Washington, DC: Catholic University of America Press, 1989.

Hilberg, Raul. *The Destruction of the European Jews: Revised and Definitive Edition.* Vol. 2. New York: Olmes and Meier, 1985.

_____. *Perpetrators, Victims, Bystanders: The Jewish Catastrophe 1933–1945.* New York: Harper Collins Publishers, 1992.

Hochuth, Rolf. *The Deputy.* New York: Grove Press, 1964.

Hughes, H. Stuart. *Prisoners of Hope: The Silver Age of the Italian Jews, 1924–1974.* Cambridge, MA: Harvard University Press, 1983.

Katz, Robert. *The Battle for Rome: The Germans, the Allies, the Partisan and the Pope, September 1943–June 1944.* New York: Simon & Schuster, 2003.

_____. *Black Sabbath: A Journey through a Crime against Humanity.* Toronto: The Macmillan Company, 1969.

Kent, Peter C. *The Lonely Cold War of Pope Pius XII: The Roman Catholic Church and the Division of Europe, 1939–1950.* Montreal: McGill-Queens University Press, 2002.

Kertzer, David I. *The Popes Against the Jews: The Vatican's Role in the Rise of Modern Anti-Semitism.* New York: Alfred A. Knopf, 2001.

Koon, Tracy. *Believe, Obey, Fight: Political Socialization of Youth in Fascist Italy 1922–1943.* Chapel Hill: University of North Carolina Press, 1985.

Bibliography

Lamb, Richard. *War in Italy 1943–1945: A Brutal Story*. New York: St. Martin's Press, 1994.

Laquer, Walter. *The Terrible Secret: Suppression of the Truth about Hitler's "Final Solution."* Boston: Little Brown and Company, 1980.

Levin, Nora. *The Holocaust: The Destruction of European Jewry 1933–1945*. New York: Thomas Y. Crowell Company, 1968, 449–454.

Luxmoore, Jonathan, and Jolanta Babiuh. *The Vatican and the Red Flag: The Struggle for the Soul of Eastern Europe*. London: Geoffrey Chapman, 1999.

Marchione, Margherita. *Consensus and Controversy: Defending Pope Pius XII*. New York: Paulist Press, 2002.

Mayda, Giuseppe. *Ebrei sotto Salo: La persecuzione anti-Semite 1943–1945* [Jews under Salo: The Anti-Semitic Persecution 1943–1945]. Milan: Feltrinelli Editore, 1978.

McInerny, Ralph. *The Defamation of Pius XII*. South Bend, IN: St. Augustine's Press, 2001.

Miccoli, Giovanni. *I dilemmi e i silenzi di Pio XII* [The Dilemmas and the Silences of Pius XII]. Milan: Rizzoli, 2000.

Michaelis, Meir. "Fascism, Totalitarianism and the Holocaust: Reflections on Current Interpretations of National Socialist Anti-Semitism." *European History Quarterly* 19 (1989): 85.

———. "The Holocaust in Italy, Areas of Inquiry." In *The Holocaust and History: The Known, the Unknown, the Disputed, and the Reexamined*, edited by Michael Berenbaum and Abraham J. Peck, 439–62. Bloomington: Indiana University Press, 1998.

———. *Mussolini and the Jews: German-Italian Relations and the Jewish Question in Italy 1922–1945*. Oxford: The Clarendon Press, 1978.

Morley, John F. *Vatican Diplomacy and the Jews during the Holocaust, 1939–1943*. New York: Ktav Publishing House, 1980.

O'Carroll, Michael. *Pius XII: Greatness Dishonored*. Chicago: Franciscan Herald Press, 1980.

Passelecq, Georges, and Bernard Suchecky. *The Hidden Encyclical of Pius XI*. New York: Harcourt Brace & Company, 1997.

Pawlikowski, John T., O.S.M. "The Catholic Response to the Holocaust." In *The Holocaust and History: The Known, the Unknown, the Disputed, and the Reexamined*, edited by Michael Berenbaum and Abraham J. Pick, 551–65. Bloomington: Indiana University Press, 1998.

Phayer, Michael. *The Catholic Church and the Holocaust, 1930–1965*. Bloomington: Indiana University Press, 2000.

Poliakov, Leon, and Jacques Sabille. *Jews Under Italian Occupation*. New York: Howard Fertig, 1983.

Ramati, Alexander. *The Assisi Underground: The Priest Who Rescued Jews*. New York: Stein and Day, 1978.

Reitlinger, Gerald. *The Final Solution: The Attempt to Exterminate the Jews of Europe 1939–1945*. New York: A. S. Barnes & Company, 1961.

Rittner, Carol, and John K. Roth, eds. *Pope Pius XII and the Holocaust*. London: Leicester University Press, 2002.

Roth, Cecil. *History of the Jews of Italy*. Philadelphia: Jewish Publication Society of America, 1946.

Rubenstein, William D. *The Myth of Rescue: Why the Democracies Could Not Have Saved More Jews from the Nazis*. London: Routledge, 1997.

Bibliography

Rychlak, Ronald J. *Hitler, the War and the Pope.* Columbus, MS: Genesis Press, 2000.
Sacerdote, Giancarlo. *Ricordi di un Ebreo bolognese: illusioni e delusioni 1929–1945* [Memories of a Jew of Bologna: Illusions and Delusions 1929–1945]. Rome: Bonacci Editore, 1983.
Sanchez, Jose M. *Pius XII and the Holocaust: Understanding the Controversy.* Washington DC: The Catholic University of America Press, 2002.
Sarfatti, Michele. *Mussolini contro gli Ebrei: Cronaca dell'elaborazione delle leggi del 1938* [Mussolini Against the Jews: A Record of the Expansion of the Laws of 1938]. Torino: Silvio Zamorani Editore, 1994.
Segre, Dan Vittorio. *Memoirs of a Fortunate Jew: An Italian Story.* Northvale, NJ: Jason Aronson, 1995.
Shelah, Menachem. *Un debito di gratitudine: Storia dei rapporti tra l'Esercito italiano e gli Ebrei in Dalmazia (1941–1943)* [A Debt of Gratitude: The History of the Relations between the Italian Army and the Jews in Dalmatia (1941–1943)]. Rome: Ufficio Storico, Stato Maggiore dell'Esercito, 1991.
Spinosa, Antonio. *Mussolini, Razzista riluttante* [Mussolini: A Reluctant Racist]. Rome: Bonacci Editore, 1994.
Stille, Alexander. *Benevolence and Betrayal: Five Italian Jewish Families under Fascism.* New York: Summit Books, 1991.
Tas, Luciano. *Storia degli Ebrei italiani* [The History of Italian Jews]. Rome: Newton Compton Editori, 1987.
Tittmann, Harold H. *Inside the Vatican of Pius XII: A Memoir of an American Diplomat during World War II.* Edited by Harold H. Tittman III. New York: Doubleday, 2004.
Tornielli, Andrea. *Pio XII: Il Papa degli Ebrei* [Pius XII: The Pope of the Jews]. Casale Monferrato: Edizione Piemme, 2000.
Toscano, Mario, ed. *L'abrogazione delle leggi razziali in Italia (1943–1987): Reintegrazione dei diritti dei cittadini e ritorno ai valori del Risorgimento* [The End of the Racial Laws in Italy (1943–1987): The Restoration of the Right of Citizens and Return to the Values of the Resorgimento]. Rome: Collana del Servizio Studi del Senato della Repubblica, 1988.
Weisbord, Robert G., and Wallace P. Sillanpoa. *The Chief Rabbi, the Pope, and the Holocaust: An Era in Vatican-Jewish Relations.* New Brunswick, NJ: Transaction Publishers, 1992.
Wilhelm, Maria de Blasio. *The Other Italy: Italian Resistance in World War II.* New York: W.W. Norton & Company, 1988.
Wyman, David S. *The Abandonment of the Jews.* New York: Pantheon Books, 1984.
Zimmerman, Joshua D. ed. *Jews in Italy under Fascist and Nazi Rule, 1922–1945.* New York: Cambridge University Press, 2005.
Zuccotti, Susan. *The Italians and the Holocaust: Persecution, Rescue, and Survival.* New York: Basic Books, 1987.
_____. *Under His Very Windows: The Vatican and the Holocaust in Italy.* New Haven: Yale University Press, 2000.

Index

Aarons, Mark 150
Acheson, Dean 93
Allen, John 33
Andrew, Christopher 79
Anger, Pier 44
Anscombe, Gertrude 150
archival access 116
Arendt, Hannah 166
Auschwitz 138

Babiuch, Jolanta 79
Battini, Michale 164
Bederia, Guido 17
Berenbaum, Michael 138
Bernstein, Barton 30
Beschloss, Michael 136
Bierman, John 20
Birn, Ruth 108
"Black Sabbath," Oct. 16, 1943 8
Blet, Pierre 179
Bloxham, David 162
Bombing 101
Bosworth, R.J.B. 78
Bradsher, Greg 125
Brown, Anthony Cacve 33
Browning, Christopher 108, 166
Bull, George 154
Bullitt, William 46
Bunzel, Martin 141
Butz, Arthur 174

Caffaz, Ugo 6
Canepa, Andrew 3
Cannistraro, Philip 4
Cargas, Harry 169
Carracciolo, Nicola 42
Carroll-Abbing, John 70, 89, 130
Cavaglion, Alberto 22
Cavalli, Fiorello 105
Census of military 15

Census of 1931 6
Ceplair, Larry 136
Chadwick, Owen 111
clemency for war crimes 161
Concordat 37
Coppa, Frank 149
Corfu's Jews 22
Corley, Felix 79
Cornwell, John 59, 120
counterfactuals 141
Croatia 18, 20, 148

Dalin, David 127
Dallek, Robert 137, 139
Darlan, Adm François 36
Davis, Jack 30
Deaganovic, Krunoslav 159
DeFelice, Renzo 64
Della Sera, Fabio 9, 63
Delzell, Charles 63
Demjanjuk, John 170
Dezza, Paolo 171
DiScala, Spenser 51
Djilas, Milovan 163
Doino, William 28, 130
Dollman, Eugen 45, 59
Dower, John 30
Dulles, Allen 35
Dwork, Deborah 23, 66

Eichmann, Alolph 94, 95
Eisenhower, Gen. Dwight 119
Eizenstat, Stuart 123
Eley, Geoff 108
Elie, Paul 153
Enciclopedia Italiana 4
Encyclicals on racism 39
Erickson, Erik 61
Evans, Richard 169
excomunication 46, 96

Index

Falconi, Carlo 102
Fargion, Liliana 8, 14
Farranacci, Roberto 113
Farrell, James 31
Favez, Jean 85–86
Finkelstein, Norman 108
Fish, Stanley 28
Foner, Eric 29
Freiwald, Aaron 106
Friedlander, Saul 132

Gariboldi, Georgio 45
Gilbert, Martin 20, 62
gold 65, 68, 69, 186
Goldhagen, Daniel 25, 41, 107, 132, 145, 166, 169
Goni, Uku 65, 160
Goodman, Peter 41
Graham, Robert 112, 183
Graziani, Rudolfo 49
Green, Philip 32
Grover, Andrea 67, 173

Hanyok, Robert 68
Hare, R.M. 152
Herzer, Ivo 15
Heydrich, Reinhard 101
Heymann, C. David 151
Hilberg, Raul 142
Hill, Leonidas 73
Hochuth, Rolf 29
Hoensch, Jorg 85, 142
Hoover, Herbert, 106
Hudal, Bp Alois 94, 97–98, 149, 165
Hughes, H. Stuart 4

International Catholic-Jewish Historical Commission 27
Irving, David 70, 118
Italian resistance 50, 51

Katz, Robert 45, 50, 70, 71
Keegan, John 138, 150
Kennan, George 93
Kent, Peter 142
Keogh, Dermot 144
Kertzer, David 7, 37, 41
Knox, MacGregor 14
Koestler, Arthur 146
Kolko, Gabriel 31
Kubovy, Aryeh 87

LaFarge, John 39
Lamb, Richard 23, 45, 154
Lang, Berel 72
Laquer, Walter 86, 136
Leiber, Robert 40, 63–66, 98, 182–183, 189
Lens, Sidney 31
Lerner, Gerda 133
Levin, Itmar 123
Levin, Nora 54, 86
Levinson, Sanford 32
Levy, Primo 130
Lipstadt, Deborah 76, 140
Loftus, John 150
Loi, Salvatore 24
Lukacs, John 36
Luxmorre, Jonathan 79

Macksey, Kenneth 147
Madigan, Kevin 62, 72
Manifesto della razza 7, 39
Manifesto di Cremona 24
Marchione, Margherita 91–92, 120, 126
Marrus, Michael 146
McCloy, John 31
McDonald, James 137
McInerney, Ralph 121, 126
McMillan, James 85, 101
Meir, Golda 172
Miccoli, Giovanni 7, 38, 47, 117
Miller, James, 115
Mitrokhin, Vasili 79
monolithic Catholicism 142, 144
Montanelli, Indro 5
Morley, John 53
Mosley, Raymond 58
Mueller, Josef 101

National Archives 122
national characteristics 109
Neufield, Michael 138
Niccacci, Rufino 42
Nobecourt, Jacques 146
Novick, Peter 110, 129, 167

Occupation of Vatican 50, 119
occupied Rome 49
O'Flaherty, Hugh 93, 130
Operation Sunrise 35
Orsenigo, Cesare 148
Orsi, Robert 151
L'Osservatorio Romano 133, 134, 173

partisan justice 164
Paselecq, Georges 41
Paskuly, Steven 141
Pavone, Claudio 108, 164
Pawlikowski, John 54, 82
Penkower, Monty 55
Pfeiffer, Pankratius 43, 60
Phayer, Michael 38, 46, 102, 121
Pipes, Richard 78, 143
Pius XII 33, 36, 54, 61, 80, 82, 87, 92, 97, 110, 135, 147, 149, 151, 152, 184
Poliakov, Leon 12
Posner, Richard 151, 153
public intellectuals 153
Pugliese, Stanislao 63
Puzzo, Dante 35

Quazza, Guido 51
Quigley, Martin 34

rat lines 164
Rawls, John 150
Read, Anthony 38, 62
Red Cross, 87
repatriation of POWs 163
Repubblica Sociale Italiana (RSI) 49
restrictions on Jews 6
revisionist history 28
Rhodes, Anthony, 37, 39, 84
Riccardi, Andrea 117
Rittner, Carol 87, 126, 141
Rose, Lisle 35
Rossi, Elena Ago 35
Roth, John 87, 126, 141
Rotta, Angelo 44
Rubenstein, Richard 55, 83
Rychlak, Ronald 90, 120, 168

Sanchez, Jose 56, 60, 78, 126
Scattolini, Virgilio 159
Schweitzer, Albert 154
"secret encyclical" 40, 41
Segre, Bruno 16
Sereny, Gitta 41, 96, 162
Sheil, Bp. Bernard 103
Shelah, Menachem 14
Sillanpoa, Wallace 135
Slany, William 123, 158
Slicer, Kevin 167
Slovak Jewish Code 104

Smith, Bradley 35
social networks 175
Spellman, Arch Bp 103
Spinosa, Antonio 68
Sterling, Eric 55
Stille, Alexander 8, 43
Sturzo, Don Luigi 144
Suchecky, Bernard 41
Sullivan, Brian 4

Tardini, Cardinal Domenico 100
Taylor, Myron, 100
Tischner, Josef 57
Tittmann, Harold 111
Tornielli, Andrea 40
trials of war criminals 162
Trieste's Jews 10
Tuterow, Norman, 117

unfortunate expendables 54, 55
University of Washington 121
Ustasha gold 125, 158

Van Beek, Franz 90
van Pelt, Richard 23, 66
Vassalli, Guliano 34
Vatican 53, 64, 77, 78, 81, 87, 100, 101, 102, 105, 128, 188, 189
Verolini, Gennaro 44
Via Rasella 58
Villari, Luigi 10
Vourkoutiotus, Vasily 87

Waagenaar, Sam 63–64
Wallenberg, Raoul 43
Warthegau 99–100
Waugh, Evelyn 90
Waugh, Katyn 90
Weinberg, Gerhard 117
Weisbord, Robert 135
Weisenthal, Simon 165
Wills, Gary 75
Wolff, Richard 85, 142
Wyman, David 136

Zahn, Gordon 145, 167
Ziegler, Jean 123
Zuccotti, Susan 58, 118, 121, 170
Zuggar, Christopher 79

www.ingramcontent.com/pod-product-compliance
Lightning Source LLC
Chambersburg PA
CBHW032053300426
44116CB00007B/716